Indigenous Writings from the Convent

Indigenous Writings from the Convent

NEGOTIATING ETHNIC AUTONOMY IN COLONIAL MEXICO

Mónica Díaz

FIRST PEOPLES
New Directions in Indigenous Studies

THE UNIVERSITY OF ARIZONA PRESS   TUCSON

The University of Arizona Press

www.uapress.arizona.edu

Library of Congress Cataloging-in-Publication Data
Díaz, Mónica, 1974–
   Indigenous writings from the convent : negotiating ethnic autonomy in colonial Mexico / Mónica Díaz.
      p. cm.
   Includes bibliographical references and index.
   ISBN 978-0-8165-2853-0 (hard cover : alk. paper)
   1. Indian women—Mexico—History—Sources. 2. Nobility—Mexico—History—Sources. 3. Nuns—Mexico—History—Sources. 4. Convents—Social aspects—Mexico—History—Sources. 5. Catholic Church—Mexico—History—Sources. 6. Indians of Mexico—Ethnic identity—History—Sources. 7. Indians of Mexico—Religion—Sources. 8. Mexico—History—Spanish colony, 1540–1810—Sources. 9. Mexico—Ethnic relations—History—Sources. 10. Mexico—Religious life and customs—Sources. I. Title.
   F1219.3.W6D54 2010
   305.800972—dc22

                                     2010018572

Publication of this book was made possible in part by a grant from the Andrew W. Mellon Foundation.

Manufactured in the United States of America on acid-free, archival-quality paper containing a minimum of 30 percent post-consumer waste and processed chlorine free.

15   14   13   12   11   10   6   5   4   3   2   1

Contents

Figures

A Note on Sources and the Appendixes

I have included substantial portions of the primary sources analyzed in the book within the body of the work. For readers interested in examining longer passages from these sources, I have also included a sample of various documents and their translations as appendixes. To make the excerpts more accessible, I have modernized the orthography but retained the original syntax as much as possible to give the reader a more accurate idea of the original version. As the nuns' writings often followed a structure more consistent with the spoken word, I have at points arranged the syntax to be more consistent with modern grammar. Finally, I included accents in accordance with modern Spanish and modified the following letters: [x] to [j]; [z] to [c]; [y] to [i]; and included [h]. In every case, my translations are intended to reflect the tone and language of the Spanish originals in modern English.

Acknowledgments

I began this project many years ago, and as with any long-term endeavor, I have accumulated numerous debts to people and institutions. Several travel grants and a dissertation research grant from Indiana University supported the early stages of my research. Later, a Faculty Research Award from the National Endowment for the Humanities allowed me to return to Mexico for additional archival work and to devote valuable months to the writing of the book manuscript. Grants from the College of Arts and Humanities and the Faculty Research Council at the University of Texas Pan-American funded the final trips to Mexican archives. I want to express my gratitude to Patti Hartman, senior acquiring editor at the University of Arizona Press, for making the publication of this book a smooth process, and to Mary Ann McHugh, manuscript editor, for her professionalism and excellent work. I also thank the anonymous reader and the no longer anonymous reader, Jennifer Eich, whose careful reading and suggestions made this a much better book.

At Indiana University, I am very grateful to Kathleen Myers, who introduced me to the field and who has mentored me ever since, and to Peter Guardino, who has always been supportive of my interdisciplinary interests. I would also like to thank my other professors, Gordon Brotherston, Arlene Díaz, Jeffery Gould, Catherine Larson, and Mary Jo Weaver, for always challenging me intellectually and providing such a supportive environment during graduate school.

I want to express special thanks to Asunción Lavrin, who encouraged me to continue with this venture from its earliest stages, as well as to Susan Schroeder, who took a special interest in my work. I was fortunate to have met Josefina Muriel in person and have listened to the many anecdotes hidden behind the manuscript of *Las indias caciques*. I am grateful to all the other people in Mexico who offered me advice and support: Manuel Ramos Medina, Antonio Rubial, Francisco Morales, Arturo Rocha, Nuria Salazar, Don Luis Castañeda Guzmán, Daniela Traffano, and Nimcy Arellanes. I want to thank Sister María Eucaristía at the Convent of Corpus Christi, Genaro Díaz at the Archivo Histórico del Instituto Nacional de Antropología e Historia, Rebeca Trejo at the Fondo Reservado of the Biblioteca Nacional in Mexico City, Alma Montero from the Museo Nacional del Virreinato, and Gabriela González-Mariscal Muriel for facilitating access to valuable documents and images for the book.

I would like to thank Hernán Vidal and Nina Scott, who read earlier versions of the book manuscript and offered invaluable comments and questions that led me to a more engaging argument; and Amanda Powell, whose careful reading of chapter 4 resulted in some significant improvements. More recently, I received words of wisdom from Rolena Adorno, whom I thank for her insightful comments.

I would have never been able to see this book through to completion without the help of friends and family. I am grateful to Marcia Caltabiano-Ponce for helping me with translations, to Pablo García for his support in the initial phase of the transcription process, and to Grady Wray, Rocío Quispe-Agnoli, and Mariselle Meléndez for their suggestions and encouragement. I am most indebted to my family: my father, who has constantly supported my academic pursuits, my mother, who has been there as a cheerful source of support at all times, and my sister. And last but not least, I am grateful to Eliot, Olivia, Alan, and Liam, who endured my long absences while I was doing research abroad and while I was writing the manuscript. Thoughts of them kept me going and helped me bring this book to conclusion. I am grateful to Ethan so much more than words can say; he is not only a brilliant academic and interlocutor but the most devoted father and patient husband. He created perfect conditions that allowed me to finish this project.

Abbreviations

ACC   Archivo del Convento de Corpus Christi

AGN   Archivo General de la Nación, México, D.F.

AINAH, FF   Archivo Histórico del Instituto Nacional de Antropología e
            Historia, Fondo Franciscano

Indigenous Writings from the Convent

Introduction

Appeals to the past are among the commonest of strategies in
interpretations of the present. What animates such appeals is not
only disagreement about what happened in the past and what the
past was, but uncertainty about whether the past really is past,
over and concluded, or whether it continues, albeit in different
forms, perhaps.
—Edward Said, *Culture and Imperialism*

Sometime around the year 1740, Sor María Magdalena, an indigenous
noblewoman living in one of only two convents in New Spain that allowed
Indians to profess as nuns, sent an undated letter to Father Juan de Altamirano asking for his help. Sor María asked Father Altamirano to write a letter to the king of Spain on behalf of all the indigenous nuns living in the
Convent of Cosamaloapan in Valladolid (today's city of Morelia), informing him of the situation in the convent. She wanted the king to know that
the prelates in charge of the cloister, which was supposed to have been
established exclusively for Indians, were allowing Spanish women into *their*
convent.[1] The indigenous women wanted to be left alone in their convent,
she argued, since the Spanish women had many cloisters and the "pobres
indias" (poor Indian women) had only two (AINAH, FF, vol. 100, fol. 166).

Colonial sources that mention indigenous women are not scarce, but
in every case it is easy to recognize colonial constructions of ambivalent
spaces filled with racial and gendered stereotypes. Documents in which
women emerge as agents who actively participate in the construction of
their own identities are rare, and Sor María Magdalena's letter is one of
those unique documents in which the voice of the subaltern can be heard.[2]

From the convents of the colonial period come writings that offer new possibilities for developing a history of Mexico's indigenous women and for recognizing their contributions to the country's literary and cultural heritage. This book analyzes the ways in which indigenous women participated in one of the most prominent institutions in colonial times—the Catholic Church—and what they made of their conventual life experience. The indigenous noblewomen who inhabited the convents studied in this book engaged in discourses that defended the autonomy of the space conferred on them and performed agency by manipulating the set of rules established by the new colonial order.[3] These women were not alone in the colonial scene, however; they followed a long list of other subalterns who grappled with the ever-changing world they inhabited. In particular, Indians from the elite class attempted to preserve their lineage with the new knowledge they acquired from the colonial order to create spaces in which they could reinvent themselves and survive.[4]

Colonial Cities and the República de Indios

The spatial scope of this book is mainly urban since the three convents that opened their doors to Indian noblewomen in the eighteenth century were located in Mexico City, Antequera (today's city of Oaxaca), and Valladolid (fig. 1). The sedentary native population of pre-conquest times was concentrated for the most part in four regional centers: the Valley of Mexico, Puebla, Michoacán, and Oaxaca. The new colony's European inhabitants also populated these regions, and they became the four central dioceses of the viceroyalty. All four regions fell under the jurisdiction of the *Audiencia* (the high court of New Spain) of Mexico. Mexico City, Antequera, and Valladolid were largely made up of indigenous peoples from different ethnic groups and a minority of Spanish colonizers.

To bring "order" to the new social and ethnic scene, the Crown created a legal system to differentiate Indians from non-Indians. The Crown instituted two independent republics, the *república de indios* and the *república de españoles*, both with distinct legal rights and obligations. The two republics were geographically separated, with the república de españoles comprising the *traza*, or urban center, built around the central plaza and the república de indios replacing the ethnic states of pre-Hispanic times, made up in some cases of *reducciones* or forced relocation of indigenous peoples into new *pueblos de indios* (Indian towns). The physical separation of peoples was unsuccessful, however, as the república de españoles depended on the indigenous population for labor and goods. Yet, through the

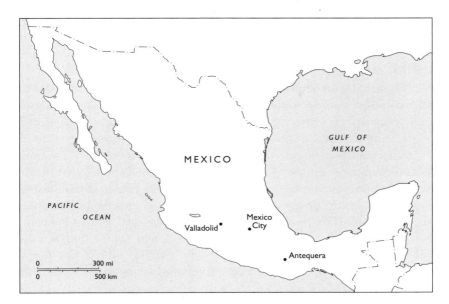

Figure 1. Convent locations in New Spain.

duration of the colony, the pueblos de indios maintained a somewhat autonomous space reinforced by the special legal status conferred by Spanish colonial law.

The success of the Spanish colonization was in part due to the use of certain institutions that regulated their subjects' lives, one being the Catholic Church. Under the aegis of the Royal Patronage, the regular religious orders received a papal dispensation to assume full power of their missionary enterprise in the Americas along with ample privileges and exemptions.[5] The Franciscans were the first to establish their "spiritual hegemony" in the Indian pueblos of central Mexico; they were also in charge of conversions, except in Oaxaca where the Dominicans dominated.

One of the initiatives of the missionary project was for friars to learn the native languages and to establish schools for Indians. The Franciscans were the leaders in the study of Nahuatl, but other missionaries learned Purépecha in the Michoacán area, Zapotec in Oaxaca, and Maya in Yucatán (Nesvig, "The 'Indian Question'" 73). The unusual arrangement of the regular Church in New Spain under the papal bull *Omnimoda* allowed them to be pastors of their churches in the Indian pueblos, which they called *doctrinas* or *congregaciones*. In the three regions of Mexico, Oaxaca, and Michoacán, the *caciques* (native lords) and *principales* (Indian notables) were quick to identify the new faith as an opportunity for "building a new religious basis for their authority," welcoming the missionaries and finding outlets to perform acts of local devotion like the *cofradías* (confraternities) and other cults like that of the Virgin of Guadalupe (Israel 7).[6]

William Taylor explains that in Oaxaca the valley's Zapotec and Mixtec caciques were rewarded for their peaceful surrender to the conquistador Francisco de Orozco in 1521. The caciques were also instrumental in modeling the ideal religious behavior that the missionaries expected of the indigenous population. Taylor describes the situation of the caciques in Antequera in much the same way Charles Gibson captures that of the Nahuas of central Mexico: "The Dominicans' first step in disseminating Christianity was to convert the Indian nobles, who then served as examples for their people, bringing them together in towns for Christian ministration" (*Landlord and Peasant* 37). At first glance, we could surmise that the missionaries were using the elites for their own purposes, which they surely were; yet at the same time, the elites also found a way to maintain their political authority by finding a place in the new religious order. Taylor adds that later in the seventeenth century, the Dominicans would support the caciques' creation of separate *cabeceras* (head towns) and the indigenous commoners' participation in local government.

In Michoacán, the conversion of natives depended on the efforts of the famous Bishop Vasco de Quiroga, the Franciscans, and the Augustinians. The first initiative for conversion began with the Indian elites: according to *The Chronicles of Michoacán*, fifteen boys from elite Purépecha families were sent to the Colegio de Santa Cruz de Tlatelolco in Mexico City in 1524. In 1526 the Franciscans, following the model of indoctrination used in the central valley, established the first doctrina at San Francisco Tzintzuntzan (Verástique 98).

The Crown and the Church worked together to develop a legal and philosophical justification for an ideology of difference that would characterize colonial society. From the state's point of view, the Indians were considered wards of the Crown, a status that granted them certain privileges. They were protected from slavery and had a certain amount of political autonomy. In religious terms, Fray Gerónimo de Mendieta, author of the *Historia eclesiástica indiana*, offers us a textual image that prevailed, at least in religious discourse, well into the eighteenth century.[7] The characteristics of the Indians, Mendieta stated, were "meekness, gentleness, simplicity of heart, humility, obedience, patience, and contentment with poverty," traits that forged a unique temperament and the need, therefore, for a social regime suited to them (Phelan 59). Although disagreement existed among the

Franciscans about this view of the natives, this was the prevailing opinion and one that helped justify their indoctrination solely by missionaries from the regular orders, particularly the Franciscans.

By the beginning of the seventeenth century, New Spain's social organization had altered considerably, particularly in urban settings. The physical division of the two republics meant little, given that the Indian population provided labor in the Spanish sector and moved about the two republics with ease. Moreover, scholars contend that by the seventeenth century many Indians had adopted cultural markers that concealed their ethnic identity, rendering the caste system of difference a malleable modality of little significance for the urban poor.[8] Yet, Indian communities still existed, and by this time they had created an identity that incorporated certain elements of Christianity. Having also learned to use the legal apparatus, they had begun to fight for their land titles and other privileges conceded to them in the early years after the conquest.[9]

With the Bourbons in power, the eighteenth century opened with new policies toward the Spanish colonies, particularly in religious matters. In 1749, for example, the Crown began secularization entrusting all the doctrinas administered by religious orders to the secular clergy (Brading, *Church and State* 62).[10] In addition to reducing the power and assets the Church had amassed in two hundred years, these Bourbon policies had another purpose: the integration of Indians through education reforms, with a prominent emphasis on Spanish language instruction.[11] David Brading mentions that the Indians' religious practices, particularly their image veneration and public processions, came under close scrutiny (*First America* 494). The indigenous population complained that the secular priests did not understand their various native languages. As Matthew O'Hara has noted, part of the agenda of reformist officials was to "eradicate Indianness" from the doctrinas; on the other hand, indigenous leaders saw the reform as an opportunity to "re-Indianize" parish life (*A Flock Divided* 58).

Native leaders knew exactly how to lobby for their cause and negotiate spaces for native autonomy, astutely aligning their requests with religious orthodoxy. As brokers between their communities and religious authorities, for instance, they asked for seminaries and convents exclusively for the Indian population. Their success was mixed: although seminaries for Indians did not materialize, three convents for indigenous noblewomen were founded in the eighteenth century.[12] In practical terms, convents, but not seminaries, were acceptable because of the roles that Indian men and women fulfilled within the ecclesiastical hierarchy. While Indian males ordained as priests would function out in the world as parish priests and spiritual leaders of a community, indigenous nuns would remain forever in the cloister, serving as examples of virtue but with little contact with the outside world. The same ideology of difference toward the social and religious authority of natives that had been established in the first years of the colony resonated with these new policies, whose goal was to make Indians less "Indian" but not to the extent that they were equal in the social hierarchy to Spaniards or *criollos*, those of European ancestry born in America. The policy of physical separation also endured: ecclesiastical officials would not allow the inclusion of Indian women in the seventeen convents that already existed in Mexico City by 1700. Instead, they were willing to open spaces of difference as long as the women expressed religious beliefs in orthodox and controlled ways.[13]

Convents for Indigenous Noblewomen

The idea of establishing a place dedicated to teaching Christianity to indigenous women began with the arrival of Fray Juan de Zumárraga, first bishop of New Spain, who petitioned the Spanish Crown to send nuns from Spain to instruct indigenous girls. He hoped to create a cloister for indigenous women where it would be easier for them to concentrate on their Christian education. His request was denied because native women were thought to lack the abilities needed for life in a convent. One of the Crown's arguments against his idea for a cloister was their recent indoctrination in the Christian faith. For that reason, the first convents founded in New Spain were planned for the daughters of the conquerors. Only Spanish women, *criollas*, and some *mestizas* (women of European and indigenous blood) were allowed to take the veil during the first two hundred years after the conquest.[14] Indigenous and mulatta women who wanted to follow a religious path were allowed to enter only as servants.

The first efforts to evangelize the female Indian nobility did not take place in a cloister. By 1529 Spanish Franciscan matrons from the Third Order were in charge of a house in Texcoco where they provided basic education to the Indian nobility (Gallagher, "Las monjas" 178).[15] But when more religious women arrived from Spain in 1534, teaching indigenous girls the basics of religious doctrine and preparing them for married life became their sole task. By 1537 there were about ten schools for indigenous girls, but they all gradually closed their doors, mainly because the teachers left to work in private homes or returned to Spain (Muriel, *Conventos* 29). The first convent, founded in 1540, was conceived for the daughters of the *conquistadores* who had traveled to the newly conquered lands.

The religious context that prevailed in New Spain was a direct result of Spain's cultural imports. At the beginning of the sixteenth century, starting with the political and religious unification of Spain, the Catholic Church began a process of internal reform meant to reinforce spirituality and improve the quality of its members' devotion. These reforms affected the convents established during the Middle Ages and paved the way for the founding of countless new religious orders and the buildings that housed them. The new monastic orders fortified the concepts of seclusion and isolation from the world, and the search for personal salvation through prayer, spiritual deeds, and physical penitence. In the religious culture of the Counter-Reformation, the founding of a convent became a symbol of prestige, and the nuns took on heightened importance based on their special role in society; their relatives, friends, and the community in general saw their prayers as a personal benefit, an intercession before God or the saints (Lavrin, "Women and Religion" 43).

The different feminine orders that came to Spanish America can be classified in two main groups: discalced orders, also called Capuchin or *recoletas*, and calced orders. The discalced were fewer in number and followed a more austere life. The calced orders housed between fifty and one hundred nuns, and admitted servants and slaves into their cloisters. The Capuchins allowed between fifteen and thirty-five nuns, depending on the specific rules of the convent. The calced orders required a dowry ranging from 1,000 to 4,000 pesos, whereas discalced convents allowed women to enter without dowries and relied on patronage and charity. City councils would usually oppose such foundations for their risk of becoming an economic burden. Nuns followed a communal rule and a ritual of canonical hours alternating periods of silence, prayer, meditation, and fasting (Socolow 98).[16]

Early on, indigenous women who had been converted to Christianity wanted to participate in conventual life, as did the criollas and, later, the mestizas. In many cases, Indian noblewomen's parents would not allow their daughters to assume the servile roles they were assigned in convents. In some cases, even if the women had a calling for religious life, class restrictions prevented them from fulfilling this desire. In New Spain, the question of ethnic difference became the principal obstacle. As Jacqueline Holler notes, female monasticism in Spain was already an exclusive option, but when transported to New Spain, the question of ethnicity made it even more exclusive (16).

Not until 1724, by the intercession of Viceroy Don Baltasar de Zúñiga, Marquis de Valero, was the first convent for indigenous women established.

Even so, when the Convent of Corpus Christi was founded, it was open only to noble or *cacica* women. Church authorities gave two official reasons for this: first, they claimed noble native women would be better educated than other indigenous women; and second, so many women wanted to take religious vows that authorities somehow had to limit the number of possible candidates. Convent life for Indians was similar to that of other nuns. Admittance to the cloister was modeled after Spanish establishments, which required *limpieza de sangre* (purity of blood) to keep the convent exclusively for native women who could prove noble lineage (Schroeder 10). The convent adhered to the First Rule of Saint Claire, a branch of the Franciscan order that allowed only eighteen to twenty-two nuns. Nevertheless, by 1769 the Corpus Christi convent was granted permission to house thirty-three nuns, and by 1822 it was known to have 110 professed nuns. According to the conventual rule, nuns were required to live by the precepts of obedience, poverty, and chastity, and in absolute seclusion (Quiñones 4).

The founding nuns chosen to govern the Convent of Corpus Christi until the Indians had the ability to rule themselves were criollas from the Convent of San Juan de la Penitencia.[17] The founding abbess was Sor Petra de San Francisco, who died in 1727. Another criolla, Sor María Teresa de San José, then held the post of abbess until her death in 1772. Not convinced that the indigenous nuns were capable of governing their own cloister, Fray Pedro de Navarrete, commissary general of the Franciscan Order, kept admitting Spanish nuns into the convent, creating an environment of animosity and delaying the day when the Indians would self-govern.[18]

Juan Ignacio de Castorena y Ursúa, a prominent Jesuit theologian who became Bishop of Yucatán in 1729, indicated in a sermon at the foundation of the nunnery that the Marquis de Valero wanted to build a convent for indigenous women as a means of celebrating the second centenary of the conquest of Mexico. Asunción Lavrin notes how ironic it is that the conversion of indigenous women became a symbol of the definitive "spiritual conquest" of the native population (*Brides of Christ* 256). The symbolic place that nuns occupied in society within the colonial imagination explains this line of reasoning. Holler contends that the enclosure of women and their admittance into religion was an important aspect of the shift of Mexico City from an Aztec into a Spanish capital (29). Holler's claim about the symbolism of cloistered nuns is supported by Castorena y Ursúa's assertion. Although this logic suggests that indigenous women should have been admitted into religious life from the beginning of the spiritual conquest, their status as neophytes in the faith undermined arguments for their place in conventual life in sixteenth-century New Spain.

Bishop Escalona promoted the second convent for Indian noblewomen in Valladolid, but it was Marcos Muñoz de Sanabria, canon of the Cathedral, who was the main patron of the foundation (Brading, *Church and State* 95). Although he sought to have the convent placed under direct episcopal jurisdiction, the Convent of Nuestra Señora de la Purísima Concepción de Cosamaloapan was founded in 1737 as another discalced Franciscan establishment. The founders arrived from the Convent of Corpus Christi and from the Convent of Santa Isabel, the latter inhabited by criolla women. In its first years of existence, this new convent was not entirely Indian, Fray Pedro de Navarrete continuing to allow Spanish novices into this cloister as he had with Corpus Christi.[19]

While the nuns of calced orders were striving to defend the privileges they enjoyed in their convents and resist the change to "the common life" that Archbishop Francisco Antonio de Lorenzana was trying to impose, the Indians were playing an active role redefining Bourbon religious reforms and functioning as brokers in the negotiations to open more cloisters for Indian women.[20] In 1743 two caciques from Antequera, Don Manuel de Aguilar and Don José López Chávez, began negotiating with the town council for another convent for the daughters of caciques and principales (Zahino 332). Bishop José Gregorio Alonso de Ortigosa oversaw the negotiation with the Crown, and in 1782 the Convent of Nuestra Señora de los Ángeles opened it doors next to the recently built church of Los Siete Príncipes (The Seven Princes). They followed the discalced Capuchin rule, but unlike the other indigenous foundations, this convent was under secular government.[21]

Caciques and Principales

In the eighteenth century, at least in the archdiocese of Mexico City, Indian caciques and principales functioned as cultural mediators. They created and re-created native gendered identities, using stereotypes in their discourses when they saw fit. Once they had negotiated spaces in which indigenous women could participate fully in religious life, the cloistered nuns took into their own hands the task of maintaining their native autonomy. Through the study of documentation produced within convent walls, I hope to flesh out the way the Indian nuns participated in the fashioning of their own identities. It will become apparent throughout these pages that Indian identity did not reside solely in cultural markers like language and dress. Ethnic lineage was also important, allowing the Indian nuns to express fully their "Indianness" while placing themselves in the ecclesiastical hierarchy as full members of the Church.[22] A key component in this conception of Indian identity is that change has been as important as continuity. This seemingly paradoxical ideology can be found in their use of written discourse that appeals to a pre-Hispanic past and at the same time incorporates new elements to legitimize their place in the social order.[23]

Louise Burkhart explores the question of Indian identity in relation to Christianity and the way Nahua people forged a religious praxis different from that of the Spanish church in part because the colonial order systematized the separation of the two. Missionaries worked at emphasizing difference for at least a century. She asserts that "Nahuas understood Christian teachings in their own terms and adapted them for their own ends, which varied through time and from place to place" ("Pious Performances" 362). The author argues that questioning the sincerity or authenticity of Christian belief among Indians is ethnocentric and pointless. In the case of caciques and principales, who moved about the colonial system with ease, they recreated their identities and worked at producing documents and histories that would legitimize their place in colonial society. Not surprisingly, while emphasizing their own origins and history, they usually evoked their early and quick conversion to Christianity, and their loyalty to Spanish conquistadores from the earliest years of invasion, thereby indicating their adherence to the dominant society.

Frances Karttunen for her part examines the way indigenous writing served as a vehicle to articulate continuity and change. She reviews the way that indigenous peoples promptly learned the new model of alphabetical literacy brought from Europe and began recording and transcribing their pictographical and oral sources to fit into the new history. She identifies covert and overt traditions that differentiated writing intended for use within the communities from writing for the scrutiny of strangers. Karttunen stresses that both traditions contain strands of continuity *and* change, and she also notes that the self-conscious work of "being Indian" has carried on to the present and can be identified in costumes and performances (434). James Lockhart goes further by asserting that the nobility of central Mexican Indian towns, in particular, were often fluent in Spanish and had an ample understanding of the configuration of Spanish colonial society and government: "The many documents left by this group bespeak a full comprehension of Spanish legal and religious concepts and procedures" (*Nahuas and Spaniards* 40). It is evident that although *macehuales* (commoners) had access to some Spanish institutions and successfully achieved some of their goals, the elite learned to move about in this arena rapidly and comfortably.

Peter Guardino makes us aware of our biases about "ethnic others" and how we usually paint a generalized picture of communities where culture does not change. He adds that indigenous subjects themselves "encourage this belief when they often justify cultural practices and even the possession of particular resources as originating in a past too distant to remember" (*The Time of Liberty* 11). The argument of this book aligns with Guardino's equally important point that indigenous people have adapted to the social and political structures of colonial hegemony while maintaining a certain continuity in their concept of Indian identity.

Scholars have subtly resisted the study of Indian elites and other subalterns who exhibited accommodation to the colonial system. Yanna Yannakakis refers to this phenomenon, explaining that because colonialism was so exploitative and violent, open resistance was usually portrayed in heroic terms, whereas native accommodation appeared as part of a process of transculturation. The author adds that the social history of the past thirty years and the almost century-old tradition of *indigenismo*, which values the culture of natives in the Americas, have had conflicting consequences—promoting invaluable original research on indigenous peoples but, at the same time, marginalizing certain groups and aspects of these peoples. Referring to native intermediaries, Yannakakis observes that "at best, scholars have perceived them as enigmatic, but more often they have portrayed them as social climbers, tragic figures, power seekers, and lesser partners in the colonial enterprise" (5).

The Indianness of the cacica nuns is usually contested, having been indoctrinated into the Catholic faith and used Spanish language and genres in their communication. As mentioned earlier, they were not the first to draw from a European humanistic tradition in order to legitimize their aristocratic standing vis-à-vis ecclesiastical institutions. As in the earlier cases of Fernando de Alva Ixtlilxóchitl in Mexico and Felipe Guaman Poma de Ayala in Peru, indigenous nuns in New Spain experienced the transculturation of the "contact zone" and chose to engage with European language and discursive formations (Pratt 7). Rolena Adorno has demonstrated that ecclesiastical rhetoric, namely, the literature of religious conversion, sermons, and catechisms, provided the noble Indian class with methods of articulation that allowed them to successfully cross cultural barriers (*Guaman Poma* 57).

This book seeks to explore the hybrid places within the colonial order where these nuns maneuvered. As Carolyn Dean and Dana Leibsohn argue, cultural hybridity should be understood as an obvious subaltern strategy for coping with dominating cultures (24). The dimension of the term "hybridity" emphasized here is that of the space (imagined and real) created by colonial subjects to buttress their identity, recovering a historical memory of their shared past with elements they have embraced from the colonizing European culture. They recreated, integrated, and interpreted all these elements to survive colonial domination.

Building on the notion of a colonial indigenous identity, we can begin to grasp the insertion of the remote Christian and Indian past in the *informaciones* compiled about the candidates entering the Convent of Corpus Christi.[24] Of particular interest are two women who became professed nuns. Both declared with great pride that they were descendents of the Indian seer Juan Diego. Gertrudis de Torres y Vásquez was not only the daughter of caciques from Xochitlan but a descendent of Juan Diego, and Doña María Antonia de Escalona y Rosas "quinta nieta del Venerable Venturoso Indio Juan Diego a quien el año de 1531 se apareció Nuestra Señora de Guadalupe" ("fifth granddaughter of the venerable and fortunate Indian Juan Diego, to whom in the year 1531 appeared Our Lady of Guadalupe"; *Gaceta de México*, qtd. in González Fernández 218).

Although indigenous nuns spoke through written genres available to them in the conventual arena, I contend that their eighteenth-century discourse of ethnic pride can be traced back to the earliest historiographical recreations of indigenous identity such as those authored by Domingo Francisco de San Antón Muñón Chimalpahin and Fernando de Alva Ixtlilxóchitl. The creation of hybrid spaces where Indian elites reinvent themselves and the kinds of discourses used for this purpose can be found over the *longue durée*. These pages will not trace this continuity in detail or the way it changed over time, but it is important to acknowledge its existence.

Gender, Race, and Ethnicity

The conceptual categories of ethnicity, race, and gender have evolved in almost parallel ways in historical studies of the past two decades, arriving at a very similar understanding of their existence in colonial life. Key works by Louise Burkhart and Susan Kellogg demonstrate that indigenous women in central Mexico before the Spanish arrival responded to a pattern of gender parallelism and complementarity.[25] That pattern collapsed with the Spanish arrival, and although women maintained their domestic roles as mothers, wives, and daughters, they lost power and authority (Kellogg, *Weaving* 63). This interpretation of indigenous women's lives pre- and post-conquest has been revised in recent times for essentializing both the alleged pre-conquest agency women possessed and their post-conquest complete loss of power with the establishment of Spanish patriarchalism. Karen Vieira Powers has criticized the paradigm that feminist historians have set forth of the "Indian woman as victim" (10). Karen Graubart, dialoguing with Powers, responds that scholars "continue to concentrate upon indigenous women as a marginal community, which they surely were, despite the gains of some" (6). Nancy van Deusen, proving even more provocative, asks: "Has gender complementarity become a tool of analytic fixity rather than flexibility?" (146).

Recent scholarship has shown the fluid and mutable nature of gender relationships, but for the most part, the paradigm of victimization and pre-conquest complementarity has remained the central model of scholarship. A good example of how this paradigm has shifted, however, can be found in the fashioning of the figure of Malintzin (Malinche or doña Marina). Camilla Townsend reviews how Malintzin went from being considered a traitor in the first half of the twentieth century to a victim and then a survivor in the 1970s and 80s. Townsend refers to this noblewoman who served Cortés as a translator and negotiator as someone with the "ability to maneuver for a number of years," someone who learned to use the tools in her reach to keep herself afloat under the most difficult of circumstances (8). Even earlier historical works on indigenous women foreshadow that space where Indian women brought into play the rhetorical apparatus of colonial power.[26] Although it has been contended that indigenous women's power was largely mediated by men and that indigenous women did not leave written records of their life experiences,[27] in other outlets of agency, academics can and have identified glimpses of their active role in forging colonial society. Elite indigenous women were more likely to challenge the paradigm of victims. These noblewomen maintained their place in society to a certain degree yet found the means to reconceptualize it to fit the New World order and did so in surprisingly creative ways.

Important scholarly contributions on indigenous women have shown the informal and transgressive ways in which these women challenged colonial hegemony through witchcraft and healing.[28] Other scholars have identified how indigenous women participated in the public arena in formal ways and through more orthodox paths. For instance, Robert Haskett show-cases Josefina María Francisca, a widowed cacica from Tepoztlán, as a very aggressive political activist, and Ronald Spores demonstrates that Mixtec cacicas were "equal in rank to their brothers and husbands and succeeded to their titles in their own right" ("Mixteca Cacicas" 195). Donald Chipman has studied how Isabel and Mariana Moctezuma were two of the most unusual cases of *encomenderas* in sixteenth-century New Spain,[29] and Edward Osowski has analyzed the participation of Ana Ventura Gómez, a member of the indigenous elite, as an alms collector for her community of devotees of Our Lady of Loreto. Lois McNay explores the concepts of gender, identity, and agency, stating that a revised understanding of gender identity does not consider it simply imposed through patriarchal structures "but as a set of norms that are lived and transformed in the embodied practices of men and women" (13). All these studies are useful for clarifying the ways in which indigenous women managed to have access to power without necessarily subverting the established order. By using legal and religious outlets, they were able to accommodate and re-create their indigenous identities as women and as members of the elite class. This book builds on the work that these and other scholars are producing to understand the participation of indigenous women in the colonial socio-political structure and the ways they challenged and at times supported ideologies of difference.

The ethnic diversity found in New Spain, coupled with the hierarchical system established by the imperial mentality of the colonizers, stimulated scholars to think about these categories in terms of racial nomenclature. In the 1980s scholars contributed to a better understanding of what seemed to be a group of racial categories linked to a system of social stratification.[30] In the following decades, studies adding the class component made it evident that these categories are merely constructs that "cut across other classificatory systems, notably those of class, estate, occupation, and culture" (Cahill 326). Douglas Cope shows not only that colonial society, particularly in urban areas, was stratified ethnically but also that social difference, which did not necessarily coincide with ethnic divisions, was put into place by a nascent plebeian class. He also argues that ethnic identification was not fixed and that it was a component in the constitution of social identity (5).

Although scholars have been cautious when using the term "race" to refer to the caste system or the classificatory division of social structure in the colony, recent awareness of it as a negatively charged term has made it difficult to justify its use without some sort of explanation of the term's origin. Kathryn Burns makes apparent how this term implying such fixity is in itself unstable. She invites scholars to historicize racial usage to better understand the term in early modern times and our own ("Unfixing Race" 189).

The Castilian politics of discrimination established with the events surrounding the expulsion of Jews and Moors from the Iberian Peninsula at the end of the fifteenth century was defined in terms of purity of Christian practice. What began as an initiative to regulate orthodox Christian belief became a matter of inheritance.[31] The ideology rooted in the concept of limpieza de sangre (purity of blood) was transported to the New World, where the ethnic variant was not the immediate reason for implementing the ideology of difference. The Crown and the Church worked together in justifying the salvation of souls, but the newly converted Indians did not have and could not possibly inherit pure Christian blood. The implementation of the "coloniality of power" illustrates how there was no loophole. People's ethnic or social self-identification meant little; in the new colonial order, they all became "Indians."[32]

The obvious relation between later emphasis on phenotype and seemingly biological explanations for this discrimination foreshadows nineteenth- and twentieth-century racism. We can almost never escape the temptation of implicating our contemporary notions of race when reading colonial difference. But the colonial ideology of difference resided in yet another concept, that of *calidad* (quality). Magali Carrera explains that this notion, found in numerous documents from the eighteenth century, refers to "skin color but also often encompassed, more important, occupation, wealth, purity of blood, honor, integrity, and place of origin" (6). In chapters 4 and 6, I will show how indigenous nobles rapidly learned this kind of discourse and adapted it to their particular needs and circumstances. The preservation of their lineage and consequent purity of *Indian* blood allowed them to make reference to and defend their calidad by using colonial constructions of ethnic difference.

A recent contribution to the study of colonial identities is Andrew Fisher and Matthew O'Hara's *Imperial Subjects*. Their book was the logical next step in the intellectual development of the categories of difference in the academic terrain. Fisher and O'Hara's introduction reviews the way scholars have thought about racial and ethnic categories in the colonial period and the way they have acknowledged and begun to study the participation of subalterns in the construction of their own identities.[33] They support a more nuanced view of identity formation that recognizes the existence of a multiplicity of constituencies in one person's identity, as well as a hybrid space where most subalterns move about. The authors admit that although the question of identity seems to be a personal inquiry, it also carries a political dimension that in this particular case is intrinsically conceived within Iberian imperialism (2).

This work relies heavily on their terminology, especially their conceptualization of "colonial ideologies of difference." The authors admit that the analytical categories of ethnicity and identity are imperfect tools; however, for my purposes, I find these appropriate and preferable to the use of "race," which has proven to be an artificial construct, as much as the stereotyped definitions related to it. "Ethnicity" here refers to the way people identify as members of a group who share a common heritage, which can be real or imagined. The focus of my study is on the fashioning of Indian identity as an ethnic construction through religious discourse. More specifically, it will not delve into the constitution of the nun's personal identity but rather the social identity of the group representing itself in the many discursive manifestations that subsist.

Methods

Drawing from the subfield of conventual writing within literary studies but embedded in a dialogue with historians who study the political, social, and cultural participation of indigenous women, this research analyzes the different genres produced in convents. From those texts, we can begin to understand the relationships established between priests and nuns and how, despite their subalternity, these women were active, viable members of the Church hierarchy.

This book contributes to the body of works dedicated to the analysis of colonial discourse and, more specifically, to the religious realm of eighteenth-century Spanish America.[34] The study of colonial discourse, particularly how it is understood today in the context of Latin American studies, is influenced in large part by methodological considerations brought to bear in the 1980s. Rolena Adorno, Walter Mignolo, and other academics coined the term "colonial discourse" as a substitute for the notion of literature, which no longer met the needs of colonial studies because it was limited to the processes of Eurocentric writings; the term "discourse," on the other hand, considers many voices previously unheard (Adorno, "Nuevas perspectivas" 11). In addition to examining marginalized textualities, Mignolo proposed studying iconography, textiles, maps, etc., a process he called colonial semiosis ("Afterword" 335). Then came the call for a paradigm shift in colonial studies: not only incorporating into the canon previously ignored discursive materials but also reading them in a different way. This scholarly quest for the decolonization of the field continues today.[35]

My research focuses on the dimension of colonial discourse that bears the authoritative enunciation and articulation of knowledge, moving from text to discourse as it establishes itself in society, history, and, ultimately, the structure of power. The notion of colonial discourse that will become apparent in the pages to come is one in which the alleged understanding of the "Other" and the power that colonial Church authorities assume are distributed through their discursive practices. Postcolonial criticism and its concurrence with subaltern studies provide certain analytical tools that shed light on the discourse imposed by Spanish colonial rule and help us rethink the "knowledge and social identities authorized by colonial domination" (Prakash, "Subaltern Studies" 1475).

Gayatri Spivak problematizes the representation of the subaltern subject in Western discourse and points out a prevailing inability to capture that subject's voice. She proposes a limiting definition of subaltern that would easily annul many of the indigenous subjects who have left a written record in Latin America. According to Spivak, elites, considered eminently privileged, would not count as the "ideal subaltern" (284). If that were the case, however, the majority of subalterns would fall beyond the scope of our research. Gyan Prakash, much as Spivak does, ponders the impossibility of preserving the feminine voice when women have not even been given a place as historical subjects. Still, according to Prakash, that should not keep the histories of the subaltern from being written ("Subaltern Studies" 1488).

The context of the early modern and colonial Hispanic world presents an alternate situation to the one suggested by Prakash. The past few decades have seen the creation of a new subfield in colonial studies, an area Kathleen Myers calls conventual writing.[36] The first important works about religious women written by Asunción Lavrin and Josefina Muriel in the 1960s coincided with feminist politics and academic interest in writing a history of women. In the 1980s the discovery of key documents written by women allowed a new space for research and analysis where the boundaries between history and literature blurred. Colonial studies have since aimed for interdisciplinary scholarship. Pivotal works published in the 1990s, such as Jean Franco's *Plotting Women* and Electa Arenal and Stacey Schlau's *Untold Sisters*, added to previous research on conventual writings in historical studies and further enriched textual analyses with historical, literary, and artistic contextualization.

Those studies revealed that the Catholic Church, by encouraging women to use certain traditional written genres (such as spiritual autobiography, hagiographic biography, etc.) and employ certain kinds of rhetoric to express themselves, ensured the creation of a written record. However, most of those writings belonged to white, socially privileged women whose confessors required they examine their own lives and write about them (Myers, *Neither Saints* 4). The indigenous nuns were of noble families and thus belonged to the elite, yet they were doubly alienated—for their ethnicity and their sex—within the colonial and patriarchal Spanish system, underscoring how important it is that texts written by them even exist.

The discursive construction of the colonial subject required the articulation of racial and sexual differences. By constructing subjects as lesser beings because of their race, colonial discourse attempted to justify the conquest itself, as well as the subsequent administrative and educational systems established to maintain colonial control (Bhabha, *The Location* 70). These are not transparent discourses but rather constructed textualities that made use of the processes of representation and language imposed by the colonial system. My research in this book does not focus solely on the few texts of indigenous authorship that exist but on a series of discourses, including sermons, letters, and official documents, that emerged not just within but also outside convent walls.

The Catholic Church system in Latin America was one of the most powerful bodies in the viceroyalty. Its power was disseminated through the production of discourses that came to heavily influence the organization of society. The discourses were fostered in the structure of monastic life, wherein resided a large portion of the criollo population, or simply dispensed from the pulpit and through evangelization. Religious discourses varied over the years. Evangelical missions became less necessary, and more men and women were accepted into monasteries and convents. Devotional literature was one of the most important forms of religious colonial discourse, along with catechisms, sermons, and the life stories of saints. These were the kinds of texts first made available by the printing presses established in New Spain in 1535 and in Peru in 1582 (Myers, *Neither Saints* 3).

My research here studies the formal organization of religious discourses into specific genres. By examining certain textual genres in the religious context, we can expand the definitions and limitations of the ideology of difference in colonial society. For example, by delivering a sermon in a public arena about an exemplary nun, priests called for spiritual and ideological conformity and enforced the dominance of a learned male elite. The biography and the letter were accessible to both men and women, although access was markedly different for each. The nuns wrote about their own lives and experiences or about the lives of other nuns in the convent, all at the behest of their male confessors. The texts were then altered by the confessor and sometimes transformed into hagiographic biographies published and circulated in colonial society. Nuns communicated privately and personally with church authorities through the letter, whose formal dictates allowed them to express their spiritual concerns or address problems experienced in the convent.

I intend to demonstrate that the most salient difference between texts produced by men and by women is their space of circulation: men's works belonged to the public space; women's works, to the private. Yet the spiritual autobiographies and hagiographic biographies written by nuns who believed they were writing within the private space could move into the public space when rewritten by priests. That fact would have influenced the style of these genres. A nun who authored the biography of one of her companions might not have expected her writing to be published exactly as written, but she would nevertheless have used a certain style and rhetoric that aspired to meet the societal demands of a colonial/patriarchal system.

In this study, "genre" is defined as a discourse that has its basis in a specific rhetoric. The classification of discourses of the colonial period presupposes a configuration that differs from those in use since the nineteenth century. The characteristics that define these discourses and allow them to be grouped together depend on a shared rhetoric, derived from Renaissance adaptations of classical rhetoric. Another important characteristic here is the clear relationship that exists between motive and effect, promoting discourse that becomes a form of social action (Miller 25). In "Genre, Intertextuality, and Social Power," Charles Briggs and Richard Bauman explain that discourse becomes genre when its structure, form, function, and meaning are identified (146), and even more critical is their observation that genre "pertains crucially to negotiations of identity and power" (148). Through discourses formally organized into genres, we can appreciate and study relationships of social power, manifest in this particular case in the microcosm of conventual life.

This study does not pretend to be conclusive but hopes rather to invite further lines of historical and literary investigation. The very existence of convents built exclusively for indigenous women leads us to wonder about their role in establishing the European Church in America. Was it the indigenous nuns who symbolically established the practices of Catholic religion in Mexico? Were the convents for indigenous women local expressions of Catholicism? Regarding cultural and social issues, were the ethnic alliances established in a cloister stronger or weaker than gender alliances? And is it possible that we might find other kinds of cultural material that will yield information about the discursive production of indigenous women in the colonial era?

Responses to these questions will shed light on the lives of the indigenous women, confessors, and colonial officials involved in the distinctive conventual experience in eighteenth-century New Spain and enlighten further readings of material of this nature. My larger aim is to make available texts thought to be inexistent and to let these materials speak for themselves by placing them in their cultural, social, and historical context.

Studying Religious Women in Mexico

Much of what we know today about the history of the Convent of Corpus Christi in Mexico City, we owe to the work of Josefina Muriel, who published the only manuscript believed to have survived from the convent, entitled *Las indias caciques de Corpus Christi* (The Indian Noblewomen of Corpus Christi) in 1963. That same year, Asunción Lavrin filed her doctoral dissertation on eighteenth-century Mexican convents. One chapter presents the history of the founding of Corpus Christi and the subsequent problems brought on by the ideology of the time.[37] Lavrin's scholarship has been fundamental in laying the foundation for most recent studies of female conventual culture in Spanish America. Less well known than the work of these two pioneering historians is that of Ann Miriam Gallagher, a nun who wrote her doctoral dissertation in 1972 on the family lineages of the nuns of Corpus Christi and of Santa Clara in Querétaro.[38]

In addition, Elisa Sampson Vera Tudela has studied how indigenous nuns were portrayed in testimonies in which priests gave their opinions about opening convents for noble indigenous women. Mariselle Meléndez examines the process of building racial identity in the *Apuntes de las indias caciques*, the original title of the manuscript published by Josefina Muriel. A similar study by María Justina Sarabia Viejo draws on materials from the General Archive of the Indies in Seville, Spain.[39]

Conventual writing has become accepted as an interdisciplinary field. Valuable contributions in the area of history—such as the works of Muriel and Lavrin—have advanced our overall knowledge of women's religious life in Latin America and the importance of convents. In recent years, works by Manuel Ramos Medina about the Carmelites and by Jacqueline Holler on the founding of sixteenth-century Mexican convents, as well as a study by Margaret Chowning on the Convent of La Purísima Concepción in San Miguel de Allende, are examples of the kind of analytical scrutiny historians are applying in order to contextualize convent life.[40] In the same vein, Kathryn Burns's *Colonial Habits*, which deals with the spiritual economy of various convents in Cuzco, Peru, has special relevance for this study because it analyzes issues of race and gender within the cloister. According to Burns, the indigenous noblewomen of Peru were accepted into convents as nuns as soon as these institutions were introduced and founded in the first years of colonial life, a stark contrast from convents in Mexico, where indigenous women were not admitted as nuns until 1724. Vows notwithstanding, however, the daughters of elected Quechua officials were relegated to the lowest levels of the conventual hierarchy because of their ethnicity, similar to the policy in Mexican convents, where indigenous women could live and serve only as servants.

The contributions of literary scholars to the subfield of conventual writing have focused for the most part on the types of rhetoric used by nuns and female lay religious in convents and the women's relationships with their confessors and spiritual directors. The many works of Kathleen Myers, a pioneer in this field, have established a theoretical and methodological basis for the close reading of conventual writings. In her book *Word from New Spain*, she offers one of the first definitions of the kind of feminine conventual writing known as *cuenta de conciencia* or *relación de espíritu* (2). This genre attests to the fact that the textual production of nuns did not stem solely from an actual impulse to write but also from the request of their confessors or spiritual directors, particularly in the case of a mystic nun.

Gender relationships, then, acquire a special place in the study of these texts, establishing clear parallels with the writing of colonial nuns who often took Teresa of Ávila as their model. It became popular to call nuns' confessional writings *vidas* (lives), mirroring Teresa's masterpiece, *Libro de la vida*, even when the texts did not take an autobiographical form and were only confessions, accounts of mystical experiences, or other specific events having to do with conventual life.[41]

Other important literary contributions in the area of convent studies include Kristine Ibsen's work on spiritual autobiography in Latin America, Kathryn Joy McKnight's work on the writings of Colombian nun María Josefa del Castillo, Kathleen Myers and Amanda Powell's study of María de San José, Jennifer Eich's study of María Anna Águeda de San Ignacio, and Stephanie Kirk's study of nuns' alliances in the conventual community. There is also Kathleen Myers's latest book, *Neither Saints Nor Sinners*, in which she analyzes the religious practices that informed the different kinds of rhetoric evident in confessional autobiographies and hagiographic biographies, and their role in the construction of the identity of six women in seventeenth-century Spanish America.[42]

In this relatively new field of study, however, the connection between ethnic identification and textual production has not yet been developed. Marginalized groups remain unrepresented—not just indigenous women but also African and mulatta women who were affected by religious institutions during colonial times. A closer analysis of the formation of discursive genres is also needed. Even though the relationship between nuns and their confessors has been studied, we have not explored in depth the correlation between the gender of writing subjects and the discourses employed in their writing, the crucial relationship between the kind of discursive genre employed and the politics of difference that affected its use. This book seeks to address that void by examining these issues as manifest in discourses produced in the convents established for indigenous women in colonial Mexico.

The first chapter, "Indigenous Nobility and Conventual Foundations," considers the historical development of the *cacicazgo* (chieftainship) in New Spain and the concept of ethnic identity put into practice with the opening and defense of the convents exclusively for indigenous women. The chapter is based mostly on ethno-histories dedicated to the evolution of the cacicazgo and the relationship of the Catholic Church to indigenous cultures during and after the time of the conquest. It addresses the manner in which the eighteenth-century cacicazgo was forged and the features that allowed for the existence of a discourse of ethnic identification that prevailed in the negotiation of conventual spaces for noble Indian women.

The second chapter, "The Idea of Corpus Christi: Discursive Effects of Colonialism," is concerned with the construction and dissemination of the colonial ideology of difference through religious discourse in New Spain. Special emphasis is given to the moment when the first convent for indigenous women was proposed. The chapter analyzes testimonies of the Jesuits and Franciscans for the Audiencia of Mexico, showing their support for or opposition to the opening of the convent for indigenous women.[43] It also studies some hagiographic narratives supporting the cause when the proposal was debated publicly in Mexico. From a close reading of various testimonies, reports, and other documentation produced prior to the foundation of the Convent of Corpus Christi, it is evident that gendered and racial constructions of colonial subjects are highly malleable. In the ideology of difference, contrasting opinions can be found about the same indigenous women who aspired to become nuns. Those discursive constructions of female indigenous subjectivities were later used by the nuns themselves to defend the ethnic autonomy of their cloisters.

"Indigenous Women and Religious Life: Stereotype and Ambivalence," the third chapter, examines documentation produced between 1724, when the Convent of Corpus Christi opened its doors, and 1762, when a hagiographic biography was published suggesting that noble Indian women could enter a *beaterio* (lay congregation) instead of a convent. This chapter continues with an analysis of discursive constructions of ethnically different and gendered subjectivities found in the foundational sermon preached at the Convent of Corpus Christi, in hagiographic biographies, and in the documents sent to the Council of the Indies. It considers, for example, the prevalence of the concepts of *miserables* (wretched) and *pobres* (poor) in the definition of indigenous peoples; as well as the accusations that indigenous nuns sent to the Council of the Indies, decrying the fact that the Franciscan government had admitted Spaniards to the convent and denied the veil to indigenous women.

The fourth chapter, "Biographies and Hagiographies: The Different Perspectives of Gender," brings together the study of the construction of ethnicity and gender in religious colonial discourse and compares a manuscript first published by Josefina Muriel that was composed by a priest, possibly a confessor of the nuns, and the original manuscript that was composed by the nuns themselves. This chapter is pivotal because it attempts to recover the voices of indigenous women, in spite of the difficulties of reading a highly mediated text. The female indigenous writers used rhetorical devices available to all religious women writers in Spain and its colonies in order to accommodate and resist patriarchal control in matters of ethnic exclusivity.

Chapter 5, entitled "Panegyric Sermons: Dialogic Spaces and Examples of Virtue," focuses on sermons, which readily reveal the relationships linking gender, religion, and society. Sermons were intended for public performance in which three spheres overlapped: secular society, church authorities, and nuns. This chapter analyzes funeral eulogies preached for three founding nuns, two from the Convent of Corpus Christi and one from the convent in Oaxaca. The former were Spanish and the latter, Indian. These sermons offer an alternate construction of the women's identities, following the conventions of religious literature of the time. The chapter also includes an analysis of the founding sermon preached for the opening of the Convent of Nuestra Señora de Cosamaloapan in Valladolid in 1737, preached by the Jesuit Juan Uvaldo de Anguita. Such sermons were delivered not just for the nuns but also for the public who participated in celebrations and funerals.

Chapter 6, "Letters from the Convent: Struggles through the Written Word," analyzes the epistolary production that originated in the Convent of Cosamaloapan in Morelia. In that convent, as in Corpus Christi, criolla nuns were admitted even though it had been established exclusively for noble Indian women. Through an exchange of letters, we glimpse the struggles created in the convent by the presence of the Spanish women. This chapter helps us understand how power relationships were established and challenged through the writing of letters, and how nuns used elements of classical rhetoric so that their petitions could be heard at the highest levels of the ecclesiastical hierarchy. They finally obtained what they sought when the Spanish nuns were evicted from the convent, leaving the Indians with a convent of their own.

In the Epilogue, I offer some reflections on the two main issues that prevailed in the various religious discourses analyzed in this research: first, the survival of an Indian identity recast in Catholic terms and through European discursive genres, and second, the change and continuity inherent in the conceptualization of identity that indigenous communities pursued through their use of colonial constructions of difference. I also consider the ways Indian noblewomen actively participated in defending the conventual spaces granted to them at a key historical moment, when Bourbon policies required the secularization of indigenous parishes. The participation of these women in conventual life in eighteenth-century New Spain shows the cohesive identity that existed for noble indigenous peoples and its close relation to religious practices. This analysis seeks to reveal the discursive interaction between genders and ethnic groups, and how women altered and on occasion used the discursive constructions of difference originally created by male ecclesiastics to maintain a social hierarchy that would bring order to New Spain.

1

Indigenous Nobility and Conventual Foundations

A prevailing notion about the Spanish colonial system of New Spain is that the entire indigenous population succumbed to the hegemonic power imposed after the conquest. In fact, there was a certain segment of indigenous society who enjoyed privileged status among the general population from early on: the nobility. The indigenous nobles, whom the Spaniards called caciques, maintained a special position of power during the sixteenth century, functioning as intermediaries between colonizers and colonized from the very beginning of the process of conquest and colony. In some cases, they were even allied with the Spanish in armed conquests.[1] As reward for their loyalty and collaboration, the Indian nobility were allowed to transfer their pre-Hispanic titles of nobility to the new colonial order, and they sometimes acquired a new series of privileges that distanced them somewhat from the macehuales.[2] Nonetheless, the colonizers were sure to establish a clear social difference between the early Spanish population and all Indians, regardless of their class.

Although indigenous nobles were quick to adopt certain cultural traits that made them seem "Hispanicized" by the end of the sixteenth century, such as religious practices, dress, and language, the colonial discourse produced in New Spain continued to place them in an inferior social position. This dynamic, sustained by the ideology of colonial discrimination, was one of the driving forces in the forging of an Indian identity vis-à-vis the Spanish colonizer. The cultural adaptation of European practices and customs was not enough to eradicate the indigenous consciousness, which continued to function as a bonding agent for the group. Textual discourse produced by noble Indians, in which ethnic pride is evident, challenges the erroneous assertion that the indigenous nobility lost their ethnic identity in the wake of alliances and favors obtained from the Spanish Crown. This discussion, along with an examination of the historical background of the convents founded for indigenous women in colonial Mexico, will serve as a point of departure for a closer look at the nature of the Indian identity of the noblewomen who entered the convent and that of their families.

Caciques and Principales

Charles Gibson distinguishes between two indigenous groups of the elite class, the *tlatoque* and the *pipiltin*.[3] The caciques were the "señores naturales" (natural lords) of indigenous society, and they were, in fact, the heirs of the tlatoque from before the conquest. The principales were the relatives of the caciques or the heirs of the pipiltin (155). James Lockhart agrees with Gibson that there was a difference in the terms cacique and principal, observing that early in the colony, *cacique* was equivalent to *tlatoani* and *principal* to *pipiltin*, but with time the Spanish increasingly generalized the use of the term *principal* to refer to an important person without a noble rank: "The Spaniards were mainly concerned with rulers and lords as figures of authority, not with nobles or nobility as such" (Lockhart, *The Nahuas* 133).

This common practice of differentiating between the caciques and the principales, which according to Lockhart seemed to be of interest only to the indigenous people, becomes evident in a document housed in the Luis Castañeda Guzmán Archive in Oaxaca regarding the opening of the cloister for cacicas, the Convent of Corpus Christi in Mexico City. It is an undated, loose sheet that conveys the existence of a distinction between the terms *principal* and *noble* regarding their admission as candidates to the convent:

> El [Exe] Patrón y fundador de este convento de Corpus Christi requiere en las que en el han de ser recibidas y se les ha de vestir el santo hábito pues dice sean nobles o principales de la pobre nación de los Naturales y no siendo como no es lo mismo noble que principal porque ambas cosas son diversas . . . se debe notar que no se requieren las dos cosas juntas en las que han de tomar el santo hábito Esto es, que sean nobles y principales pues basta lo uno o lo otro. (n. pag.)

> (The most excellent benefactor and founder of this convent of Corpus Christi requires that the women who would be received into the convent and who would don the holy habit state whether they are nobles or principales of the poor nation of Naturales, since it is not the same

thing to be noble as to be principal because both things are different
. . . it should be noted that those about to take the holy habit will not
be required to be both; that is to say, it is enough that they be either
nobles or principales, one or the other.)

The caciques, referred to in this document as nobles, were defined as the
legitimate descendants of those who governed in pre-Hispanic times, those
who early on were the equivalent of the Spanish ranks of duke, marquis, or
count. On the other hand, the principales, the descendants of pre-Hispanic
nobility, were equated with *hidalgos* or *caballeros* (Katzew 43). Although the
indigenous nobility clearly upheld a difference between one term and the
other, according to Gibson, for some of the Spaniards the overlapping
usage between the two was generalized.

While the indigenous people accepted the definition of nobility that
the Spanish bestowed on them in colonial times, they did not reject its pre-
Hispanic connotation. There is evidence that until the eighteenth century
and even into the beginning of the nineteenth, the practice of preserving
their lineage continued, including the purity of bloodline that allowed them
to continue demonstrating their legitimacy as nobles.[4] Another important
reason for caciques to continue guarding their lineage was their interest
in conserving their territorial rights in the newly established repúblicas
de indios.[5] Moreover, as the indigenous elite had been the primary focus
for the teaching efforts of the first missionaries, the nobility had learned to
transcribe and translate the oral and pictographical tradition of their past
into the written form, developing a literature and a history in their own
language that permitted them to maintain their cultural and social identity.
As David Brading notes: "Nowhere was the defense of cultural identity
more obvious and successful than in the attempt to retrieve the historical
record" (*First America* 117).

For the Spaniards, the social system of the indigenous people, organized into social classes much like those of European society, was not difficult to understand. However, the colonizers, who eschewed the traditional
names indigenous people used, translated indigenous names into Spanish
(implying a Christian status) and transferred connotations of Spanish systems to indigenous cacicazgo. An example of this would be the considerations brought to bear on the cacicazgo as an institution equal to the
Spanish *mayorazgo* (entailed estate) (Menegus 15).

The Crown was clearly interested in protecting the status of indigenous nobles and in granting them privileges, favors, and goods. The Spanish
colonial system based itself on the pre-established native American order

without bothering much about its origins; it was clear that it could not survive without these important intermediaries, on whom the task of collecting taxes and maintaining order and obedience to the colonial power fell (Gruzinski 64). Their role as intermediaries and their close relation to Spanish officials have yielded the image of an acculturated people, when in reality the Indian elites owed their place in the social hierarchy to the rest of the Indian population who legitimized their power. Because of this ethnic loyalty, they preserved their Indian identity throughout the colonial period.

Charles Gibson asserts that over time, the caciques and principales became Hispanicized culturally while maintaining their status as privileged indigenous people (156). This opinion emerges from his study of their apparent use of Hispanic cultural markers: these two indigenous groups had the right to dress in Spanish styles, display their coat of arms, and ride on horseback; they were also exempt from paying taxes.[6] Jonathan Israel describes the class tension that the alleged Hispanization of indigenous nobles may have caused, given that the macehuales or lower classes likely did not hold this group of privileged indigenous people in high regard, an argument based on considerable evidence suggesting they were "domineering and even corrupt" (44). Israel invokes a stereotyped image of caciques, however, without considering how "native intermediaries bound native pueblos to the colonial state and its right arm, the Catholic Church" (Yannakakis 11). Rodolfo Pastor, using the example of the Mixteca, claims that although the caciques even in precolonial times were no longer regarded as "señores todopoderosos" (all-powerful lords), they still "reclamaban un legítimo liderazgo como autoridades étnicas, con el peso de una tradición todavía viva." (They still "claimed a legitimate leadership role as ethnic authorities, with the weight of a living tradition"; 307).

Until recently, the prevailing position on the cacicazgo was one recovered from research on sixteenth-century Indian elites in which caciques were depicted as the "vanishing nobility" (Chance, "Indian Elites" 46).[7] The focus of this pioneering scholarship on cacicazgo was its relationship to land tenure, as well as its political and economic dimensions, but little concern was shown for the process of identity construction.[8] In the past thirty years, however, research on Indian elites has significantly changed this picture. Ethnohistorians have shifted their attention to the eighteenth century, proving that Indian elites continued to occupy an important place in Indian communities and that the cacicazgo institution changed with time and varied from one region to another (Chance, "Indian Elites" 45).

Cacicazgo in New Spain

The volume edited by Margarita Menegus Bornemann and Rodolfo Aguirre Salvador is a notable effort to develop a more complete understanding of the cacicazgo as a colonial institution and to revise earlier arguments put forth by specialists on the subject. It begins by noting the negative effects of the traditional historiography on cacicazgo, which tended to define the cacicazgo institution through property, leaving out other sorts of income such as tribute, personal service, and *terrazgo* (land holdings). It also mentions the need to refocus attention on the way estates and assets were handed down and on those who inherited the rents of an estate. Lastly, the authors emphasize the negative effect of Charles Gibson's conclusions about the cacicazgo as a declining institution throughout the colony and the ultimate separation between the cacique and his position of governance (17).

The cacicazgos did not remain static during the three centuries of the colony. Until the seventeenth century they were held together with singular strength, and in cases in which the caciques started to lose their rights to their lands, it often was due to a failure to produce heirs, the death of direct successors, or usurpation (Spores, "Mixtec Cacicas" 187). Rodolfo Aguirre Salvador notes that it is understandable for Gibson to have mistakenly supported the notion of a declining cacicazgo because of early scholarly efforts to equate the power of the cacique with that of the pre-Hispanic tlatoani, which we now recognize as erroneous. It is critical, he asserts, to acknowledge the ability of the colonial caciques to articulate their power position within the new Hispanic structures (88). This more recent development in the study of cacicazgos does not deny the existence of some Hispanicized and poor caciques in the eighteenth century. Rather, it means that we need to delve much deeper into the broad panorama of the cacicazgo to define its tendencies in the eighteenth and nineteenth centuries (Aguirre Salvador 89).

Laura Machuca, in her study on the cacicazgo in Tehuantepec, claims that the great cacicazgos of the Mixteca survived thanks to the absence of Spanish haciendas, but she adds that although cacicazgos survived well into the nineteenth century, their nature was very different from the ones conceived in the sixteenth century (167). For his part, Aguirre Salvador explains that we can observe a strengthening of the cacicazgo in regions that underwent a demographic and economic recuperation after the Bourbon politics of the eighteenth century. A case in point would be the cacicazgo of Panoaya, created in one of the ancient *señoríos* (lordship) of Amecameca (105).

In order to have an accurate idea of the cacicazgo, its evolution and nuances, Menegus contends that we must understand the entire array of possibilities present in colonial Mexico. To begin with, the Hispanic concept of nobility could be of two kinds: by blood or by privilege. The first pertained to one's lineage; the second was created at the will of the monarch to reward merits and services performed on behalf of the Crown (36). There were caciques who defended their ancient rights and the patrimonial lands inherited from their forefathers, and those who acquired material assets and privileges in return for services rendered to the Crown. It should be noted that the cacicazgo took on different characteristics in each region, depending not only on the variations of pre-Hispanic customs but also on the presence of colonial representatives in each region (54).

Based on the information yielded by recent studies dedicated to the cacicazgo, we can conclude that, contrary to what was previously thought, cacicazgos still existed in the eighteenth century. Society held a clear concept of the institution, especially in the case of those conceived as colonial cacicazgos, and even when not all cacicazgos maintained a link to the power of the pre-Hispanic past, they did in fact possess an ethnic pride that set them apart from the rest of the population. This ethnic pride maintained by indigenous nobility had an impact on the conceptualization of Indian identity. The importance indigenous nobles ascribed to maintaining the purity of their bloodlines is closely tied to the system of land inheritance, since the cacicazgo system of inheritance followed a pattern of direct-line succession (Muriel, *Las indias caciques* 32).

Indian Solidarity

The existence of cloisters exclusively for Indian noblewomen debunks the commonly held idea that by the eighteenth century caciques and principales had lost their indigenous ethnic identity through transculturation and their noble lineage through intermarriage outside their ethnic group. Indeed, the candidates and their families showed great pride in identifying themselves as Indians and in displaying and demonstrating their noble lineage in legal and religious documents.

Scholars have argued that the colonizers were intent on maintaining the indigenous people as a subordinate class, condemned by their "indianidad" (Indianness) to remain subjects of the Crown and to occupy certain economic roles such as rural producers, merchants, or artisans in urban centers.[9] The system of *castas*, institutionalized in Mexico City by the mid-seventeenth century and reaching maturity between 1660 and

1720, propagated notions of racial difference that distinguished the Spanish from the rest of the population (Katzew 42–43). But although categories of difference and discrimination existed in the political discourse as a way to establish "order," these discourses had little impact on the way people moved about in the colonial space.

Douglas Cope refers to the Hispanization of Indians, arguing that although the caciques completed this process much more rapidly than the macehuales, the macehuales were not exempt from that influence. Acculturation, according to Cope, happened at all levels of the social scale, especially in cases where the indigenous people had more contact with the Spanish population. Indigenous people who worked in the república de españoles developed patron-client relationships, which pressured them to adopt Hispanic cultural markers like clothing, bearing, and speech. That kind of cultural adaptation was closely related to the urban center in Hispanic society and economy (55). The conditions of transculturation manifested themselves in very different ways in the rural areas, where indigenous people found themselves more isolated from the Spaniards. Still, there were cases in which Indians and castas from these areas adopted Spanish cultural markers. The adoption of cultural traits, however, did not seem to affect their identification with their ethnic group, and they were successful in keeping an Indian identity.

As a matter of daily practice, racial determinants for the most part were ignored, and the majority of the people were guided by social attributes. Although in theory a clear ethnic hierarchy existed in colonial Mexico, it was not so in practice. The social reality in New Spain in the eighteenth century was the result of a variety of economic factors. Starting in 1650 with the establishment of the hacienda as a dominant rural institution, the bilingualism of indigenous people grew more generalized. Indeed, various ethnohistorical studies on ethno-racial relationships in the colony provide a nuanced picture of the kinds of alliances established among colonial subjects. Two issues become apparent: first, there was an Indian identity shared by people of different pueblos but whose colonized condition promoted solidarity regardless of class. And second, there was also solidarity of class among plebeian Indians and castas from the urban centers who moved continuously between the two repúblicas. In the case of the convents for indigenous women, we can glimpse the existence of a consciousness that is not purely class based. Rather this consciousness owed its formation to a broad Indian solidarity preceded by class oppression and divorced from any "tribal" allegiance but which clearly existed in opposition to Spanish colonial officials (Knight 123).

The concept of calidad (quality) appeared frequently in eighteenth-century documentation, merged with the rhetoric of purity of blood (*pureza de sangre*) (Carrera 6). The convents first founded in the Americas for daughters of colonizers and later for criollas required proof of purity of blood in the women's informaciones—that is, that they were free of Jewish or Moorish blood—and their witnesses usually made reference to their family's calidad as well. The same standard of purity of blood was adapted for the monasteries for indigenous noblewomen in New Spain, where the candidates had to prove purity of blood, but in this case, it had to be purely Indian (Gallagher, "The Family Background" xiii).

The notions of lineage and calidad adapted from the Iberian context and put into effect in the first years of the colony for the indigenous nobility set in motion the creation of a discourse of ethnic identification that promoted group cohesion. The caciques and principales did not openly resist the racial categorization and separation imposed by the colonial order. On the contrary, they created a hybrid space in which they re-created their historical past and felt pride in their indigenous noble lineage. Based on her work on the *Crónica mexicana*, a text written by Indian noble Hernando Alvarado Tezozomoc, Rocío Cortés offers an explanation for the ability of indigenous groups to adapt and adopt elements of the new culture in the pre-Hispanic conception of the cosmos they knew. Cortés argues that the native Mesoamerican cosmovision focused on a constant transformation of the cosmos, which gave different ethnic groups the flexibility to integrate, appropriate, and adjust cultural and religious practices (69). This may very well be a factor that allowed indigenous people to quickly and efficiently understand and appropriate elements of European ideology for their own purposes.

The indigenous nobles and principales maintained their ethnic pride and cohesive identity by preserving the cacicazgo institution until the end of the colonial period.[10] However, the meaning that these colonial subjects conferred on their ethnic identity remains largely misunderstood by scholars.[11] Given the forcefulness with which colonial hegemony was instituted, it is commonly expected that the Amerindian intermediaries, to whom certain powers had been granted, would resist the system openly. In any case, the indigenous noble class did resist Spanish colonization from within that very system, displaying high levels of adaptation while at the same time accentuating the difference between themselves and the Spanish and criollos. The study of the convents for Indian noblewomen nuns offers a clear example of this phenomenon.

The occupations of the parents of the cacica candidates were included in the informaciones. In some cases, losses of land properties and political status are recorded, while others affirm the preservation of the cacique and principal as figures of power and social privilege. Josefina Muriel reports that of the 58 caciques whose occupation is mentioned, 48.2 percent of them still held authoritative positions, such as governor, mayor, *fiscal*, and town councillor, and 51.5 percent were artisans, laborers, farmers, and merchants (*Las indias caciques* 31).

The group of caciques and principales related to the cacica nuns viewed itself even in the eighteenth century as a social elite with distinct cultural markers. Nevertheless, it continued to occupy a subordinated position in the larger colonial scheme established with the conquest and propagated over the years through an ideology of difference. When some of the ecclesiastical officials allowed criolla nuns into the convents founded exclusively for indigenous women, the discursive dispute that gave rise to the nun's epistolary production and other official documentation was constructed using the rhetoric of a solid Indian identity. The Hispanicized cultural qualities the Indian nuns used, particularly those conferred by the Catholic religion, did not make them less Indian. Their ability to integrate the Hispano-colonial culture did not erase the ethnic awareness their social class had bestowed on them. Héctor Díaz-Polanco explains that the ethnic identity of the indigenous groups in Mexico allowed the group not just to define itself as indigenous but also to establish difference or contrast with respect to other groups (qtd. in Soriano 81). When engaging in religious discourse production, the group of Indian nuns had forgone pre-Hispanic religious practices and beliefs, as well as their native language, but they maintained with the rest of the Indian population the bonds of solidarity of their shared history and colonial subjugation.[12]

Indigenous People and Catholicism

One of the main concerns of the Crown was establishing its religious hegemony in American territories through the presence of missionaries charged with the evangelization of the "infidels." Missionaries, like the rest of the conquistadors, buttressed the class difference found among Amerindians by distinguishing the nobles from the macehuales. The children of the Indian aristocracy were treated differently and with special care as future leaders of the territory (Ricard 98). The Crown's initial interest in teaching the Catholic religion, the Castilian language, and the main European arts to the first generation of Indian nobles produced a generation of bicultural and bilingual youths with great intellectual ability in New Spain.[13] Perhaps due to their pedagogical success and the colonial official's fear of creating a powerful indigenous intellectual class, the schools dedicated to this undertaking were closed a few years later, redirecting their teaching efforts to the new population of criollos and Spaniards who continued to immigrate to the New World.

There was a keen interest in teaching noblewomen the principles of Catholic religion by virtue of their social status, but they did not have the opportunity to be educated in the same way as their male counterparts, mainly due to the Spanish gender ideology transferred to American territory.[14] In the *Historia de los indios de la Nueva España* by Fray Toribio Motolinía, we find the Indian nobles described as examples of perfection due to their rapid conversion: "Las hijas de los señores, se recogieron en muchas provincias de esta Nueva España, y se pusieron so la disciplina de mujeres devotas españolas, que para el efecto de tan santa obra envió la Emperatriz" ("The daughters of the lords were gathered from many provinces of this New Spain, and they placed themselves under the discipline of the devout Spanish women, which was the holy work the Queen had sent them to do"; García Icazbalceta 225). Motolinía stresses how these girls learned to be Christians and to live according to Catholic teachings, adding that their future was not to become nuns or to be consecrated in the religion, but to get married.

Although indigenous peoples were excluded from participating in priesthood and conventual life for most of the colonial period, their participation in other religious outlets, such as confraternities and brotherhoods, was significant. Their involvement in the churches of the república de indios is also worth noting. In the community, the main religious official, a *fiscal*, acted as assistant to the priest and handled the finances of the church and part of the religious instruction. Another official was charged with the choir and with preparing the music for masses and festivals. A woman could hold the position of *cihuatepixqui*, the "guardiana de mujeres" (guardian of the women), who was supposed to make certain that all the girls and women attended religious services (Burkhart, *Holy Wednesday* 81).

For two centuries, Indian women were not able to participate fully in convent life as professed nuns and could only enter the convents as servants. There was a singular exception in 1606 when a cacique gathered support to found a convent where his daughter Luisa could profess as a black-veiled nun. Diego de Tapia was the son of Captain General Don Fernando de Tapia, an Otomí cacique from Querétaro who had helped with the pacification of the Chichimeca and Otomí Indians during the conquest, earning his coat of arms and the title of captain general. He also became the owner of a number of gold and silver mines and large expanses of land in San Luis

Potosí and Querétaro. With the support of the Franciscan Provincial Fray Miguel López, Diego de Tapia succeeded in founding the Convent of Santa Clara de Jesús, where the first cacica took the nun's habit. No other Indian woman was ever accepted there as a novice throughout the long history of the convent; only criollas were admitted (Gallagher, "The Family Background" 78). It was not until 1724, when the first foundation for indigenous women was agreed upon, that Indian noblewomen could enter a cloister as novices and eventually take the veil.

Some of the Bourbon reforms of the eighteenth century were directed at restructuring monastic life. There was an attempt to reform the way of life within the convents, particularly the most relaxed, which were known as convents of *vida privada* (private life) because of their extravagance and luxurious ways.[15] Although many clergymen, especially Archbishop Francisco Antonio de Lorenzana, supported the king's reformation initiatives, the ensuing discontent was so great that these types of convents were allowed to continue to function, especially if they had been conceived as convents of private life since their inception (Gallagher, "The Family Background" 63).[16] Yet new establishments founded in the eighteenth century adhered to much stricter religious orders, the discalced. These followed the *vida común* (common life) detailed in the First Rule of Saint Claire, the rule that all convents for indigenous women had to follow. Conventual life in the eighteenth century ceased the steady growth it had experienced in the previous century. Even so, at the beginning of the nineteenth century in New Spain, there were nearly 2,400 religious women living in convents, and roughly 900 nuns in Mexico City alone (Socolow 93).

The archival work conducted by Sister Ann Miriam Gallagher in the Convent of Corpus Christi in Mexico City yielded important information about the origins of some of the families of noble Indian nuns in New Spain living in the convent. Between 1724 and 1775 ninety-five nuns were admitted into Corpus Christi, and seventy-four eventually professed there. Of that number, 79 percent belonged to the Diocese of Mexico and were mainly from the barrios of San Juan Tenochtitlán (26) and Santiago Tlatelolco (12). There were also nuns whose families came from Puebla de los Ángeles, Oaxaca, Michoacán, and Guadalajara ("The Family Background" 152–53). Concerning their lineage, eighty-four of the nuns declared that both parents were caciques. Two nuns had fathers who were caciques and mothers who were principales, and there were four more whose mother and father both were principales (158). Gallagher explains that they proved their nobility by mentioning they were exempt from paying taxes or by presenting copies of their titles of nobility. Some nuns claimed to be descendants of Moctezuma, others of the kings of Tlaxcala, and others of King Chimalpopoca; some nuns identified the origin of their family's cacicazgos in the contribution of their ancestors to the pacification wars (159).[17]

In trying to ascertain the reasons the indigenous nuns could have had for entering the Convent of Corpus Christi, Gallagher found that the mothers of eleven of the nuns had died before they went into the convent, the fathers of twenty other nuns had died, and another seven had been orphaned before entering the convent. Gallagher also considered to what degree having other family members who were priests or nuns had influenced a candidate's decision. Twenty-three nuns reported having relatives who were priests. Three acknowledged uncles who were priests, and some said their brothers were. Fifteen percent of the ninety-one nuns had sisters or aunts in the convent who were nuns (173–174).

Josefina Muriel described the activities of nuns in the Convent of Corpus Christi, who were of a contemplative order and dedicated themselves mainly to prayer: "Sin embargo en las horas de labor que exige la regla, las monjas se empleaban en bordar ornamentos, frontales, cortinas y otros objetos" ("However, in the hours of labor that the conventual Rule demanded, the nuns occupied themselves with embroidering accessories, frontlets, curtains, and other objects"; *Conventos de monjas* 244). In the biographical manuscript *Las indias caciques de Corpus Christi*, there are references to the daily activities of the nuns, although framed in the hagiographic style. The narrative of Sor Magdalena de Jesús recounts that "a prima noche, se iba al coro, en donde permanecía hasta que venían las religiosas a media noche a rezar los maitines, los que concluidos, seguía ella en los ejercicios de su oración hasta prima, sin tomar más descanso" ("At nightfall, she would go to the choir, where she would remain until the nuns would come at midnight to pray matins, and when that was concluded, she would continue with her exercises of prayer until sunrise, without any more rest"; Muriel 271). The same nun would also leave after matins, go to the orchard, and carry a very heavy cross, enacting the Way of the Cross.

The *Suma manual de las ceremonias que deben observar las señoras religiosas descalzas del convento de Corpus Christi* (Essential Manual of the Rituals to be Observed by the Discalced Religious Women of the Convent of Corpus Christi), written for the convent in 1737, lays out the rules that must be observed "fuera y dentro" (inside and outside) of the convent. Some of the issues explained in this document concern daily life inside the cloister, including the application of discipline, the order to be maintained when the nuns left the choir, and the acts of penitence that should be practiced, such as living on nothing but bread and water, kissing the feet of the entire community of sisters, or maintaining permanent silence. The manual explains that "éste es todo el ser de las religiosas, pues mientras menos hablaren estarán más quietas sus conciencias, pues el desmedido desorden en la lengua no acarrea mas que vicios e imperfecciones y continuos escándalos" ("This is the core of religious life, as the less they speak the more at ease their consciences will be, since the unchecked running of the tongue causes nothing more than vices and imperfections and constant scandals"; Seoz 38).

The guidebook also reviews the most solemn occasions, like the rites for the dead, the method of assisting sung Masses, and how and when to prostrate themselves: "Estas acciones son dirigidas de la verdadera humildad la cual nos trae al verdadero conocimiento de los que somos para que en todas nuestras acciones seamos muy humildes y rendido como lo debemos ser: éstas se hacen hasta llegar a tocar con la cabeza o la frente a nuestro primer origen que es la tierra" ("These deeds are directed by true humility which brings us to the true understanding of who we are, so that in all our actions we may be humble and surrender as we should: this is done by touching the head or forehead to our first origin, which is the earth"; 10).

With regard to prostrations, it mentions that "se hacen siempre que la prelada corrigiere, esto es, mientras esta en culpas la religiosa, que no se levantan hasta acabada la corrección que entonces se mandará levante; mas si la Prelada quiere mortificarla la puede dejar postrada todo el tiempo que quisiere para mayor mérito de la religiosa y ejemplo de las demás" ("They are always done when the abbess chastises, that is, when the nun is at fault, and she should not rise until the reprimand is completed and she is told to rise; but if the abbess wishes to mortify her further, she can leave her prostrated as long as she wishes for the greater good of the nun and as an example for the others"; 10). This document allows a glimpse of daily activities inside the convent and exemplifies the kind of prescriptive literature produced for religious feminine communities by male clerics. This kind of document exemplifies the degree of conformity that religious authorities required from their spiritual daughters, who in this case were to be their colonial subjects as well. The *Suma* tells us more about what was expected from the community of nuns, however, than what actually happened behind cloister walls. In this manual we can perceive the discursive structures used by the Church to "contain and control convent communities" (Kirk 14).[18]

The Convent of Corpus Christi was subject to the Franciscan Order and followed the First Rule of Saint Claire, the same one followed in the Convent of San Juan de la Penitencia, where some of the indigenous women who later entered Corpus Christi resided as servants (Muriel, *Conventos* 194). But the nuns in the Convent of Corpus Christi were not allowed to have servants or slaves. While the Indian nuns were under Franciscan jurisdiction and would have followed the same rule as the other three discalced convents that already existed in Mexico where servants were indeed allowed, ecclesiastical authorities specified that the Indian noblewomen could not admit servants into their convent. Although a foundation for Indians was finally established, the ideology of difference remained. Through subtle acts, like prohibiting servants, and a considerable display of discourses, colonial officials made it clear that even if indigenous women were allowed to be nuns, they were not equal to Spanish women. The Convent of Corpus Christi was established exclusively for the women of the indigenous nobility, but despite their noble class, they were expected to follow a life of stricter poverty, obedience, and prayer.

Conventual foundations in New Spain mirrored the hierarchical social structure imposed by the colonial order. When female foundations were open for Spaniards and criollas, Indians and members of the castas were admitted in the convents to fulfill the lowest position on the conventual social scale: they were servants or slaves. Many Indian girls entered the convent to receive an education but were relegated to positions of servitude. Later in the eighteenth century when Indian women were allowed to profess as nuns, it was decided that they could not do so in the convents that already existed for criolla and Spanish women. The Convent of Corpus Christi and subsequent convents for Indians functioned in a fashion similar to that of the repúblicas de indios; that is, the colonial system created a unique space for them based on ethnic difference, which according to the colonial mentality was equated with social distinction. Still, this symbolic division effected in conventual establishments would not be entirely observed.

In 1737 three priests who attended the nuns at Corpus Christi wrote a letter to the King of Spain, asking him to issue a royal decree that would expel the Spanish nuns who had been admitted into the convent by priests who doubted the Indians should have a convent of their own. They maintained that the presence of Spanish nuns prevented peace in the convent and based their letter on the following argument:

> La real sangre de sus ascendientes que con tanto amor ardimiento y lealtad abrazaron nuestra fe católica luego que el glorioso Hernán Cortés Marqués del Valle se la manifestó y dio a entender dejando olvidada la doctrina que profesaban por que clara y distintamente conocieron era falsa y sólo creyeron la de Jesucristo. (AGN, Reales Cédulas, vol. 52, fol. 21)

(The royal blood of their ancestors who with so much love, bravery and loyalty embraced our Catholic faith when the glorious Hernan Cortes, Marquis del Valle, introduced it to them and helped them understand it, leaving behind the beliefs that they had followed, because they clearly and distinctly knew it to be false and they only believed in Jesus Christ.)

The priests who defended the cacicas in this document fell back on the past history of the conquest and recalled the testimonies of the missionaries who had declared, as in the case of Motolinía, that the noble girls had had the easiest time embracing the Christian faith. When it became necessary to defend the spiritual integrity of the indigenous women in the cloister, they reverted to the first images created by the missionaries in which the nobility were given special status for their role in the propagation of the faith throughout the Indian republics.

In various documents, Carlos de Sigüenza y Góngora, one of the most influential criollo intellectuals of the seventeenth century, defended the nature of indigenous women as entirely suited for the Catholic religion. In a 1684 document entitled "Noticias de las vestales mexicanas" (News of the Mexican Virgins), Sigüenza y Góngora tries to construct an indigenous past preceding Christian religion that can be explained in the same ortho-dox terms. In this text he speaks of women who were cloistered and lived a life of humility and chastity during the Aztec empire. The women in this group were trained to be priestesses of some sort, yet Sigüenza y Góngora describes these virginal women using conventual imagery and language, even calling the places where they were confined "convents": "Desde este punto, sin que se hiciese reparo en su edad, comenzaba la rigurosa vida, que allí se hacía reducida a un perpetuo ayuno. . . . Su cotidiano ejercicio (des-pués que se desocupaban en el espiritual que adelante diré) era según lo había prevenido la superiora, hilar y tejer las mantas necesarias para el ves-tuario de los sacerdote" ("From this point, without concern for their age, they began a rigorous life which from there on was reduced to a perpetual fasting. . . . Their daily routine (after they completed their spiritual obliga-tions, which I will speak of later) was, as their superior had directed, sewing and weaving the coverings needed for the clothing of the priests"; AGN, Historia, vol. 14, fol. 154).

It becomes apparent that the language and activities of the priest-esses are presented in terms related to monastic life. Sigüenza y Góngora refers to one of the priestesses with the most experience and authority as the "superiora," as if she occupied the highest position of authority within the convent. In the same vein, the activities of the indigenous women related in the narrative are similar to those of many nuns inside the colonial cloister.

Another argument put forth in the Audiencia in the early eighteenth century by the ecclesiastical authorities who supported the indigenous women becoming nuns was that they would serve as an example for the rest of the indigenous population and, in that way, propagate the "true" religion among them: "En concederles separadamente y sin intervención de españolas un convento, o monasterio en que pudieran hacer vida penitente y ejercitarse en devotos ministerios para que a su ejemplo todos los de su nación abracen con más fervor nuestra fe católica" ("In granting them a separate convent without the intervention of Spanish women, or a monastery in which they could live a life of penitence and practice devout ministries so that by their example all the people of their nation could embrace our Catholic faith with more fervor"; AGN, Reales Cédulas, vol. 52, fol. 20). The isolation of the Indian women was seen as protection from the vices of Spaniards, who would not allow them to live a life of perfection, just as the Franciscans missionaries had argued for the separation of the repúblicas. According to the great majority of their defenders, the indigenous nuns were to function as advocates of their pueblos who would demonstrate that Indians were suited for religion and whose prayers would aid in the salvation of the rest of the indigenous population.

Final Considerations

Not all the caciques and principales who were granted benefits during the sixteenth century experienced the same economic and social advantages throughout the colony in New Spain. Their privileged role in the indigenous population faded as the years passed, and by the eighteenth century the social differences in indigenous society were minor. The most important aspect of conserving the tradition of the cacicazgo was the ethnic consciousness maintained by the indigenous groups who either were descended from the ancient tlatoque and their relatives or who had obtained a colonial cacicazgo by means of their loyalty. In any case, the Indian identity and cohesive meaning accorded their belonging to an ethnic lineage became evident in the opening of convents for Indian noblewomen. In addition, the possible erosion of social difference among indigenous people brought them closer to their origins and helped forge their ethnic identity, in opposition to the dominant groups.

Nuns and their families adopted and reinvented the aspect of difference imposed by the colonial system. Their ethnic identity did not respond to the hierarchical system of castas but rather involved the group's perception and definition of the terms "Indian" and "noble."[19] The group of indigenous women who lived in the three convents founded for them maintained a clear Indian identity regardless of the level of Hispanization they had acquired. Belonging to an ethnic group is a question of attitudes, perceptions, and feelings through which one identifies oneself with one group or another. An ethnic community can share a historical memory, cultural elements, and a sense of solidarity, among other characteristics (Anthony Smith 20–21). When the Indian nuns saw the ethnic autonomy of their cloister affected, they were quick to articulate their difference through discourse. Those nuns who engaged in religious discourse presented an Indian identity that reinforced some of the stereotypes of colonial discourse by defining themselves clearly in opposition to the Spanish nuns.

The perception we have acquired of the cacicazgos as antecedents of present-day political bosses has obscured our appreciation of these native intermediaries. The preservation of their noble lineage was tied to economic interests and social prestige, but when the native autonomy of the convent was threatened, the indigenous women defended it using the very tools the colonial system had given them. The historical separation in distinct republics where ecclesiastical authorities catered differently to Indians and Spaniards—and the special role that Indian elites fulfilled as intermediaries between their people and colonial officials—allowed them to forge an Indian identity. Contrary to what some scholars have believed, the caciques and principales developed solidarity with the rest of the Indian population rather than Spanish elites, at least in ideological terms. The Indian nuns used the same language of the colonial Church to differentiate them from the Spaniards, this time to defend the space conferred to them. The indigenous nobility learned to use rhetorical strategies in the early days of the colony, when they had to appeal to colonial officials in order to legitimize their power. The Indian nuns were skilled communicators; they appealed to the Crown using the same rhetoric of difference that had supported the isolation of indigenous populations in their own pueblos. This time, they used the colonizer's rhetorical weapons to their advantage.

The Idea of Corpus Christi

Discursive Effects of Colonialism

Colonizers identified differences between themselves and the people they conquered in the Americas, establishing a system of power that entailed maintaining the supremacy of knowledge.[1] The drive for power led them to produce discourses, such as the one used for their evangelization missions, through which indigenous peoples were viewed as Others. In discrediting the epistemological system sustained by the native cultures of the New World before the conquest, the colonizers granted themselves the authority to govern and institutionalize a colonial system of domination over the native population.[2] Although this ideological hegemony appeared to be a singular entity, the production of discourses was not monolithic and responded to the interests of the various colonizing factions on the continent. It is important to note that the colonial subjects themselves participated in this process, at times as agents and at other times as of discourse.

The idea of opening a convent for indigenous women in Mexico during the eighteenth century unleashed an immense production of representations of the women involved, not all of which affirmed the ideology of difference disseminated by the colonial system. The contradictions that existed paved the way for women to use discourse to exercise autonomous ethnic authority years later in those same convents. A convent for indigenous women was highly controversial in colonial society, especially in religious circles and with those who doubted the intellectual and spiritual abilities of native women. The groundwork for opposition originated in the theological debate that arose when the colonizers had to define the conquered Other. Although a generalized consensus of opinion about natives already existed toward the end of the sixteenth century, debate emerged again before the Corpus Christi convent opened its doors, when the idea of a cloister for indigenous women was just an unfulfilled possibility.

Baltasar de Zúñiga, Marquis of Valero and Viceroy of New Spain (1716–1722), proposed to the Crown a convent for Indian women of the noble class. The Audiencia, the City Council of Mexico, and the Council of the Indies conducted the required investigation prior to approving the idea. All the priests and nuns asked to testify came from the San Pablo, San José de los Naturales, Santa María la Redonda, Santiago Tlatelolco, San Sebastián, Santa Cruz, and Soledad parishes located in the indigenous sector of Mexico City. Priests who testified were from the Franciscan and Jesuit orders. Even though some important Jesuit figures in the eighteenth century defended the rights of indigenous men and women to participate in the Church, the proposed Convent of Corpus Christi encountered clear opposition from other Jesuits at that time.[3] Written testimonials remaining from the investigation that preceded the opening of the convent permit us to appreciate the clear diversity of opinion expressed by the two religious orders.[4] The debate, which arose in 1723 and continued strenuously for a number of years, reveals how Spanish colonists viewed the socio-racial category of Indian and its weight when deciding whether native women had the abilities to participate in conventual life.

Colonial religious discourses produced ambivalent spaces of difference. The Spanish Church, by using diverse discursive strategies (such as ambivalence, stereotypes, and hybridity) to single out the Indians as different, actually created tools for resistance, which in turn affirmed the indigenous people's ethnic consciousness and allowed them to defend their autonomy, as much as possible, from the colonization of which they were already subjects. Through a number of documents that illustrate the tensions of the theological debate in eighteenth-century New Spain, I will illustrate the complexities of defining an inferior Other while demonstrating the indigenous woman's capacity for participation in the Catholic faith.

Homi Bhabha, in a critical analysis of the work of Charles Grant (1792), warns that, with respect to the evangelization efforts in India, the colonizers produced a knowledge of Christianity that was used as a tool for social control, which provoked a kind of hollow mimicry obligating the subjects of the imperial order to continue under its protection (*The Location* 87). The social conformity required for participation in a religious community represents the kind of control to which hegemonic systems have recourse. Even more interesting is the concept of hollow mimicry that Bhabha notes, inherent in the discursive construction of the colonized.

This does not mean that mimesis of religious practice on the part of indigenous nuns was unreflective. Rather, it means that colonial discourse about indigenous nuns—as in the case of testimonials, sermons, and hagiographic biographies—conveyed images that copied the European model because they had to imitate the norm, even while deviating from it just enough to be able to justify colonial control and the hierarchical order that placed Indians and Africans in the lowest place in society. This effect of colonial discourse is evident in all the materials analyzed throughout this book.

The Discourse of Difference and the Missionary Undertaking

By the mid-seventeenth century the imperial order in America instituted a caste system made up for the most part of invisible divisions supported by the colonial mentality. As Walter Mignolo explains, the justification for appropriating land and exploiting indigenous workers in the colonial process required the ideological construction of racism (*The Idea of Latin America* 15). The invention of a classificatory system, considered analogous to that of nineteenth-century race conceptualization, constituted for the Europeans of the sixteenth century a revelation of the differences that existed between themselves and Others. Mignolo states that this notion of discrimination gelled in seeing those differences and deciding that not being like Europeans automatically made Others inferior (17). The concepts of race and ethnicity were joined in this systematic discrimination, which came to a head during colonization and was affirmed by the practices that Catholicism brought to these conquered lands, although this discrimination became more nuanced in the years that followed.

For the colonizers, ethnic differences boiled down to binary issues. The classification of Indian thus bore an inherently negative connotation with regard to social and cultural difference. Those who exhibited certain cultural or physical characteristics were specifically defined as Indian and were allowed to move only within certain spaces like the república de indios. The conventual space was not one in which indigenous people could move about until the eighteenth century. The issue of accepting indigenous women as nuns and equal members of the Catholic Church community was a quandary that created bitter conflicts for all parties involved.

The Catholic Church was instrumental in the conquest and colonization of America, in addition to playing a leading role in establishing Spanish culture on the newly discovered continent. In 1933 historian Robert Ricard coined the term "spiritual conquest" to define the clergy's

participation in the conquest of America. This concept has been challenged for its falsely monolithic sense of the religious conquest of native
groups, portraying the evangelization process as uniform, rapid, and complete. Conflicting reports of informants make apparent the disconnect
between the political agenda of missionary religious orders and the actual
results of evangelization. While sources produced by friars tend to be
highly optimistic about the results obtained just a few years after establishing the colonial system in Mexico, information provided by the censuses
shows more clearly the way in which Christianity was imposed on the
native population of New Spain.[5] Jorge Klor de Alva explains that the
missionaries' optimism was a phenomenon generated by the disposition
of Nahua Indians toward adopting elements of Catholic teachings in their
own spiritual repertoire (174).

The first Franciscans arrived in Mexico in 1524, followed by the
Dominicans in 1526 and the Augustinians in 1533. These regular religious
orders had obtained a special papal bull known as the *Omnimoda*, which
granted them extraordinary apostolic powers quite different from those
they held in Europe. In addition to their missionary functions, they could
administer the sacraments, a privilege that would eventually cause rivalries
with the arrival of secular priests in the New World. The Christianizing
fervor that the first Franciscans presented to the indigenous people, as well
as their ethnographic interest in educating themselves in indigenous languages and cultures, was a response to an ancient vision of the Abbot
Joaquín de Fiore (1145?–1202), a mystical prophet who divided human history into three ages. De Fiore's third age was his version of the millennial
kingdom of the Apocalypse, which for many coincided with the discovery
of the New World (Phelan 14). Viviana Díaz Balsera explains that according to Franciscan discourse, those final years would be "an era of freedom,
of love, of childlike simplicity, when the Holy Spirit would confer *plenitudo
intellectis* (full understanding) with which humankind would be able to see
truth without mediations or substitutions" (164).

The missionary friars charged with the conversion of the indigenous
population dedicated themselves to defining the new subjects of the Spanish Crown and the Catholic Church, establishing the natives as different
from themselves and the rest of Spanish society. For example, Fray Gerónimo de Mendieta wrote that the Indians made up the best race in the world
because they were already humble, innocent, and simple, yet he added that
"por su docilidad, infantilismo y apocamiento distan mucho de ser los amos
de este mundo, pero sin duda serán como son, los señores del orbe celestial"
("Because of their docility, their childlike nature and their timidity, they are

far from being the masters of this world, but without doubt, being as they are, they will be lords of the celestial realm"; qtd. in González y González 84). The portrayal of Indians as children is a common theme, one repeated often in religious chronicles, especially in those of the Franciscan Order. According to Luis González y González, Fray Gerónimo de Mendieta did not exclude indigenous people from being priests because he believed they held a secondary position in Christianity; rather, he considered the Sacrament of Holy Ordination unnecessary for them because their purity was already sufficient to achieve Holy Ordination in the next world.

Just a decade after Spain had gained military control of the original inhabitants of Mexico, debate arose over the indigenous people and their relationship with the Catholic Church. In 1536 the Colegio de Santa Cruz de Tlatelolco was founded for the education of noble indigenous men. The Colegio had several goals, such as making secular Catholics of young indigenous men, training them as translators, and ultimately ordaining them as priests. Martin Austin Nesvig believes the Franciscans adopted the indigenous education model of the *calmecac*.[6] The aim of the Colegio de Santa Cruz de Tlatelolco, however, was to educate and shape these young men as future priests, not restore them to society, the goal of the calmecac (77). Louise Burkhart explains that the education of the indigenous elite in this college gave them an advantageous position due to their knowledge of Spanish and Latin, as well as Nahuatl. They also learned to reason with both Western and Nahua logic, allowing them to build arguments based on the rhetorical arts of the West and the Nahua alike (*Holy Wednesday* 59).

By 1537 Pope Paul III had issued the bull *Sublimis Deus*, which established the humanity, reason, and liberty of indigenous people (Rivera 5). In 1539 the *Junta Apostólica* declared that the better educated Indians and mestizos could be admitted into the four minor religious orders, laying the groundwork for future ordination, and in 1543 the Franciscan Alfonso de Castro wrote a treatise defending the education and ordination of indigenous people.[7] Nevertheless, by the First Provincial Council of 1555, we see a sharp reversal of opinion, and indigenous people are again portrayed as weak and fickle, with a natural inclination toward vice.

Although the clergy, and in particular the first Franciscan missionaries, initially considered indigenous peoples capable of becoming Christians and of converting completely to Spanish customs, their position shifted, marking a setback in the advances gained in the first years of colonization. Specific circumstances encouraged this change of opinion. Stafford Poole explains that half a century of war, slavery, culture shock, epidemics, and economic hardships had left the indigenous population in a deplorable state, all of which contributed to a cycle in which the Spanish blamed the Indians themselves for their miserable condition: "It is an eternal situation with oppressed minorities that the oppressors blame the oppression on the natural flaws of the oppressed" (15).

Jorge Klor de Alva argues that the Church's change in attitude toward the Indians stemmed from problems the friars had to confront since the second half of the sixteenth century, when their privileges granted by the Vatican in the first years of the conquest were questioned. At the same time, there was a clear shrinking of the indigenous population and growth of the Spanish and mestizo populations, along with a clear indifference and resistance of indigenous peoples to many teachings of the Church (174).

The arrival of secular priests who demanded spiritual control of the people caused an internal rift in the Church as an institution, leading Archbishop Alonso de Montúfar, with the support of the Dominicans, to prohibit ordaining Indians as priests in 1565. By 1570 the Colegio de Santa Cruz de Tlatelolco, which had concentrated on the education of noble indigenous men, closed its doors. There were clearly contrasting Church opinions concerning the development of Indians in religious matters. The restraints set on ordaining indigenous men as priests lasted only until the Third Mexican Council in 1585, whose documents do not, however, openly promote Indian ordination but rather recommend "great caution" in admitting Indians, mestizos, and mulattos into the priesthood (Poole, "Church Law" 644). Interestingly, the Third Provincial Council at the same time proclaimed all Indians "neophytes in the faith" and validated the paternalistic treatment of indigenous peoples for their coarseness and limited capacity ("gente ruda y de poca capacidad") (Llaguno 117).[8]

In 1574 the Spanish Crown enacted the *Ordenanzas del Patronazgo*, a series of decrees meant to limit the parochial obligations of the regular clergy and support secular priests, thereby increasing the Crown's absolute power over the entire ecclesiastical system. The king had power over the diocesan hierarchy but not over the mendicant religious orders. Once the regular clergy were under the control of the archbishop, they automatically came under the power of the Spanish Crown. In spite of that, it would be two centuries before the complete secularization of all rural parishes (Schwaller 254).[9] The close relationship being forged between political and religious powers in the colony is evident in these Crown initiatives. Bishop Juan de Palafox y Mendoza (1640–1655) subsequently secularized all the *doctrinas* (Indian parishes) in Puebla de los Ángeles. The secularization of the remaining Indian parishes administered by religious orders would begin in 1749 with the institutionalization of the Bourbon reforms.

Indigenous communities interpreted the secularization of the doctrinas in their own way. Matthew O'Hara indicates that "important Indian leaders suggested that secularization offered an opportunity to develop a robust Indian clergy to replace the outgoing mendicants" (*A Flock Divided* 58). Native leaders also proposed the opening of convents for elite Indian women. Spanish officials opposed the opening of a religious center exclusively for the sons of the Indian elite, however, questioning their spiritual abilities just as Indian women had been the objects of scrutiny before the cloister was agreed upon. Thus, a reading of both the discourses and the actions of the Church, as they wielded hegemonic power, reveals the way in which the imperial state tried to manipulate and redefine its colonial subjects.

The negative opinions the Church expressed regarding indigenous abilities were formulated by the population of friars, who were more vocal and had more power within the system. Yet there were also those who defended the abilities of the Indians, to the extent of declaring them equal to the Spaniards. The controversy surrounding the spiritual nature of indigenous people and how it differed from that of the Spaniards spurred animated debates during the early years of the conquest and colonization of America, disputes that would resurface in the eighteenth century with the introduction of a proposal to open a convent exclusively for indigenous women.

Convents founded in sixteenth-century Peru, unlike those in Mexico, accepted indigenous women. Kathryn Burns explains that in the eyes of the colonizers, convents acted as places that could promote the acculturation of young indigenous girls or, in the majority of the cases, the mestizas, adding that over the years it became harder to accept indigenous women into convents established for criolla women. Nevertheless, until 1713, indigenous women were still novices in the Convent of Santa Catalina, something not seen in Mexican convents. The fact that indigenous women were not allowed to be black-veiled nuns Burns views as evidence of a racial bias in the convents, but in Cuzco indigenous women were at least permitted to be novices and not just servants, as was the case in Mexican convents. Still, these Peruvian novices were not given the right to vote in conventual elections or take part in the decisions of the community. Beyond this, they were limited to the most humble positions inside the convent (125).

The ideology of gender further influenced ideas about ethnic difference. Although indigenous women were not allowed to become nuns until the eighteenth century, their participation in religious life since the inception of colonialism responded to the gender ideology transplanted from Spain. Kristine Ibsen indicates that, in Spain as much as in Spanish America, "man was associated with the soul, spirit, and reason, and woman with the body, carnality, and sinfulness" (1). In the ongoing eighteenth-century debate about the nature and qualities of indigenous women, they found themselves doubly discriminated against in the spiritual hierarchy for both their gender and their Indianness.

These cultural constructions of difference appear in both external discursive representation and self-representation. Teresa de Lauretis writes that "the sex-gender system, in short, is both a sociocultural construct and a semiotic apparatus, a system of representation which assigns meaning (identity, value, prestige, location in kinship, status in the social hierarchy, etc.) to individuals within the society" (5). The gender burden is as relevant as the ethnic one in colonial discursive representations that construct the subjectivity of indigenous women. These women, as objects in the debate among religious factions, are presented as either absolutely perfect or absolutely imperfect for religious life. Consistent with de Lauretis's argument regarding the semiotic construction of the system of sex-gender, the language found in the testimonials presented to the Audiencia concerning the suitability of indigenous women for conventual life resonate with symbolic meanings entrenched in the colonial ideology of ethnic difference and gender.

Nuns or Lay Sisters?

The contrasting arguments regarding indigenous spirituality and intellect are evident in the testimonials given by various Franciscan and Jesuit priests to support or refute the idea of opening the Convent of Corpus Christi. In *Colonial Angels*, Elisa Sampson Vera Tudela states that these testimonials were written in the hagiographic style. I contend that their style aligns even more clearly with judicial defense and specifically uses rhetoric present in forensic debates. As demonstrated by Rosa Perelmuter Pérez in the analysis of the *Respuesta a Sor Filotea de la Cruz* by Sor Juana Inés de la Cruz, these testimonials are intended as a defense illustrating an argument. The testimonials of the Jesuit and Franciscan priests about opening an indigenous convent focused on whether indigenous women were capable of being nuns and employed the structure of prelude, narration, analysis, and peroration (Perelmuter 150). The Audiencia asked those who testified to inform them of the utility and convenience of founding such a convent. In doing so, priests drew on examples of their daily exchanges with Indians of the ecclesiastical area in which they worked and lived.

An early testimonial dated 1723 and written by Antonio Gutiérrez, chaplain of the Colegio and Parish of Santiago Tlatelolco, located in one of the oldest indigenous barrios, supports indigenous women in their bid to become nuns. Gutiérrez calls them "nacionales" (from the concept *nación de indios*),[10] and when formulating his defense, he defends the women first as Indians: "Son las naturales sujetos idóneos, y capaces para entrar, y profesar en religión; porque son por su naturaleza constantes en sus propósitos, muy observantes en las tradiciones, en que las pusieron en la nueva conversión . . . viviendo como viven en el santo temor de Dios, de donde infiero: son sujetos capaces para el voto solemne de Religión" ("They are fitting native subjects, and have the ability to enter and practice the religious life; because they are by nature constant in their intentions, very observant of the traditions into which they were placed during the new conversion . . . living as they do in the holy fear of God, from which I infer: they are subjects capable of taking the solemn vow of Religion"; AGN, Historia, vol. 109, exp. 2, fol. 22). Later, Gutiérrez's defense focuses on gender: "siendo ellos buenos, son mejores ellas, por ser mas humildes, mas pobres, mas recogidas, mas trabajadoras ("if the men are good, the women are better, because they are more humble, poorer, more retiring, harder workers"; AGN, Historia, vol. 109, exp. 2, fol. 23). Gutiérrez identifies five theological requirements for taking religious vows, testing and giving evidence as to how the indigenous women met those conditions: the vow must be taken voluntarily, by a capable subject, who gives herself to God, and she must be a free subject for whom the vow would be a better choice than its opposite, matrimony.

One of the recurring arguments against indigenous women, present in the earliest debates about indigenous people and resurfacing in the eighteenth century, was their purported lack of chastity. According to Allan Greer, questions of sexual impurity were related to the violence perpetrated against subaltern women in the early days of Spanish conquest, when white men sexually abused them, a practice that continued once the colony had been established (250).[11] Colonial discourse advanced vastly different characters for indigenous and Spanish women; while the vows of poverty and humility would not be a problem for indigenous women because that was their nature, the vow of chastity could be a serious obstacle. Questions have endured about whether certain characteristics of these women were inherent in their Indianness. For example, even just a few decades ago, Sister Ann Miriam Gallagher, in her study of the Convent of Corpus Christi, states that "the Spanish and Indian temperaments were so unlike that one wonders whether a 'mixed community' would ever have succeeded," a statement that illustrates this kind of colonial legacy ("The Family Background" 95).[12]

Gallagher's opinion concurs with the ideology supported by the Franciscan Antonio Gutiérrez. Although in favor of the convent, he clearly upheld the alleged differences between the Spaniards and the Indians. Having consulted at length with various doctors about the self-restraint of indigenous women, he discovered that "they are warm by nature" (a reference to the theory of the four body humors),[13] but he also believed this would not be an obstacle to entering religious life because these are sins of the flesh for indigenous women. They even have a word for it, he explained, which is *tlatlacole*, and when they go to confession, they say: "'No lo quiera Dios que no lo he cometido, ni quiero cometer;' y así digo que aunque son de naturaleza cálida, son muy puras, y muy castas" ("'God forbid that I have committed this sin, nor do I want to commit it'; and in this way I say that although they are hot by nature, they are very pure, and very chaste"; AGN, Historia, vol. 109, exp. 2, fol. 24). The testimonial of Gutiérrez supports the opening of the Convent of Corpus Christi, asserting that many of the indigenous women who wanted to enter the convent spoke Latin better than their native language. They also all knew how to read and write, according to what Gutiérrez was told by Sor Petra de San Francisco, with whom the first candidates prepared to enter the convent and who would become its founder and abbess.

Another testimonial in favor of indigenous women becoming nuns was written by Fray Antonio Miranda, who, reducing spiritual matters to political concerns, contended that permitting indigenous women to become nuns could only bring glory to "our Catholic monarch and the Spanish nation" ("a nuestro católico monarca y nación española") because the convent would be proof of the gentle yoke of faith over a nation of barbarians (AGN, Historia, vol. 109, exp. 2, fol. 25). In other words, that which for many appeared to be an aberration and a mistake is, for Miranda, an action that does not inconvenience but instead benefits the Spaniards, one more sign of their domination over a conquered and colonized nation.

Indigenous women for their part believed that being elevated to the level of nuns in the religious hierarchy placed them in a space not of domination but of clear resistance to a system that had denied them status equal to that of Spanish and criolla women. Miranda and those who wanted Corpus Christi to open its doors were right, given that the convent itself would become an ambivalent space. Clearly, it was a means of social control over the group upon which colonial hegemony was imposed, directed at the same time at a particular class-conscious group that had maintained a certain autonomy, power, and, above all, a clear understanding of their ethnic lineage which they continued to preserve. The term *nepantla*, a word used in the sixteenth century by those who spoke Nahuatl to refer to their circumstances during the Spanish colonization, could define the situation in which the caciques and principales found themselves during the colonial era. It meant to be "in between" or "in the midst of," as illustrated by the Dominican priest Diego Durán, who wrote that the Indians told him they were still nepantla, or "en medio," meaning that they believed in God while keeping some of their old rituals and beliefs (237).

Asunción Lavrin notes that the core of the opposing arguments raised by the Jesuits of San Gregorio involved the intellectual ability and emotional readiness of Indian women for conventual life (*Brides of Christ* 258). Franciscan friars not surprisingly supported the foundation of the Convent of Corpus Christi as it was intended to be a Franciscan foundation. Yet, the reasons for the fierce opposition of the Jesuits seem less evident, particularly given that several Jesuits wrote in defense of Indians during the eighteenth century, notably the Vicar General of the Indians of New Spain, Juan Ignacio de Castorena y Ursúa, and later in that century, Francisco Javier Clavijero.

In one of the testimonies given against the foundation, the Jesuit Joseph María Guevara of the Colegio de San Gregorio explains and attempts to prove his belief that the founding of a convent would not be useful for the spiritual well-being of the souls of indigenous women. He declares that almost all the natives are unstable and change their minds constantly, adding "Lo pruebo con la experiencia que tengo: más de diez y seis años que me he ejercitado en ayudar a todos los indios de esta ciudad, y sus contornos."] ("I prove it by my own experiences with them: for more than sixteen years I have worked to help all of the Indians in this city and the surrounding area"; AGN, Historia, vol. 109, exp. 2, fol. 29). In proof of this supposed fickleness and indecisiveness, he notes that indigenous women do not last very long as servants in the convents and come and go for the most "trifling annoyance." There is irony in the proof on which Guevara relies to prevent indigenous women from advancing from the status of servants to nuns, showing that Indian women are indeed treated as inferiors, which he himself supports. He also adds that because they are short on understanding, they would only waste attempting contemplative prayer. Finally, he contends that indigenous women lack chastity.

These opposing descriptions of indigenous women—the one by Gutiérrez in favor of the foundation of the convent and the second one by

Guevara against it—reveal images of aspiring nuns at the proposed Convent of Corpus Christi that result from discursive constructions of colonial subjects. Their representation reveals a semiotic play of dissimilar meanings in two subjective and highly politicized portraits of difference.

We find yet another testimonial against establishing the convent signed by the Jesuit Alejandro Romano and dated May 20, 1723. One of his central arguments is that indigenous women are not inclined to live in a community setting, evidenced in their ancient and still extant habit of living in the mountains and on small ranches, separate from one another. Romano writes: "Siempre han conservado y conservan en gran parte su natural oposición a la vida sociable y civil" ("They have always maintained and for the most part still retain their natural opposition to a civil and sociable life"; AGN, Historia, vol. 109, exp. 2, fol. 32). Similar to other testimonials against establishing the convent, he declares that Indians lack the constancy of spirit to maintain their good intentions, and their attention span is "very short," so short, says Romano, that they cannot meditate or reflect on the truths of the faith. His final argument focuses again on the Indian women's inability to keep a vow of chastity. In summation, he argues that all the shortcomings found in indigenous people are worse in women because they are the more imperfect sex. As noted earlier, if the abilities of indigenous peoples were in doubt, indigenous women were viewed with even greater skepticism.

Two testimonials suggest that instead of establishing a convent, a *beaterio* (lay congregation) should be set up for indigenous women. Another Jesuit, Andrés García of the Colegio de San Gregorio, basing his opinion on experience gained during ten years of spiritual ministry to the Indians, states that indigenous women lack the necessary virtue of constancy and are not suited for community life. He uses as an example the beaterio for lay indigenous women in the city of Guatemala: "que con un gran provecho suyo y no menos edificación de todos, años ha que se instituyó y florece en la ciudad de Guatemala" ("A great benefit for the Indian women and no less [spiritual] edification to all, it has been years since it was instituted and flourishes in Guatemala City"; AGN, Historia, vol. 109, exp. 2, fol. 38).

The city council in Mexico City expressed concern for financial issues, as the convent would have to rely on charity for its maintenance. The Audiencia opposed the foundation because the city had too many convents and did not need a new one. Attorney Pedro Malo de Villavicencio, aligned with the Jesuits' opinion, believed that indigenous women lacked the constancy needed to successfully maintain a religious and perpetually cloistered life, and for that reason he recommended that Corpus Christi be established not as a convent but rather as a beaterio or a *recogimiento* (AGN, Historia, vol. 109, exp. 2, fol. 53). The documents considered in the debate also include several narratives written in the hagiographical style dedicated to the exemplary lives of indigenous women who served in nunneries in New Spain. Even these works, however, support the idea of a beaterio because, although it could be demonstrated that indigenous women had the spiritual abilities to live a religious life, until that moment none had professed, and therefore they lacked a model.

The documentation presented to the Audiencia also includes the opinions of two nuns. Sor Petra de San Francisco of the Convent of San Juan de la Penitencia, who became the founder and abbess of the Convent of Corpus Christi, refuted an attempt to portray indigenous women negatively, denying claims that some of the women selected to become nuns were already promised in marriage, which merely proved their inconstancy. Moreover, she affirmed that the Indian women who had been in her charge were "aptas y capaces para el estado y por su virtud, recogimiento y buena crianza es que serán muy buenas religiosas" ("suited to and capable of the religious life, and because of their virtue, solitariness and good upbringing, they will be very good nuns"; AGN, Historia, vol. 109, exp. 2, fol. 43–44).[14]

Other documents written by priests identify indigenous women they had known in convents and speak well of them. Father Joseph Ribera, vicar at the Convent of the discalced nuns of Santa Isabel, states that he knew and for many years heard the confessions of the Indian woman Joana de la Concepción, who was raised in the convent serving Isabel of Santa Clara and died at the age of eighty without ever having left the cloister. He also mentions other Indian women who had lived in the convent: "Nicolaza, Magdalena, María de la Cruz and María de la Trinidad" (AGN, Historia, vol. 109, exp. 2, fol. 49). The vicar of the Convent of Santa Clara, too, reports that he had known indigenous women who lived in the convent: "Se han educado asistiendo a algunas religiosas seis naturales caciques, que son: Doña Joana Phelipa Gonzalez de la Peña, que entró de cinco años y tiene ya cuarenta, Doña María Gregoria Bernal, que tiene veinte y cinco años . . . " ("They had educated themselves by assisting the nuns, these six noble indigenous women, they are: Doña Joana Phelipa Gonzalez de la Peña, who entered the convent when she was five years old and is now forty, Doña María Gregoria Bernal, who is twenty-five years old . . . "; AGN, Historia, vol. 109, exp. 2, fol. 50).[15] The six Indian women mentioned were servants of Spanish nuns in that convent.

In the midst of the debate, royal approval to open the convent for indigenous women reached Mexico City. The Audiencia, therefore, had to support the foundation of the Convent of Corpus Christi, which opened its doors in July of 1724. Following the First Rule of Saint Claire, it required no dowry from the novices. Public opinion maintained that the First Rule of Saint Claire, which was particularly austere, would not pose a problem for the indigenous women because the capacity to endure severe conditions was in their temperament.[16]

According to Josefina Muriel, once the founding of the Corpus Christi convent was approved, Sor Petra de San Francisco began to receive requests for admission and proceeded to gather information about the candidates and their families. That information would then be summarized by a Franciscan friar, citing four or more residents of the city or town where each young woman lived, and sometimes interviewing the residents to determine if the candidate was noble, if she was a pure-blooded Indian, if her relatives had ever committed a despicable act or had ever been tried before the Inquisition, if she was the daughter of a legitimate marriage, if she was being forced to enter the convent, if she was already promised in marriage, and if she was in good physical condition so as to withstand the rigors of religious life and its rule (*Las indias caciques* 62).

Ann Miriam Gallagher includes a fragment of information about the purity of blood required to be a candidate at the Convent of Corpus Christi. The information requested of this particular candidate did not address the physical conditioning needed for life as a nun, only that she be healthy and free from contagious disease ("The Family Background" 280). The adaptation of this common practice for Spanish convents—obtaining information about candidates and proving their purity of blood or lineage—supports the idea of mimicry as a strategy in colonial discourse. A sign of double articulation, mimicry, on the one hand, is a strategy of regulation and, on the other hand, functions as a mechanism for "normalization" (Bhabha 86).

Limpieza de sangre (purity of blood), a phenomenon that surfaced in Castilian culture around 1492 under the absolutist reign of Isabel and Ferdinand, was an element of orthodox religious practice and belief that also allowed a special emphasis on inheritance. Resulting from Spain's political and religious history, the pure-blooded status required of Spanish women for their entrance into convents also became a requisite in the Americas. Candidates to convents intended for indigenous women had to prove that they were of pure Indian blood without any mixing, a practice accentuating the indigenous character of the convents that those same nuns and their families later defended. As María Elena Martínez illustrates, the establishment of European values of nobility and traditions of inheritance in Spanish America "resulted in a recasting of the native past, in indigenous histories and genealogies increasingly framed in European and Christian terms" (113). The "new" value system brought from Spain provided the original inhabitants of New Spain with a different language and terminology that the nobility ably used to maintain their pre-Hispanic power as much as possible. Religious colonial language and the political organization of the two repúblicas empowered noble Indians to rewrite their dynastic histories and demonstrate their worth through the discourse of limpieza and calidad.

In Defense of a Colonized Nation

In the midst of public debate about the ability of indigenous women to be nuns, yet another document appeared, which argued that they were, indeed, capable of participating in religious life. In 1724, as a counterpoint to the negative campaign of opposition to the convent, Juan de Urtassum published a hagiographic narrative titled *La gracia triunfante en la vida de Catharina Tegakovita, india iroquesa* (Grace triumphant in the life of Catharina Tegakovita, an Iroquois Indian) about an indigenous woman from New France.[17] Francisco Colonec wrote the original narrative, which Jesuit Juan de Urtassum translated from French into a book with three volumes. In the first part, Juan Ignacio de Castorena, who was appointed vicar general of the Indians of New Spain, writes a *parecer* (opinion) in which he extensively defends the aptitude of New Spain's indigenous women to become nuns. His post as rector of the university and advisor of the Holy Office gave him the authority to issue his opinion on the debate. The second part contains Catharina's biography composed in the hagiographic style. The last section includes a series of short narratives of indigenous women in New Spain who had lived exemplary lives. The first and last parts of the Spanish version of *La gracia triunfante* are most relevant to the specific founding of the Convent of Corpus Christi. The hagiographic biography of Catharina Tegakovita appears as an exemplary life story of an Indian woman in support of the agenda shared by Urtassum and Castorena. Its translation resulted from the efforts of these two men who presented convincing evidence about the capacity of indigenous women to keep themselves chaste and pure and, thus, fit for conventual life.

Elisa Sampson Vera Tudela and Asunción Lavrin both note that primarily the Jesuits opposed the convent, while the Franciscans were largely in favor of it, assertions based on the documents discussed earlier in this chapter. Yet, when all the documents and events concerning the opening of the convent are considered, it becomes more difficult to extrapolate from the attitude of a particular writer to that of the larger religious order or other involved party. The following facts, for example, undermine the view of Jesuit opposition and Franciscan support. Two Jesuits took on the task of defending the indigenous women in their effort to open the convent by publishing *La gracia triunfante*, and it was a Franciscan who created problems within the convent by allowing the entrance of Spanish novices. On *La gracia triunfante*, Antonio Rubial remarks: "Pareciera que el impreso se presentaba como un acto de contrición o como una declaración de principios de algunos jesuitas proindígenas frente a la actitud negativa mostrada por sus hermanos del colegio de San Gregorio" ("It would seem that the printed material was offered as an act of contrition or as a declaration of principles on the part of some pro-indigenous Jesuits in the face of the negative attitudes shown by their brothers in the Colegio de San Gregorio"; "La exaltación de los humillados" 3).

It was particularly significant that the key argument in favor of, or against the convent's foundation, centered on the indigenous women's sexuality. The priests' testimonies present clear evidence that the level of spirituality required of indigenous women entering the convent was determined mainly by chastity, purity, and moderation in matters of sexuality. The principal point of controversy became the issue of chastity, or the lack thereof, an issue Castorena cites directly in the first part of the book: "La razón parece convincente como es notoria, fundada en las Sagradas Escrituras, y Padres, en lo que dedicó el Espíritu Santo a la pluma del Sabio: Ninguno puede ser puro, si Dios no lo hace casto. El don de la continencia sólo se debe a tu misericordia" ("Reason is a convincing argument because it is obvious, based as it is on the Holy Scriptures; and Fathers, in that which the Holy Spirit entrusted to the pen of the Wise One: No one can be pure if God does not make him chaste. The gift of moderation is due only to your mercy"; "Parecer" n. pag.). In this paragraph, Castorena argues that God's favor is necessary in order to be able to be chaste. If God grants that gift to men and women in all parts of the world, he contends, then there is no reason for God to withhold it from Indian women. Chastity and moderation do not stem from the free will of the human being but rather from God's grace; no one, he affirms, can exclude a racial group or a gender from what God wishes for them.

In the third part of the *apología*, Castorena refutes the criticisms and reasons given for opposing the convent's foundation. Arguing against the idea that indigenous women could not understand the true meaning of monastic life, Castorena poses a rhetorical question to his readers: "Pregunto, ¿tuvieron entendimiento, para pasar de la ignorancia de nuestros santos misterios al conocimiento de ellos? Pues ¿por qué no lo tendrían para pasar del conocimiento de los misterios y obligaciones de Cristiano al conocimiento de los consejos Evangélicos?" ("I ask you, did they not have the intellect to be able to conquer their ignorance of our holy mysteries and gain an understanding of them? Then, why would they not have the intelligence to go from an understanding of the mysteries and obligations of Christianity to an understanding of Evangelical matters?"; "Parecer" n. pag.). Castorena establishes here that indigenous women were capable of understanding the mysteries of Christianity in order to voluntarily become Christians, an ability that also allowed them to understand the duties of monastic life. Even as the debate was occurring, the indigenous women in question had been Christians for generations, and there was little chance of finding a false Christian among them.[18]

The second section of La gracia triunfante recounts the life of Catharina Tegakovita. Urtassum situates the province of the Iroquois on the border with New Mexico, east of the land of the Apaches, and also contends that the Iroquois were never conquered by the French.[19] Catharina's chief virtue emphasized in the hagiographic narrative is purity. So strong was her inclination to keep herself pure, she resisted her parents' efforts to persuade her to enter into a marriage contract. The hagiography states that she was persecuted for this choice and forced to leave her village. It was then that she took her first vow—that of chastity. While the narrative also references other common elements of female hagiography, such as the suffering and pain Catharina endured with patience and happiness, purity remains her highest virtue.

The life of Catharina Tegakovita served as an occasion to write at length about and give specific examples of the virtues of indigenous women. The third and final section includes short narratives on the lives of various indigenous women from New Spain who were considered to have lived an exemplary life, "y en especial de la Continencia, que profesaron, y se mantuvieron hasta su dichosa muerte" ("And especially lives of sexual moderation, which they practiced and upheld until their blessed death"; La gracia triunfante 211). Urtassum takes these exemplary life stories from other texts, the most easily recognizable being those of Petronila de la Concepción and Francisca de San Miguel, included in Paraíso occidental by Carlos de Sigüenza y Góngora.[20] No indigenous woman mentioned is a nun because they were not allowed that privilege. Yet like Catharina, they were women who followed the model of perfection found in hagiographies and who embraced the secret vow of perpetual virginity. The experiences of Magdalena de Pátzcuaro, for example, were similar to those of Catharina. Magdalena was ill and offered to take a vow of chastity in exchange for good health. Later, her parents tried to marry her off, but she refused because of the vow she had taken: " . . . concluyó su oración, haciendo voto de perpetua virginidad a su Santísimo Hijo, proponiendo en honra, e imitación suya, conservar entero y sin mancilla su cuerpo, por todo el discurso de su vida" (" . . . she concluded her prayer, offering a vow of perpetual virginity to the most Holy Son, proposing with honor, and by your example, to keep her body whole and unsullied, for all the days of her life"; *La gracia triunfante* 217).

Two brief stories about indigenous women previously published in *Paraíso occidental* (1684) function as early recreations of the defense of Indian women in colonial religious discourse. Chapters 14 and 15 of Book Three feature Petronila de la Concepción and Francisca de San Miguel, who both worked as servants in the Convento Real de Jesús María in México. Petronila was the servant of María de la Concepción while she lived in the convent, and according to Sigüenza y Góngora, it is "justo que también aquí la acompañe, pues a lo que debemos creer se gozan ahora juntas en las delicias del cielo" ("fitting that she accompanies her in this space, and we can only believe that they are now sharing the delights of heaven"; 283). With this solemn affirmation, it became apparent that in the eyes of God, both María and Petronila, nun and servant, were equal in that they shared the same heavenly destiny. Nonetheless, while they lived, a clear difference existed between the two.

Taking into consideration Kathleen Ross's opinion that the *Paraíso occidental* is a rewriting of the discovery of America from a later perspective and uses the convent as a metaphor for colonization, I propose that the indigenous element had to be present in the account, with clearly symbolic significance: the Indian women are servants of the Spanish women and subjects as loyal to Catholicism as the professed nuns, who are of the more privileged socio-ethnic group. The text indicates that it was not known who Petronila's parents were, only that she was born in the city of Xochimilco and ran away from home to enter the convent between the ages of ten and twelve (283). She lived there a few years until she developed a "cankerous" ("cancrosa") sore, which forced her to return to her home town for fear of being contagious. The author writes that the sore healed rapidly, but when she returned to the convent, the women guarding the entrance "la repelieron con grande enfado" ("turned her away, greatly annoyed"; 283). Later, when she went to church to ask God for help getting back into the convent, the Virgin Mary appeared to her, accompanied by Mary Magdalene and Saint Catherine, saying: "No te aflijas ni llores por lo que te ha pasado; vuélvete a la portería, que yo te aseguro el que te reciban" ("Do not be concerned or cry about what has happened to you; go back to the front gates, and I assure you that they will let you in"; 284). And, indeed, when she returned to the convent, they welcomed her very agreeably and allowed her to take the vows of the lay sisters.

After this passage, her virtues and penitences are described in much the same way as those of the nuns: "Su silencio fue grande, sus penitencias muchas, el ayuno austero, la oración instante, la presencia de Dios continua, la independencia absoluta" ("Her silence was complete, her penitences many, her fasting severe, her prayer continuous, the presence of God never-ending, her independence absolute"; 284). To conclude the life story of Petronila, Sigüenza y Góngora describes one of the young indigenous woman's mystical trances: "No tuvo Petronila otra ocupación en toda su vida sino amar a Dios, siendo lo que más la persuadía a ello la pasión de Cristo. . . . En esta meditación se le suspendían los sentidos, quedándose extática por muchas horas y con tanto extremo, que no sólo no veía ni oía en estos casos, pero ni aun sentía" ("Petronila had no other goal in her entire life than to love God, and the passion of Christ was that which most tied her to him. . . . In meditation, she would abandon all her senses, which left her for many hours in a state of ecstasy so extreme that not only did she neither see nor hear, but she was not aware of anything"; 285). The author's word choice evokes an approving tone, and the narrative clearly portrays her exemplary character. For example, in the previously cited passage, Petronila, in addition to being touched by God in order to achieve a state in which her senses are suspended, also uses meditation, just as Teresa of Ávila's teachings advised.

At the beginning of a second narration recounting the biography of the Indian woman Francisca de San Miguel, Sigüenza y Góngora's comments equate Francisca with Petronila: "Hecha ya mención de Petronila no hay razón para no hacerla de otras humildes y pequeñitas que hoy, en la Corte del supremo Rey de los reyes, serán muy grandes" ("Having said what has been said about Petronila, there is no reason not to do the same for other humble and lowly women who today, in the eyes of the court of the supreme King of kings, have attained great status"; 286). Indigenous women may be lowly and humble in the eyes of the Spanish, but not in God's eyes. This Indian woman shares with Petronila (and with all nuns who follow the model of perfection) not only having been "very afflicted, very humble, very abstinent, very penitent," ("muy mortificada, muy humilde, muy ayunadora, muy penitente"), but in addition, "God endowed her with the spirit of prophecy" ("Dios la dotó de espíritu de profecía"; 286). Francisca de San Miguel also experienced apparitions much like Petronila's. When she fervently desired an image of the crucified Christ, three Indians dressed in white brought her a beautiful image of Christ on the cross, and no one ever knew where they had come from or who had sent it.[21] Sigüenza y Góngora emphasizes the miraculous nature of this event because Francisca, as an Indian who desired to live a holy life, was very poor and lacked the earthly means to have bought the image herself.[22] Unfortunately, nothing more is known of the life of Francisca, who—along with Petronila and María, a black woman who was also a *donada* (community servant)—brought "honor" to the convent even though they were not nuns (288).

The purpose of *Paraíso occidental* was didactic: the exemplary life stories of the featured nuns were meant to be models for other nuns and women who read the work. Kathleen Ross, however, does not believe that these two chapters about the indigenous servant women of the convent function as such, and she does not pursue any detailed analysis of the conventions used to describe them, stating that "alongside the nuns, who represent purity and virginity in the western Paradise, the women of color who serve them stand for the success of the conquest in converting indigenous (or imported) groups or *naciones*" (142). The reason Sigüenza y Góngora decided to include the *vidas ejemplares* (exemplary lives) of two indigenous servants is unknown. Ross's theory may be in part correct. Yet in addition to showing the author's obvious interest in and admiration for indigenous Mexican culture, his description of these women serves as a historic forerunner to a time almost a century later when indigenous women would be legitimized by being allowed to take the veil.

Textual evidence does not indicate whether Sigüenza y Góngora's stories about Petronila and Francisca directly entered the public debate into which advocates for the Convent of Corpus Christi found themselves drawn. Nevertheless, it is important to highlight their inclusion in *La gracia triunfante*. Certain kinds of proof were needed to demonstrate the aptitude of indigenous women for convent life and the existence of female precursors who could serve as their models. *La gracia triunfante*, then, provided favorable depictions of indigenous women and also established chastity as one of their virtues, a central issue in the debate about the foundation of the Corpus Christi convent. Presenting the indigenous woman as chaste, like any other woman who led a religious life, this religious text challenged the stereotypes many priests perpetuated. Its Jesuit authors, Urtassum and Castorena, presented new images of these women that influenced the decision to establish the first convent for indigenous women in colonial Mexico.

Examining a broader range of testimonies, reports, and other documentation in this debate reveals a diversity of images. It is evident here that power relations, as Foucault would maintain, are practiced through discourse (*Power/Knowledge* 93). Those who held the power to decide whether indigenous women should be able to take the vow to become nuns were, for the most part, the white men who made up the Catholic Church, and they exercised, through their written discourse, the inherent power afforded them by that institution. Priests who created the discourses controlled the power and the representations of the colonial subject, which in the case of indigenous women were expressions of Otherness and difference. Those who defended these women, and even those who did not, were diving into foreign and unknown waters where it was important to either exalt or dilute the *différance* of the subaltern.[23] We have begun to see that gender and race are malleable cultural constructions directed and modified by those who exercise the power of discourse.

Through written discourse, different constructions of the same subject can be created and contradictory forces of power can be unleashed. In the drive to establish a convent for indigenous women, particular depictions of their character and qualities entered the realms of religious and secular discourses in early testimonials and reports on the convent, which would appear time and again in later discursive constructions, such as sermons or biographic and hagiographic texts. Once the nuns became active participants in the construction of their subjectivities, however, discursive representation became more fluid.

To this point, I have referred only to writing clergymen as active agents of power and indigenous women as recipients of that power. This chapter has addressed discursive images that do not necessarily capture real subjects but, rather, imagined constructions of colonial Others. Subsequent chapters will attest to the discursive participation of the indigenous women themselves, who surprisingly will not dramatically contradict the colonial construction of their subjectivities but will instead emphasize certain traits of their Indianness in defense of the ethnic exclusivity of their cloister.

The mechanisms of power exercised through the written word with regard to the foundation of the Convent of Corpus Christi were located in a system of rhetorical reciprocity and cultural correlation. The relations of domination and contestation that filled the soon-to-be-realized indigenous conventual space gave rise to a series of conflicts and discursive practices that modified and on occasion affirmed the strategies of everyday colonial religious discourse. The ideological debate about indigenous issues did not end when the Convent of Corpus Christi opened its doors. The real conflict was just beginning.

Indigenous Women and Religious Life

Stereotype and Ambivalence

One of the rare available writings by an indigenous nun to which we have had access is a biographical account of the founding abbess of Corpus Christi. This anonymous account, addressed to the author's confessor, ends with a strange anecdote recounting how the father of one of the Spanish novices in the Corpus Christi convent had been planning to kill all the indigenous nuns living there. But after setting up a ladder to climb the garden wall, he was killed instead by the very men he had invited along to help him do the butchering ("la carnicería").[1] This disturbing episode exemplifies the conflicts caused by the ethnic exclusion stipulated for the founding of this cloister. Just as the convents established for Spanish and criolla women did not allow the profession of Indians and other castas as black-veiled nuns, the convents of Corpus Christi, Cosamaloapan, and Nuestra Señora de los Ángeles did not admit Spanish, criolla, and mestiza women; although this exclusion was more theoretical than actual, as Franciscan prelates continued to accept criolla novices in the Corpus Christi convent and later in Nuestra Señora de Cosamaloapan convent.

Once Corpus Christi's doors opened, some religious authorities, with the support of certain powerful Indian leaders, voiced their displeasure that Spanish novices had been admitted into a cloister that a papal bull had established as exclusively for indigenous women (AGN, Reales Cédulas, vol. 65, exp. 78, fol. 186).[2] The inclusion of Spanish women created conflict rooted in the two-century-old theological and legal debate on the suitability of indigenous people for religious life. The antagonism between the Indians, and the Spaniards and colonial officials who were allowing this to occur, generated a series of discourses that constructed the female colonial subject. These discursive productions had a direct effect on the subjectivity of noble indigenous women and on the way they defended the autonomy of their conventual space in their written communications.

In the forty years after the Convent of Corpus Christi opened, different religious authorities fashioned and reinforced racialized female subjectivities through sermons and hagiographic biographies. We can identify strategic rhetorical devices and language employed to convey to Church authorities and the rest of colonial society the image of Indian women that they wanted to prevail. Beginning with the sermon that the eminent theologian Juan Igancio de Castorena y Ursúa[3] preached on the occasion of the convent's opening and continuing with hagiographic biographies, like those of the Otomí Salvadora de los Santos, who lived in a beaterio in Querétaro, and of the Spanish nun Sebastiana Josefa de la Santísima Trinidad, who was allowed to enter Corpus Christi, these texts functioned as models of social conformity.

In this discursive corpus, we will also consider the documents sent to the Council of the Indies with accusations of the indigenous nuns sent to the Council decrying the Franciscan governance for having admitted Spaniards into the convent and denied the habit to Indians. Ambivalence in the discursive construction of the feminine indigenous identity in male-authored texts functions to signify the colonial condition of all parties involved, and the appropriation of stereotypical images for these colonial subjects becomes crucial in the negotiation of the ethnic autonomy of their conventual space.

Ambivalent Representations

Religious discursive production in early modern Spain and colonial Latin America was particularly prolific. Questions of debate were handled by means of the publication of philosophical or theological treatises, letters, hagiographic biographies, or sermons.[4] We have many sources of this kind, but they tend to ignore subaltern agency and their responses to ecclesiastical power and the imperial state. Documents containing lengthy discourses about the Indians largely respond to the imperial agenda of the colonial Church. Conflicts between Franciscans and Jesuits, and between those who supported and opposed the convent, contributed to the discursive production concerning indigenous issues, a discussion that did not cease after the convent for indigenous women became a reality.[5]

One such discourse is the hagiographic biography of an Otomí Indian woman,[6] published in 1763: the "carta edificante en que el P. Antonio de Paredes de la Compañía de Jesús, da noticia de la exemplar Vida, sólidas virtudes, y santa muerte de la Hermana Salvadora de los Santos, India Otomí, Donada del Beaterio de las Carmelitas de la Ciudad de Querétaro" (the "edifying letter in which Father Antonio de Paredes of the Company of Jesus gives witness to the exemplary Life, sound virtues and holy death of Sister Salvadora de los Santos, an Otomí Indian, Lay Sister of the Carmelite Beaterio in the City of Querétaro").[7] The narrative about Salvadora de los Santos indicates that many indigenous peoples of New Spain, even years after the conquest, still retained much of their "nativa rudeza: la excepción de algunos que avecinados en las ciudades, comunican con los Españoles, aprenden la lengua castellana" ("native coarseness: the exception being that some of those taking up residence in the cities, communicate with the Spanish, learning the Castilian language"; 2). From the beginning of the narrative, Paredes advances an argument based on a Manichean dichotomy, mirroring the ideology of discrimination that defined indigenous peoples in contrast to the Spaniards or by their relationship with them.[8] Abdul Jan-Mohamed warns: "Motivated by his desire to conquer and dominate, the imperialist configures the colonial realm as a confrontation based on differences in race, language, social customs, cultural values, and modes of production" (18). This type of discourse tends to simplify differences between colonial social groups that were in practice much more complex.

For instance, Antonio de Paredes contends the Otomí Indians were hindered by their complicated language, which had kept them from being indoctrinated into the Catholic faith. Yet, Charles Gibson asserts that in 1576 the priest assigned to the curate of the doctrina of Tequixquiac, in the northern part of the valley of Mexico, was officially instructed to learn to speak Nahuatl as well as Otomí and be able not only to preach in those languages but also to hear confessions in them (114). Paredes's reference to the "savagery" of the Otomí operates as a rhetorical device that elevates Salvadora and affirms her religious perfection distinguishing her from the other Otomíes. Gibson explains that when the Spanish arrived, the Otomí Indians were scattered about and lived under the control of other groups of Nahua peoples, and it was this very dynamic that allowed their culture and language to be preserved throughout most of the colonial period (30).

Salvadora was born in Fresnillo in 1701, the daughter of an *indio principal* father and a noble Indian mother; consequently, Salvadora could have been a candidate for the Convent of Corpus Christi. Yet the Jesuit Antonio Paredes had another reason for mentioning this: Salvadora chose to live as a lay sister, and that was what made her exceptional. Following the conventions of the hagiographic narrative, he begins with Salvadora's childhood, noting that her parents influenced her to follow a life of rectitude. Her godparents were Spanish, which could have given her some advantage in the social hierarchy of the colony. Close ties with a Spanish family would have made her more amiable in the eyes of the colonizer. The narration continues in the hagiographic style, relating that Salvadora had wanted to fast since she was five years old. If ill, she would learn prayers and Christian doctrine, in the belief that would restore her health. She would read the lives of the saints and pray novenas. She even made herself a habit and decided to live in seclusion. Paredes writes: "Despreció al mundo, vivió pobre, hacía guerra a su carne, reprimía sus apetitos, frecuentaba la oración" ("She rejected the world, lived in poverty, waged war against the flesh, repressed her appetites, and prayed fervently"; 14). These details in the narration of Salvadora's life are rhetorical devices common in the composition of exemplary life narratives during the colonial era. Often used to describe mystic nuns or saints, this kind of narrative also contributes to the political and theological debate about the lives of indigenous women.[9]

According to Paredes, Salvadora had gone to Querétaro one Christmas, where Sor María Magdalena del Espíritu Santo informed her of a newly founded Carmelite beaterio. Salvadora volunteered to serve in it and beg for alms. She was accepted into the new community because "era alta de cuerpo, fornida para el trabajo, de notoria virtud: y la nueva fundación necesitaba una sirviente, que atendiese a los ministerios domésticos, saliese a la calle a las diligencias ocurrentes, y fuese el alivio todo de las nuevas Carmelitas, que se retiraban del Mundo" ("She was of sound body, well built for work, of evident virtue: and the new establishment needed a servant who would take charge of household matters, go out in public to run errands, and in general ease the burden of the new Carmelites, who had withdrawn from the world"; 17). Paredes stresses Salvadora's physical characteristics and the beaterio's need for a servant, an emphasis that suggests her admittance into the Carmelite beaterio was not based on her exceptional virtue. Although Paredes identifies her as a lay sister, she was accepted not as such but as a servant, maintaining the socio-ethnic hierarchy considered appropriate for secular society and in the feminine space of the beaterio.

The author stresses that Salvadora took a vow of chastity in spite of not having taken the formal vows of the lay sisters. Paredes observes that even before entering the beaterio, she had maintained her chastity without any formal obligation to do so (18). The same virtue of chastity highlighted with Catharina Tegakovita is underscored with Salvadora, especially as neither woman was following a religious rule that required a vow of chastity. At another level this argument responds to one of the most salient contentions presented by those opposing the convent for Indians. Elisa Sampson Vera Tudela notes that keeping their virginity became metaphorically associated with the integrity of their bodies, "an integrity that came to have an exceptionally charged significance" (*Colonial Angels* 82).

Salvadora de los Santos lived in the beaterio for twenty-six years: "Sin faltar a los ejercicios espirituales que le pertenecían, continuando sus penitencias, y sirviendo como una esclava a las beatas" ("Without missing the spiritual exercises that she was supposed to do, she kept up her acts of penitence, and served as a slave of the lay sisters"; 35). Paredes observes that God gave Salvadora the gift of healing, and by merely laying on hands and praying the *Magníficat*, she was able to heal the sick and women having difficulty giving birth. The author recounts numerous anecdotes about Salvadora's saintly life and how she worked tirelessly at grueling tasks despite her age, until she fell gravely ill with fever and died at the age of sixty-one on August 25, 1762.

Why would Father Antonio Paredes, almost certainly with the support of other Jesuits, decide to write and publish the life of Salvadora de los Santos? In the case of Catharina Tegakovita, the dates of publication coincide with the debate on the Convent of Corpus Christi. Salvadora, however, was twenty-five years old when the convent was founded and already living as a servant in a beaterio. Consequently, the publication of this text does not appear to have contributed to the campaign in support of the convent's opening; rather, it supports the opinion of other Jesuits that indigenous women did not need to become nuns to lead exemplary lives, since they could do so in a beaterio.[10] Nevertheless, the Jesuits who argued that indigenous women should enter beaterios did not indicate they should do so as servants relegated to subordinate positions.

From Paredes's account of Salvadora's experiences, the reader can perceive a life much like that of any exemplary religious woman, except that she was Indian and neither a nun nor a lay sister. The creation of an exemplary narrative with a colonial subject as its model did not guarantee the veneration of this particular woman. As Kristine Ibsen incisively notes, the fact that women were included (and re-constructed) in the discursive order had no bearing on their position in the public sphere; they were present in exemplary texts in an "abstract and commodified sense" (12). Asunción Lavrin observes that "Paredes still presents Salvadora as a 'wonder,' a baffling example of God's will to humble the proud" (*Brides of Christ* 254). Yet the fact that Paredes notes Salvadora's parents were Indian nobles clearly suggests his belief that other noble Indian women considered candidates in some capacity for the nunnery should live as Salvadora did, serving Spanish lay sisters in a beaterio or serving the Spanish nuns in a convent, as was already the custom.

The ideology of discrimination reveals itself in the palimpsest of written discourses included in documents released by religious authorities. The official opinions of priests in 1723, analyzed in the previous chapter, make clear their position concerning the suitability of indigenous women for life in the cloister, but from this biography of Salvadora de los Santos, we can infer that Paredes rejects the possibility of Indian nuns. Ironically, Paredes's hagiographic biography elevates an Indian woman to a level of sainthood, provided she maintains the status quo in the socio-ethnic hierarchy. His religious order also stood in opposition to other members of the same Jesuit order—such as Urtassum and Castorena—who did indeed support the idea of a cloister for indigenous women in writings like *La gracia triunfante en la vida de Catharina Tegakovita* and the foundational sermons of the Convent of Corpus Christi.

The ambivalence Paredes conveys through his narrative is significant, given that his text also defends the abilities of indigenous women. It juxtaposes Salvadora's virtues with her weaknesses, following the conventions of a discourse that sought to maintain subordination of the colonial subject. Homi Bhabha explains this type of discursive ambivalence with the concept of colonial mimicry, "the desire for a reformed, recognizable Other, as a subject of a difference that is almost the same, but not quite" (*The Location* 86). Religious discourse achieves this by establishing analogies between Spanish and indigenous women, followed by an immediate disassociation of the "civilized" referent and an opposition of the two groups' characteristics. The discursive construction of difference, while establishing the near-equality of indigenous women, is implemented by relegating them to a stage of religious "adaptation," thus imposing a cultural disparity that inevitably confers an inferior status.

In chapter 2, we considered the hagiographic text *La gracia triunfante en la vida de Catharina Tegakovita* as an example of a document supporting the opinion of one faction in the public debate about the founding of a convent for noble Indian women. At this point, we have yet to consider the discursive constructions of the indigenous women in a hagiographic biography that, while serving as a vehicle to articulate colonial ideology, purports also to defend their spiritual abilities.

Juan Ignacio de Castorena y Ursúa, author of the parecer preceding Catharina's life story, describes the indigenous women with three qualifiers in a single phrase that epitomizes imperial Spanish colonial discourse: "las *pobrecitas miserables virtuosas* Indias, de que abundan mucho los crecidos Pueblos de estos Reinos" ("the *poor wretched virtuous* Indian women, of which there are many in the growing towns of these realms").[11] Castorena makes use of biblical teachings and aphorisms that exalt the poor and wretched, especially in opposition to the prosperous and wealthy. But at the same time he reinforces the colonial order grounded on the ideology of difference. Alejandro Cañeque identifies the idea of the Indian as a "wretched person" *(persona miserable)* as the defining element of the imperial state's discourse on the indigenous population (187). The Crown's rationale for maintaining a paternalistic presence toward the Indians was precisely consistent with their definition as wretched people. The condition of *miserable* in which the Indians fit, according to the colonialist mentality, can be interpreted as both a legal and a biblical concept.[12] The Indians were placed in the same category as minors, who, as such, needed to be protected from abuse. Nevertheless, they needed to work in exchange for this protection.

The Crown and the Church worked together to establish the imperial supremacy of Spain. The social system of unequal reciprocity seemed to work very well, at least for the colonizers, and had a robust discursive structure (religious, philosophical, and legal) that justified their initiatives toward the Indians. The origin of the ideas that fed the Crown its "rhetoric of wretchedness," not surprisingly, came from the early discourse of the missionaries, particularly that of the Franciscans. Fray Gerónimo de Mendieta was especially influential to the Crown: he defined the Indians as poor, weak and feeble, and defended their "privileges" with the Crown. The king had to fulfill the role of father to the Indians. Being *miserables* prevented the Indians from governing themselves, and according to the definition (legal and religious) of wretched, they needed assistance.[13] Cañeque notes that the discursive construction of Indians as wretched peoples hid the project of domination behind the discourse of protection, an integral part of Spanish colonial discourse (193).

The origin of Mendieta's opinions can be traced to biblical teachings in which God protects the wretched and the poor. Castorena y Ursúa was thus in accordance with religious discourse and state policy when he brought into play those three epithets to describe Indian women. One of the Bible verses supporting this view in the Old Testament states: "But he shall judge the poor with justice, and shall reprove with equity for the meek of the earth" *(Douay-Rheims,* Isa 11:5). If the Indian women were the meek of the earth, how were they also going to be virtuous?

Castorena constructs a semantic field supported by ecclesiastical rhetoric with the use of the words "poor," "wretched," and "virtuous," three adjectives of complementary significance in a religious context.[14] The first two words are easily placed in the semantic field of Indian, beginning with the earliest productions of missionary discourse, yet the third word, "virtuous," falls into a different category. A struggle for the semantic borders of the three terms occurs in the description of indigenous women. The meaning of a sign is the result of a positive semantic field—what it signifies—and a negative field—what it does not signify. Still, a sign's meaning is not limited to these two semantic fields but rather includes the entire linguistic system, and semantic borders are determined by the constant semantic battles produced in any society (Majfud 61).

Definitions of the words "poor" (*pobre*) and "wretched" (*miserable*) in the *Diccionario de autoridades* (1726) convey the same sense of humility and lack of strength; more significantly, these definitions also refer to a person who lacks value, if we understand value as a grade of utility or aptitude. Both definitions include "desdichado, infeliz y desafortunado" ("ill-fated, unhappy, and unfortunate"). The three epithets were uttered in the context of defense of indigenous women's aptitude to follow the religious life as nuns. However, the final word Castorena chooses in his description is "virtuous," which conveys strength, vigor, and courage, connoting the opposite of the image established with the adjectives "poor" and "wretched." The word "virtue" is defined as "hábito y disposición del alma para las acciones conforme a la ley cristiana" ("behavior and disposition of the soul for all actions conforming to Christian law"). The contrasting images presented in Castorena's phrase suggest ulterior motives. The defense produced through ecclesiastical discourse and its rhetorical devices are clear, but it also becomes evident that the colonized group was defined by its difference from and opposition to the colonizers. The Spanish nuns in convents throughout New Spain were defined as virtuous, but not as poor or wretched. Castorena y Ursúa attributes a different meaning to the term "virtuous" by using it in conjunction with certain linguistic signs with particular historical meanings (Majfud 78).

Castorena defends the virtues of the indigenous women by constructing an ambivalent image of them rooted in early religious stereotypes.[15] Castorena praises the Indians, who "conceden la inclinación natural a otras virtudes, como la humildad, la pobreza, el desinterés, la obediencia, y la mortificación" ("They have a natural inclination to other virtues, like humility, poverty, unselfishness, obedience, and penance"). Still, he doubts their ability to keep the vows of chastity and enclosure ("Parecer" n. pag.).

Castorena defends the aptitude of Indians to be nuns, but when he constructs his discursive defense, he contrasts the image of wretched with that of virtuous, establishing the ambivalence required to create the stereotype. Discourse is fundamental in coloniality to articulate the wide range of differences and discriminations informing the political and social practices that build cultural hierarchy (Bhabha 67). In Castorena's assertions as well as in the discourses of the nuns themselves, examined at greater length in chapters 4 and 6, we can appreciate the struggle over semantic borders in the terms chosen to define and self-define the female subject. Although Castorena defends the participation of indigenous women in monastic life, he constantly uses rhetoric common in colonial discourse to maintain control and establish difference. Even when the indigenous women of New Spain could take their vows to become nuns, distinctions still needed to be maintained: all nuns in New Spain were virtuous, but only the noble Indian nuns were poor and wretched.

Although the intellectual ability of indigenous women was seldom questioned in the debate about whether they should enter the convent, Castorena includes a passage indicating that he and "other people of distinction and character" found themselves admiring the way in which the indigenous candidates who had been under the instruction of Sor Petra de San Francisco at the Convent of San Juan de la Penitencia had learned to read Latin in such a short time and with an accent and pronunciation so correct they could compete with "the most skillful Spanish women"("más hábiles Españolas"; "Parecer" n. pag.).[16] Again, we observe the discriminatory defense with which Castorena supports yet, at the same time, subordinates indigenous women, imposing upon them a Spanish model of skill. Ambivalence is the central discursive strategy Castorena employs in his writings, one that resurfaces in his founding sermon of the Convent of Corpus Christi.

The binary dynamic at play in this particular colonial creation of indigenous subjectivity becomes most evident when Indian women themselves adopt the same stereotyped constructions in their own writings. Since being "different" allowed them to have a convent with ethnic exclusivity, their writings use the same language that had been used to defend their "wretched" nature. As part of the elite group of natives who had learned to move about in the colonial arena with the same rhetorical tools imposed by the colonizer, they quickly learned that images of the Indian woman as poor and wretched were powerfully charged. Indian women knew that being poor and wretched did not preclude being virtuous as well, knowledge that granted them the authority to invoke such rhetoric later, when they had to defend the autonomy of their conventual space.

Preaching and Conformity

Baltasar de Zúñiga y Guzmán, the Marquis of Valero and Duke of Arión, obtained a royal certificate for the founding of the Convent of Corpus Christi after his tenure as Viceroy of New Spain (1716–1722). Upon his return to Spain, he presided over the Council of the Indies and continued to support this cause until his death in 1727. The convent was located facing the plaza of the Alameda in Mexico City, where what is left of the original building can still be seen.[17] The Church was blessed on July 10, 1724, and on that day the Marquis of Valero offered, as a gift to the church's convent, a chalice and a monstrance with emeralds (Amerlinck and Ramos 126).

Jesuit Ignacio de Castorena y Ursúa preached the founding sermon on July 16, the first of four days in which the dedication of the Convent of Corpus Christi was celebrated. Titled *Las indias entendidas, por estar religiosamente sacramentadas, en el convento, y templo de Corpus Christi de esta imperial corte de México*, Castorena's sermon begins with a rhetorical play on the word "entendimiento" (intellect), included in the title of the sermon. The "entendimiento" or "intellectual and spiritual capacity" of the indigenous peoples was a key element in the prolonged debate on the abilities of indigenous women to fully participate in religious life. Intellect, in Christian rhetoric, is not limited to intellectual comprehension but also includes the actual soul. Teresa of Ávila refers to intellect as the ability of the soul to elucidate, or better, to reason.[18] The sermon opens with a reference to the intellect of the Indian women: "Bendito sea Dios, que ya los entendimientos de las Indias persuaden, que en las Indias hay muy buenos entendimientos, como hay finas voluntades . . . las Indias se edifican espiritualmente *entendidas*, para ser unas Indias Religiosamente Sacramentadas" ("Blessed be God for the intellect of the Indian women persuade us, that the Indian women have fine intellects, just as they have excellent wills . . . the Indian women are blessed with being spiritually intellectual, that they may be Indian women ordained into religious Sacraments"; 5). The ambiguity evoked with the word "entendimiento" (intellect), understood as both noun and adjective ("entendidas"), establishes the double meaning of the concept and the rhetorical play of the sermon. Castorena implies that indigenous women possess a double virtue that has been debated: the ability of the soul to understand the mysteries of the faith and the mental capacity to reason (fig. 2).

Despite delivering this sermon well into the eighteenth century, Castorena refers to pre-Hispanic times: "En tiempo del Emperador Moctezuma, eran escogidas unas doncellas de las más hermosas Indias, para que en sus cúes (así llamaron sus adoratorios) animando las llamas al soplo de su fervor

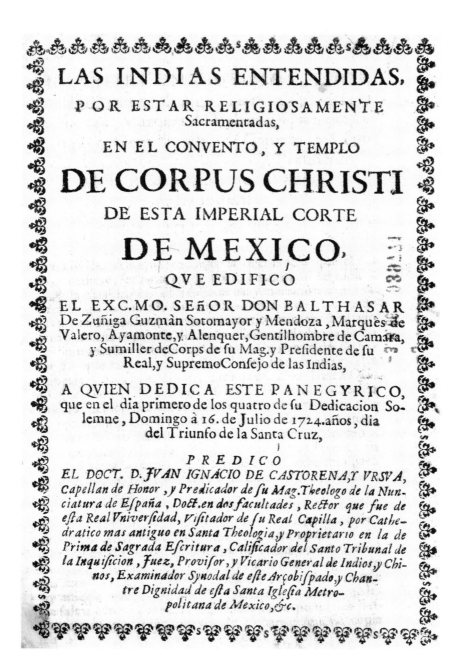

LAS INDIAS ENTENDIDAS,

POR ESTAR RELIGIOSAMENTE
Sacramentadas,

EN EL CONVENTO, Y TEMPLO

DE CORPUS CHRISTI

DE ESTA IMPERIAL CORTE

DE MEXICO,
QVE EDIFICO

EL EXC.MO. SEñOR DON BALTHASAR
De Zuñiga Guzmàn Sotomayor y Mendoza, Marquès de
Valero, Ayamonte, y Alenquer, Gentilhombre de Camara,
y Sumiller deCorps de su Mag.y Presidente de su
Real, y SupremoConsejo de las Indias,

A QVIEN DEDICA ESTE PANEGYRICO,
que en el dia primero de los quatro de su Dedicacion Solemne, Domingo à 16. de Julio de 1724.años, dia
del Triunfo de la Santa Cruz,

PREDICO

EL DOCT. D. *JVAN IGNACIO DE CASTORENA,Y VRSVA,*
Capellan de Honor , y Predicador de su Mag.Theologo de la Nun-
ciatura de España , Doct.en dos facultades , Rector que fue de
esta Real Vniversidad, Visitador de su Real Capilla , por Cathe-
dratico mas antiguo en Santa Theologia,y Proprietario en la de
Prima de Sagrada Escritura , Calificador del Santo Tribunal de
la Inquisicion , Juez, Provisor, y Vicario General de Indios,y Chi-
nos, Examinador Synodal de este Arçobispado,y Chan-
tre Dignidad de esta Santa Iglesia Metro-
politana de Mexico,&c.

Figure 2. The first page of *Las indias entendidas por estar religiosamente*.

quemando aromas incensaban sus sacrificios; aquel ardor se terminó . . . "
("In the time of the Emperor Moctezuma, some of the most beautiful Indian
maidens were chosen, so that in their *cúes* (as their shrines were called) stir-
ring the flames with the breath of their [spiritual] fervor, burned incense
over their sacrifices; that ardor ended"; 4). Castorena establishes a parallel
between the indigenous virgins dedicated to religious life in pre-Columbian
times and the indigenous women now chosen to enter the convent. We
can identify an argumentative logic originating in the sixteenth century
when Franciscan missionaries like Mendieta and Motolinía created their
discourses on the quick conversions of the Indians.[19] In the seventeenth
century, Carlos de Sigüenza y Góngora, in his narrative on the "Vestales
Mexicanas" (Mexican Virgins, chap. 1), builds on the narratives of contrasting religious beliefs and the indigenous peoples' salvation through the
"true" religion. And Juan Uvaldo de Anguita later refers to the rapid conversion of the native leaders of Valladolid in regard to the opening of a
convent for Indians in that city in 1737 (chap. 5). Clearly, this comparative
argument and the rhetoric of the salvation of people's souls reinforced the
empire's justification of the conquest, particularly by vividly contrasting the
violence of pre-Hispanic sacrifice with the goodness and peaceful nature of
Catholicism.

According to Castorena's sermon, Christian religion was the proper
vehicle of salvation for these "diez y ocho doncellas indias de distinción
nobles caciques que se ejercitaron vírgenes para graduarse de ángeles" ("eighteen Indian maidens of noble Indian families of distinction who remained
virgins so that they could move on to be angels"; 4). Their salvation was
not based on questions of theology, in which the soul naturally would be
saved for having found the "true" religion, but rooted rather in the indigenous peoples' ability to avoid the "terrible" sacrifices that pre-Hispanic religion demanded of them. The reiteration of Otherness, deftly manipulated
by the colonizer, has a double function. As JanMohamed explains, while the
textual surface takes care to represent different encounters with that racialized other, the subtext will always reaffirm the superiority of the European
culture (19). Although in this case the discourse is dedicated to defending
indigenous women, the final product reinforces the system of inequality.
Subjugating the epistemology of the indigenous past affirms the social place
in which colonizers wanted to keep these women and denies the space in
which natives could exercise their ethnic autonomy. Perhaps most important, the discourse clearly seeks to situate them as colonial subjects who
had adapted and assimilated the Hispanic culture by their own rejection of
their indigenous past.

The preacher's rhetoric employs biblical symbolism and often uses metaphorical language. Castorena subsequently introduces the central metaphor that will define the noble Indian women who were about to enter the convent, that of the eagle: "En cualquier lugar que se colocase el Cuerpo, allí formarán su Congregación de las Aguilas . . . porque esta Congregación de las Aves ha de ser de las Aguilas" ("In whatever place they should find the Body, there would they form the Congregation of Eagles . . . because this Congregation of Birds must be that of the Eagles"; 9). The eagle imagery continues, even including the convent as the eagles' nest. Castorena employs eagle imagery in his sermon in three ways: as a biblical symbol, as a symbol of colonial power, and as a symbol of the place of origin of the candidates for nuns in Corpus Christi.

In the Old Testament, the eagle was a symbol of royalty, of fierceness, and of fortitude (Ezechiel 17:3–7), much like a foreign nation with a foreign language (Deuteronomy 28:49). Other biblical passages refer to the eagle watching over its nest, achieving great heights through flight, and launching itself onto its prey with great speed (Job 9:26). Biblical eagles are an image of majesty and, at the same time, of rapacious barbarity, ambivalent constructions in the religious discourse, as are the indigenous candidates for the veil.

Castorena's sermon notes two imperial Mexican eagles: the first, "en tiempo del primero" ("in the time of the first"), which refers to the eagle poised on the cactus, symbol of the founding of Tenochtitlán;[20] and the second, "en el del último Emperador Moctezuma" ("in the time of the last emperor Moctezuma"). Castorena adds that this second eagle, a portent of divine providence, preceded the conquest (11). The second eagle may refer to the "como grulla" ("like a crane") mentioned in two of the presages that announced the arrival of the Spaniards: the first taken from the *Códice Florentino* and the second from the *Historia de Tlaxcala* by Muñoz Camargo.[21] In Solange Alberro's study of the recovery of the symbolic synthesis of the eagle and the *nopal* (cactus), she notes that the second eagle appeared thirty-five years after the conquest of Tenochtitlán on the coat of arms of Alonso de Montúfar, the second archbishop of Mexico (395).

The sermon continues to reference the symbolism of the imperial double-headed eagle, which again plays a role in the ambivalence of the linguistic sign in the colonial context. The bicephalous eagle was a symbol adopted from the Byzantine Empire that signified the secular and religious sovereignty of the emperor: one eagle was portrayed looking to the east, and the other to the west, signifying dominion over the entire territory. The double-headed eagle was featured on the coat of arms of the Hapsburg

Charles V (also known as Charles I of Spain, 1500–1558) as a symbol of the Holy Roman Empire, which he ruled from 1519 onward. Of the two-headed eagle in the colonial context, Castorena writes: "Una es de los excelentísimos virreyes que la gobiernan, la otra la de los ilustrísimos arzobispos que la dirigen" ("One belongs to the most excellent viceroys that govern it, the other to the most illustrious archbishops who guide it"; 13). Thus, the preacher begins to disassociate the traditional significance of the two-headed eagle in order to grant importance to the colonial Church together with the Crown and establish that both be respected equally.[22] He subsequently extends the semantic border of the eagle symbol, adding that the two heads also represent the majesties of Spain and Mexico but that both belong to the same king: "son como el simbolo de la Águila, de dos cabezas, dos alas, dos manos; pero un sólo pecho, un sólo corazón, una sóla alma . . . las Águilas como los Reyes, una de dos, dos en una" ("[They] are like the symbol of the Eagle, of two heads, two wings, two hands; but of one breast, a single heart, a single soul . . . the Eagles like the Kings, one of two, two in one"; 13).

Castorena's founding sermon for the Convent of Corpus Christi established the basis of what would constitute the cultural character of the convent. The building itself would fuse the very characteristics of the Hispanic culture that signified the means of control and dominance (religion) with the recognized *difference* of the group of noble indigenous women. This reinforcement of distinctive character and culture resulted in the preservation of the Indian nun's ethnic identity inside the convent. The noble Indian women had Castorena's blessing as "rational Mexican eagles," which included them in the language and imagery of the Church. By calling them rational, he established an analogy between them and the Spanish women, but they were and would continue to be singularly Mexican.

Conventual Strife

When the abbess Sor Petra de San Francisco died in 1727, only three years after the convent opened, Franciscan officials decided that it was too soon to allow the Indian women to govern their own convent. Instead, another criolla, Sor María Teresa del Señor San José, took over the role of abbess. The selection of a Spanish abbess was not the only cause for concern, however: Commissary General Fray Pedro de Navarrete continued allowing Spanish novices to enter the cloister founded solely for the Indian nobility.

The hagiographic biography of Sor Sebastiana Josefa de la Santísima Trinidad, composed by one of the nun's confessors, the Franciscan Fray

Joseph Valdés, and published in 1765, six years after Sebastiana had died, provides a partial vision of what was happening inside the Convent of Corpus Christi, as Sebastiana was one of the Spanish novices allowed to enter the convent. The argument in defense of ethnic difference is present but more subtle in this document than in *La gracia triunfante*, given that the goal of the biographer was different from that of Urtassum and Castorena. The vida was not written expressly for the debate on the suitability of indigenous nuns for religious life, but it does contain a chapter that elaborates on the tension Sebastiana's presence caused in the Convent of Corpus Christi. The vida of Sebastiana reveals that the predominant ideas about indigenous women had not evolved much during the colonial era and that conflicts of discrimination continued, even after the Convent of Corpus Christi had opened its doors (fig. 3).

Although composed by Valdés, *Vida de la venerable madre* is based largely on letters and notebooks written by Sebastiana at the request of the various confessors she had during her lifetime. In the prologue of the vida, Valdés acknowledges his use of Sor Sebastiana's letters and his role as commentator on the "truth the letters enclosed" (Sampson Vera, *Colonial Angels* 44). The content of the vida is important not only for the text selected from Sebastiana's writings but also the subtext in which it becomes evident that Fray Joseph Valdés takes sides in the conflict. He rewrote Sebastiana's experiences, leaving the reader with a modified version of what the nun originally wrote.[23] Chapter 14 of the vida describes Sebastiana's entry into the Convent of Corpus Christi, and chapter 15 briefly explains her stay in the convent and her eventual expulsion.

Sebastiana Josefa was born in 1709 in Mexico City, according to her life writings. She had a clear religious vocation, but her family could not provide her with a dowry, making her entrance into a convent very difficult. In Kristine Ibsen's opinion, Sebastiana had been used by Fray Pedro Navarrete as a political pawn, part of his plan for "strengthening" the Indian community through the presence of Spanish novices (86). Because Navarrete was against allowing indigenous women to govern themselves in the convent, he wanted more Spanish women housed there.[24]

In 1732 three Franciscan supporters of the Indian nuns of Corpus Christi wrote a letter to the king of Spain that asked him to issue a royal decree expelling the Spanish women who had been admitted into the convent. They contended that from the time of the conquest, indigenous women had been scorned and mistreated by the Spaniards, who had not made any distinction between the nobles and the commoners, and in this case, because the Marquis of Valero had decided that the convent would be

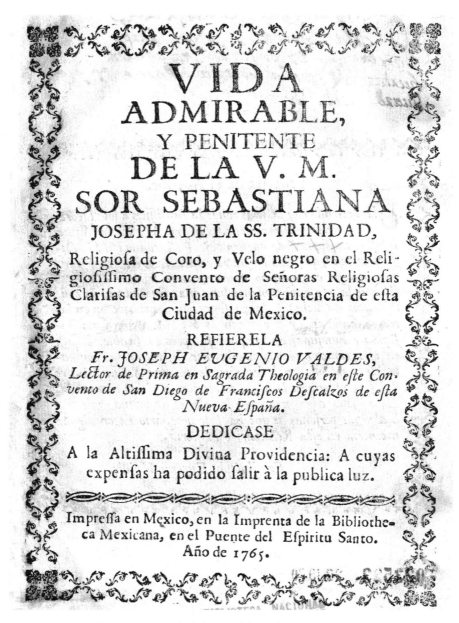

VIDA
ADMIRABLE,
Y PENITENTE
DE LA V. M.
SOR SEBASTIANA
JOSEPHA DE LA SS. TRINIDAD,

Religiosa de Coro, y Velo negro en el Religiosíssimo Convento de Señoras Religiosas Clarisas de San Juan de la Penitencia de esta Ciudad de Mexico.

REFIERELA
Fr. JOSEPH EUGENIO VALDES,
Lector de Prima en Sagrada Theologia en este Convento de San Diego de Franciscos Descalzos de esta Nueva-España.

DEDICASE
A la Altíssima Divina Providencia: A cuyas expensas ha podido salir à la publica luz.

Impressa en Mexico, en la Imprenta de la Bibliotheca Mexicana, en el Puente del Espiritu Santo. Año de 1765.

Figure 3. The first page of *Vida de la venerable Madre Sor Sebastiana Josepha*.

for noble indigenous women, they should have been treated better rather than mistreated by the Spanish women allowed entry (AGN, Reales Cédulas, vol. 52, exp. 9, fol. 20). They argued that they did not need nuns from other convents to instruct them and guide them "por el camino de la virtud: es porque es práctica establecida en dicho conservatorio, que no haya de entrar cacica alguna a recibir el hábito sin que primero estén muy diestras, expertas y hábiles en escribir, contar, leer y rezar" ("along the path of virtue: this is because it is an established practice in this place of learning, that no noble indigenous woman would be able to take the veil without first being very adept, expert, and skillful at writing, counting, reading and praying"; AGN, Reales Cédulas, vol. 52, exp. 9, fol. 21).

In 1733 a royal decree was issued, ordering the Spanish nuns to leave the Convent of Corpus Christi and establishing that, from that moment on, only noble indigenous women be accepted there. In various documents, we observe Pedro de Navarrete's insistence on questioning the abilities of the indigenous women to govern for themselves, as in the parecer he sent to the viceroy in 1743 concerning the need to admit three more Spanish nuns to the Convent of Corpus Christi "so that the noble Indian nuns can learn to administer their convent" (AINAH, FF, vol. 120, 3222, fol. 86). Some time later, in 1745, another royal decree was issued, ordering that the three Spanish novices who had taken the habit at the Convent of Corpus Christi leave the convent, along with any other Spanish women, even if they already had taken their vows. It adds that no other women be admitted unless they are elite noble Indians (AGN, Reales Cédulas, vol. 65, exp. 78, fol. 187).

It is difficult to know the exact date when Sor Sebastiana entered Corpus Christi, but she was surely one of the Spanish women who caused the controversy within the community and provoked the royal decrees. All we know is that she entered the Convent of San Juan de la Penitencia in 1744, after having been expelled from Corpus Christi, and took the veil in 1746 at age thirty-seven. The text of the vida recounts that Sebastiana entered the Convent of Corpus Christi the same day as three other Spanish nuns. A notation in the margin, however, clarifies that whoever had written that had made a mistake because on that day, only Sebastiana had entered the convent—which merely suggests that admitting Spanish women into Corpus Christi, outside of novices or professed nuns, was a more or less common practice during the convent's first years.

Although Fray Joseph Valdés expresses concerns about Sebastiana's leaving Corpus Christi in his account, he portrays the convent and its nuns as models of perfection and virtue. Supportive of the indigenous nuns, Fray

Joseph did not voice any opposition to Sebastiana's expulsion from the convent. His combination of loyalties to the indigenous nuns as well as to the Spanish nun (Sebastiana) is surprising. Elisa Sampson Vera Tudela observes that Valdés frames his reaction to the cacica nuns "not in terms of the Devil setting obstacles in the way of our pious heroine" but as a very understandable request on their part, based on the social context in which, historically, each ethnic group belonged to a different *república* (*Colonial Angels* 50). Accordingly, Valdés recounts this unfortunate chapter of Sebastiana's life in Corpus Christi without portraying the indigenous nuns in a negative light.

Valdés begins his story by praising the convent: "El convento, digo, religioso, penitente, austero, y ejemplar de señoras religiosas nobles de Corpus Christi, en donde viven al cielo, muertas al mundo, las naturales caciques, que de todo este reino vienen, como cándidas Palomas, volando a este nido, y Real Palomar" ("The convent, I say, is religious, penitent, austero, and an exemplary place because of the noble religious women of Corpus Christi, a place where they live for heaven, dead to the world, these noble native women, who come from throughout this realm, like true Doves, flying to this nest, the Royal Dovecote"; *Vida* 100). Valdés suggests that the indigenous nuns achieved perfection because of the extremely austere and disciplined life they led, a life that Sebastiana tried to emulate. He notes that the cloistered nuns' practice of severe penitence and corporal mortification was all the more admirable for their being of the "weak sex." His description of the spirituality of indigenous nuns does not mention chastity; as is traditional in this type of work, suffering and mortification are the pivotal elements of his narrative.

When the cloister for indigenous women was founded, there still existed strong opposition among some clergymen, even within the same Franciscan order that had previously supported the women for their abilities. For that reason, Corpus Christi appeared to be the solution when Sebastiana found herself in need of admittance to a convent that did not require a dowry. Sebastiana had the support of the Marquis of Salvatierra in addition to that of the commissary general of the Franciscan order: "Dando las licencias el Comisario general, aunque con resistencia, y con repugnancia de las Religiosas, que no querían recibir Españolas. Pero al fin, a instancias de varias personas, y persuasiones de los prelados, admitieron tres en aquel entonces, y entre ellas a nuestra venerable Sebastiana, de cuya virtud tenían muchas noticias" ("With the approval of the commissary general, although with the opposition and repugnance of the religious women, who did not wish to admit Spanish women. But finally, at the insistence of various people and the persuasion of the prelates, they admitted three at that time, and among the women was our venerable Sebastiana, about whose virtue they had heard much"; *Vida* 102).

As Valdés mentions, it is possible that the nuns did not want to admit Spanish women because they were afraid that their convent would be converted into one more place for the criollas and that over time they would stop admitting indigenous women, as had happened before in the Convent of Santa Clara in Querétaro. Diego de Tapia, an Indian cacique who had inherited great wealth from his father, served as the principal benefactor of Santa Clara, where his daughter had been accepted as a black-veiled nun. Hernando de Tapia, Diego's father and one of the caciques who had contributed to the pacification of the region, had received land grants and other recognitions. Diego de Tapia's plan was for the Convent of Santa Clara to become an institution that would accept indigenous women not as servants but rather as professed nuns; however, no other indigenous women were accepted, and it remained a convent for criolla women. Founded in 1607, the convent was also under Franciscan jurisdiction.[25] Valdés mentions this historical event as a reminder that the Indian nuns were concerned for good reason because they could lose their convent "as they had lost that other one" (108).[26] In a subsequent dispute taken up before the Council of the Indies, it was clarified that neither the Concepción convent (where Isabel de Moctezuma lived) nor the convent in Querétaro was founded exclusively for indigenous women, despite the fact that to the latter "sí se le permitió a una india entrar junto con otras tres españolas" ("permission was granted for an Indian woman to enter along with three Spanish women"; AINAH, FF, vol. 108, fol. 101).

In 1742 the commissary general of the Indies, Fray Mathías Velasco, asked for clarification on the continued presence of the Spanish nuns in the Convent of Corpus Christi. The defense of the three Spanish women to whom entrance had been granted holds that they possessed "ability, honesty and virtue" (AINAH, FF, vol. 108, fol. 88). Support still clearly existed for Spanish nuns living in the convent with the indigenous women. The same document states that "habiéndose puesto a religiosas caciques por maestras de novicias se reconoció no tener suficiencia para el ministerio, pues las mismas novicias y jóvenes se quejaban de la falta de educación y enseñanza monástica echando de menos las de las religiosas españolas" ("Having put the religious cacicas to the task of teaching the novices, it was noted that they did not have the ability to fulfill the ministry, given that the novices themselves and the young women complained about the lack of education and monastic learning and missed that of the Spanish nuns"; AINAH, FF, vol. 120, fol. 88). The document contends that it was best more Spanish women be admitted, even then, because of the noble Indian women's lack of ability and suitability to govern.

Around 1751, the Council of the Indies received a document from the nuns of Corpus Christi accusing the Province of Santo Evangelio, on which the convent depended, of having again admitted Spanish women into the Corpus Christi convent and also of having denied the veil to Indian women. One of their complaints indicated that in more than ten years, not one of the indigenous candidates had been allowed to take the habit. Another point of contention focused on the number of indigenous women admitted in the cloister: although in the past there had been up to thirty religious Indian women in the convent, at that time there were only twenty-three. The report also claims that "aunque hay abadesa india sólo en el nombramiento, porque el mando lo tiene una religiosa española llamada Sor Teresa de San José que fue abadesa por 9 años seguidos y siéndolo permitió el ingreso de las niñas españolas contra lo que decía la bula" ("There is an Indian abbess in name only, because the one really in command is a Spanish nun named Sor Teresa de San José, who was abbess for nine consecutive years and who, as such, allowed Spanish girls into the convent, despite the orders of the Bull"; AINAH, FF, vol. 108, 2630, fol. 93).

The panegyric sermon preached on the death of Sor Teresa de San José states that when she was fifteen years old, she took the veil in the Convent of San Juan de la Penitencia and that at age nineteen she left there to accompany Sor Petra de San Francisco in founding the Corpus Christi convent.[27] The sermon also reveals that Sor Teresa was abbess four times and lived in Corpus Christi for forty-seven years until her death in 1772. Among the accusations sent to the Council of the Indies, however, was the charge that when Sor Teresa arrived at Corpus Christi, she had no experience in religion, and "se nutrió juntamente con las religiosas indias en su regla y constituciones" ("She nourished herself along with the religious Indian women in the precepts and fundamental tenets of her order"). Despite this, "es muy adversa a la fundación y trata a las doncellas pretendientes sin alegría, y sin caridad" ("She is very averse to the establishment and treats the indigenous candidates without joy, and without compassion"; AINAH, FF, vol. 108, 2625, fol. 93). It was also alleged that for nineteen years this same founding nun had had a mulatta servant who frequently humiliated the religious Indian women and mistreated the indigenous postulants. Clearly, the textual construction of the subject varies with the document's purpose. The complaints delivered to the Council of the Indies tried to illustrate how Sor Teresa had continued to govern the convent contrary to the orders of the royal decree, whereas the funerary sermon sought to construct for society and the convent community an idealized feminine figure, a perfect role model in the person of Sor Teresa.

Another of the notable charges presented to the Council of the Indies was that the Convent of Nuestra Señora de la Purísima Concepción de Cosamaloapan, founded in 1737 in Valladolid, was having the same problems as the Convent of Corpus Christi because Spanish nuns had been admitted there too. The problems did not stem solely from the fact that Spanish women had been allowed into a cloister that was supposed to be only for indigenous women. From the documents available, it is apparent that cohabitation in the convent was, in general, fraught with conflict. An important reason for the series of confrontations that arose in the two convents was the meddling of the prelates and confessors in the affairs of those establishments and their insistence on maintaining hierarchies within the convents based on ethnic differences.

The Spanish nuns responded to the accusations made by the Indian women in Corpus Christi, defending themselves point by point in a document sent to the Council of the Indies. To the complaint about the admission of Spanish women into a convent that should have been exclusively for Indian women, for example, they argue: "Era conveniente se criasen juntamente algunas españolas que después pudiesen ser fomento para la guarda del instituto . . . y que criadas desde novicias con las religiosas indias fuese más íntimo el amor y las mismas indias tuviesen ejemplar en las novicias españolas" ("It was advisable that some Spanish women also be trained there who later could provide a model for running the institute . . . and that being raised since their novitiate with the religious Indian women there would be a more intimate love among them and that these same Indian women would have the Spanish novices as role models"; AINAH, FF, vol. 108, fol. 98). This system of instruction was necessary because the Indian women came from a nation of "natural pusillanimity" (fol. 98), an assertion that reveals how deeply rooted the use of stereotype was in the discourse and in the practice of inter-ethnic social relations. The argument elaborates that, as the founding nuns had already died, Spanish novices must be let in and be very young upon entry so that the instruction of the Indian women could last longer; the running of the convent could not be left to the Indian women alone (AINAH, FF, vol. 108, fol. 98).

This document defending the "good will" of the Spanish nuns clearly considers the indigenous women less capable than the Spaniards, even after that subject had already been debated and supposedly abandoned. If we consider that the Spanish women, like the indigenous women, were just about to begin their religious lives as novices, why should they be expected to serve as role models for the Indians? This document denies the veracity of all the accusations made against the Spanish nuns, and it distinctly backs Sor María Teresa de San José from the charges made directly against her and her mulatta servant. Another excuse the document offers for not accepting indigenous candidates was that the convent building was very small, requiring that a number of its cells be used as offices. It also notes a candidate whose purity of bloodline they had not been able to trace, and although her entry had been taking longer than expected, she had not been rejected (AINAH, FF, vol. 108, fol. 100). Moreover, the document clarifies that when Sor Teresa no longer held the post of abbess, the subsequent nuns who occupied the position governed the convent, and if she took on the charge of *maestra de novicias* (mistress of novices), it was because the prelate had ordered it (AINAH, FF, vol. 108, fol. 101).

The anecdote at the beginning of this chapter is taken from the hagiographic biography that one of the Indian nuns wrote about the founding abbess, Sor Petra de San Francisco. The anonymous female writer notes in her narrative that the founding nuns were not the ones who created problems for the indigenous nuns but, rather, the novices whom Fray Navarrete allowed into the convent after Sor Petra died. She explains that those two Spanish nuns complained constantly to Fray Navarrete that the indigenous nuns were failing in their religious practices, accusations for which Navarrete chose to punish the indigenous nuns and, on occasion, even take away their veils.[28] This text demonstrates that the indigenous nuns found the means to make their complaints heard, showed agency by writing about their conflicts in acceptable religious genres, and formed alliances with religious authorities outside the convent to denounce the conflictive situation within.

The debates that surrounded the opening of the Convent of Corpus Christi and the conflicts that continued once the convent had begun to function engendered a substantial discursive production. Each party defended its perspective, but they all made use of the same language and the same rhetoric that the religious colonial system had established. The suppressed voices of the Indian women gained support within their own communities, and their complaints traveled across the Atlantic. They never challenged their image as *miserables* and *pobres indias;* to the contrary, their alleged conformity with the established order enabled alliances that could help them defend the autonomy of their convent.

Biographies and Hagiographies

The Different Perspectives of Gender

Pioneering works devoted to female conventual writing focused, for the most part, on autobiographical writings in which the female biographical voice merges with the representation of mystical or visionary experience.[1] As a feminist endeavor, these critical studies have analyzed the writings of nuns in colonial times for their self-inscription in a tradition of female conventual writing, as well as for the evidence they present of resistance to the patriarchal control exercised by their confessors. Through their writings, nuns expressed their subjectivity and, in some instances, their resistance to the ecclesiastical institution. A gendered perspective further develops our analysis of these texts by considering the writer nun as one member of a binomial pair in which the male confessor fosters the "spiritual daughter's" writing in a socio-political and religious context where a dialogue of power is established.[2] Kathleen Myers and Amanda Powell have explored this more complex approach to reading nuns' writings, calling for a more comprehensive and complex view from which both resistance to and cooperation with clerical authorities can be appreciated (*A Wild Country* 298).[3]

The survival of female autobiographical and biographical writings, as well as texts written by men, whether of their own authorship or as rewritings of female texts within the convent space, allows us to understand the role that gender played in the production of discursive genres from the convent. By deconstructing the relationship established between confessors and their spiritual daughters over the writings each of them produced, we can appreciate how women used the written word at times to subvert the gendered order of things or resist their confessor's power and, at others times, to enlist confessorial support in their writing projects. This power relation that existed between the writer-biographer and the nuns makes us question critical assumptions both of the supposed freedom and the alleged abjection of writing nuns.

Kathleen Ross, in her study of Sigüenza y Góngora, suggests that the lives of Spanish American nuns should be studied in the context of other forms of colonial narrative (153). I would add that not only the vidas but all forms of narrative produced inside and around the convents should be analyzed in this context. Walter Mignolo describes what we generally call "colonial literature" as a body of narratives seldom written with the intention of conforming to a specific literary genre. Although these discourses could be classified according to stylistic elements of composition, Mignolo proposes two criteria of classification: textual formation and discursive type ("Cartas, crónicas y relaciones" 58). I find Mignolo's double criteria particularly useful in analyses of the vida and the hagiographic biography as religious discourses. The grouping of colonial discourse into genres is a relatively recent development. Studies like those of William F. Hanks in linguistic anthropology yield important contributions to our understanding of colonial textual constructions. Hanks contends that texts produced within the colonial context should not be read in isolation but situated, rather, within the broadest of their discursive formations (275).[4]

After some theoretical reflection on the formation of the vida (or life writing) and the hagiographic biography as religious genres, this chapter considers the biographies of the indigenous nuns published by Josefina Muriel in the book *Las indias caciques de Corpus Christi* (The Indian Noblewomen of Corpus Christi) and contrasts those versions with the original manuscript entitled *Apuntes de algunas vidas de nuestras hermanas difuntas* (Notes on Some of Our Deceased Sisters), located in the archives of the actual Convent of Corpus Christi. The style of the hagiographic biographies included in Muriel's book diverges to a great extent from those found in the convent's archive. The former were clearly written by a priest, while those found in the convent have clear linguistic markers that indicate they were written in a female and indigenous voice. Although the narratives are not spiritual autobiographies that developed a nun's authorial voice but rather biographies composed in the third person about other nuns in the convent, the dynamic between genres and genders is evident and relevant.

Vida, Biography, and Hagiography

Electa Arenal and Stacey Schlau in their now classic *Untold Sisters* explain how the environment of the convent furnished an arena for female literary production: "Sisters wrote Lives, letters, chronicles of convent founding, accounts of spiritual experience, and plays" (13). Scholars in the fields of colonial, gender, and feminist studies have shown increased interest in the study of the written genre known as vida or life writing, which, as noted earlier, allows us to appreciate women's subjectivity and some key ways in which they handled the imposed power of the ecclesiastical institution. The genre also displays the nuns' use of rhetorical devices and their creation of a space in which they could voice a discourse of resistance without being punished. For Kathryn Joy McKnight, the genre of the vida, or spiritual life, as she calls it, "emerged out of the relationship between confessors and the women whose spiritual lives they directed" (18). McKnight also notes its resemblance to the confessions that people accused of heresy wrote to Inquisitorial judges. This quality of the vida shows how the genre not only adopts the Catholic model of the confessional but also assumes a legal character. Kathleen Myers offers a definition of the vida centered on the relationship between the nun and her confessor: "At times, confessors requested that a nun record in a written form her innermost thoughts, often called a cuenta de conciencia or relación de espíritu, as a method of advancing this process of self-examination and of extending the confessor's knowledge of his spiritual daughter" (*Word from New Spain* 18).

Within the religious arena, these texts form a kind of hybrid discourse. The vida, when composed as a nun's autobiography, has in itself a confessional voice that allows for long digressions about mystical experiences or, in some instances, spiritual reflections. Occasionally, a spiritual account with no autobiographical details is wrongly called vida. Most of the nuns in New Spain followed the model established by Teresa of Ávila, whose *Libro de la vida* (Book of Her Life) was in turn influenced by Saint Augustine's *Confessions*, which had been translated to the vernacular in the early sixteenth century. We can also glimpse influences of the Inquisitorial process that informed the production of the text and its genre: the judicial confession (Slade 17). Nevertheless, the positions that men and women occupied in the ecclesiastical hierarchy were far from equal, and although Saint Augustine's book offered a formal model for Teresa's writings, hers needed to be framed in a different way. Textual purpose, rhetoric, and language varied with not only the gender of the writer but also, as Kathleen Myers suggests, his or her position in the Church ("Sor Juana y su mundo" 36).

Saint Augustine wrote the account of his life as a confession addressed directly to God without having to be subject to someone else's authority. Teresa of Ávila, on the other hand, wrote the *Libro de la vida* at the request of her confessor. At the beginning of her writing, she states: "Quisiera yo que, como me han mandado y dado larga licencia para que escriba el modo de oración y las Mercedes que el Señor me ha hecho . . . " (7). ("Since my confessors commanded me and gave me plenty of leeway to write about the favors and the kind of prayer the Lord has granted me . . . "; *Teresa of Avila* 1). In contrast, Saint Augustine's *Confessions* declare: "Yet grant me to plead before your mercy, grant me who am dust and ashes to speak, for behold, it is not a man who makes mock of me but your mercy that I address" (45). Many nuns clarify that they have received orders to write not only from their confessors but also and more important from God himself. And we see instances when the nun portrays the role of the confessor solely as intermediary between herself and the divine message of God.

Before Teresa of Ávila, other women had already written mystical reflections as well as spiritual and theological treatises, such as Mechthild of Madenberg, Hadewijch of Brabant, Julian of Norwich, and Saint Catherine of Sienna, among others. According to ecclesiastical authorities, these women were able to create a discourse that was considered correct. Yet, Teresa of Ávila's literary skill, rhetorical talent, and her privileged position in the Church as a reformer and saint made her an exceptional figure.

Libro de la vida blends autobiographical writing with mystical teachings. In the tenth chapter Teresa stops her autobiographical account to introduce what is almost a doctrinal treatise. Alison Weber, referring to the genre in which Teresa's text can be categorized, explains: "The text is clearly nonautobiographical in the sense that Teresa lacks a modern autobiographical motive—the desire to have others observe her uniqueness as an individual; hers is a document produced in response to an order from her confessor to describe her suspect practice of mental prayer and defend the authenticity of the spiritual favors received through it" (43). The text more closely resembles and performs the functions of a "religious/legal" confession, framed by the writer's need to defend herself. Weber analyzes the author's various rhetorical devices, which soon became stylistic resources for most nuns who wrote vidas in Spain and its colonies. She posits that although Teresa did not formally study rhetoric, she was able to learn it from the sermons she had heard and from conversations with "learned friends" (51). Weber's mention of the sermonic genre supports the idea of continuous dialogue between malleable genres, apparent when a writer appropriates and reworks a genre as necessary to achieve a desired purpose.

Gillian Ahlgren has identified particular rhetorical strategies Teresa used to build authority and legitimize both her teachings and her mystical experiences, which were commonly employed by nuns and beatas (lay sisters) as a commonplace in the construction of vidas during the seventeenth and eighteenth centuries. These narrative strategies include the rhetoric of humility and obedience, which can be found in almost all autobiographical narratives written by nuns. Carole Slade makes an important contribution to the study of Teresa's narrative strategies by identifying Teresa's use of other discourse genres, such as the soliloquy and the conversion narrative, employed by Saint Augustine in his *Confessions*, as well as the autohagiography (16). Slade notes Teresa's strategic ability to manipulate the autobiographical genre and merge other genres in her narrative to construct her own kind of discourse (16). Kathleen Ross situates vidas between legal and Christian discourse. She also makes evident the way in which they blend life stories with mystical experiences: "The vidas, however, often blurred into subjective life stories, blending public and private spheres of experience and attributing events to mystical forces outside the scope of conventional religious doctrine" (155). The vida clearly exemplifies the discourse of colonial hybridity.

Gender evidently influenced the production of texts within the convent. Comparative studies of autobiographical accounts written by men and women show significant differences in style and subject. Male narratives do not comment on the author's sex, assume little internal conflict, and are not based on a confessional relationship (Myers, "Sor Juana y su mundo" 55; McKnight 56). Also significant is the fact that many men, in contrast to women, clearly prepared their work for future publication (McKnight 57). Men were considered part of the public sphere in this period, while women were relegated to the private. The vida written by a nun when requested by the confessor remained in the private sphere of the convent, and while it may have circulated among priests, in order to see the light of publication, it needed to be revised and edited by a priest-biographer who would then transform the text from an autobiographical female-authored text into a biography with edifying purposes.[5]

Clergy also used discursive genres that women were prohibited from using, like sermons or theological treaties. An important but not sole exception is Sor Juana Inés de la Cruz, a consciously literary writer who explored themes and genres considered erudite and thus exclusive to university-trained men. To compose her *Answer to Sor Filotea*, she used the epistolary genre not infrequently employed by women as well as men. But she reworked it as Teresa of Ávila had done with the autobiography, opening up the epistolary discourse to a dialogue with other written genres like the autobiography, the theological treatise, and the legal defense, among others.[6]

The genre of the vida is closely related to the biography of a nun because even if the latter was composed by a man, it was generally based on a vida written by the nun herself.[7] The relationship between confessors and their spiritual daughters entailed mutual dependency.[8] The nuns were constantly overshadowed by the Church's unattainable model of perfection and usually affected by the anxiety of having to write as commanded by their confessors. Nonetheless, they depended on their spiritual guidance and even, at times, on their advice in matters pertaining to conventual governance. The priests monitored their spiritual daughters and concentrated on those whose life stories could be rewritten and become models of perfection.

Asunción Lavrin analyzes the genre of biography in colonial Spanish America, focusing on the role of what she terms the "writer-confessor." Lavrin argues that the didactic and exemplary goal of such biographies justified the intellectual appropriation and disclosure of confidences exchanged in a relationship that was assumed to be direct, personal, and confidential ("La vida femenina" 31). Jean Franco also explores the dynamic in which nuns' texts were appropriated, edited, and later published by a priest without acknowledging the original source. The biographer usually recomposed the narrative, inserting clear examples of the necessary virtues of religious perfection such as chastity and obedience: "The culminating point of the story is the 'good death,' usually accompanied by extraordinary signs and miracles" (13). This dynamic moved private writing into the public arena, but not in its original state. Rewriting the original text also entailed some alteration of its original language.

Religious women, most of whom had access to no more than a basic education, generally reproduced spoken language in their writing instead of the highly adorned language of clerics, who were trained in the rhetorical arts. Teresa of Ávila modeled the use of speech in writing, and although she was familiar with "high" language, she "pioneered a down-to-earth yet spiritual style" that did not threaten the gendered, rhetorical status quo and quickly became popular among women religious on both sides of the Atlantic (Arenal and Schlau, "Stratagems" 34).

Given that most nuns' texts, if they were printed at all, did not appear as originally written but were instead published under the name of a man and in a greatly modified style, where do we situate either the literary or cultural value of such writings? Darcy Donahue, taking on this challenge, incisively notes the different ways in which nun writers of vidas and confessor-editors of biographies inscribed their subjectivities in their written discourse (230). Not until we uncover the nuns' original versions and place them side-by-side with the male-rewritten versions can we accurately assess when and to what degree these women were capable of challenging and negotiating their position in a tightly controlled arena. Extant texts from indigenous nuns of the Corpus Christi convent reveal a diverse range of rhetorical and stylistic strategies used both to frame religious discourse and to hide pointed subtexts in commonly accepted formulae of the period. Untangling the discursive thread of their written language allows us to perceive the power and meaning of "the tricks of the weak."[9]

The biographical texts of nuns bear an intrinsic relation to another discursive type, the hagiography. As hybrid texts, religious biographies merge elements of different genres to create a life narration intended to appear more exemplary than real (Donahue 231; Greenspan, "Autobiography" 219).[10] The genre that evolves from this adaptation of nuns' writings has also been labeled "biohagiography" or hagiographical biography. These kinds of texts emerged from a priest's edition of a nun's autobiographical vida emphasizing those instances where a simple life story can be transformed into an exemplary text. Drawing on the centuries-long popularity of the saints' hagiographic lives, compiled in volumes like the *Flos sanctorum*, vidas from before and after Teresa of Ávila generally follow themes characteristic of the hagiography, as well as a similar narrative structure of events: the subject's childhood, education, metaphorical fall, and conversion. The narrative stresses their desire to live outside the secular world to dedicate their lives to God, culminating with a prolonged description of their virtues. The structure of vidas was consistent with the demands of the beatification process (McKnight 51).[11]

Significantly, when the vida of the nun is transformed in the hagiographic biography, the subject surpasses her female condition. Described with virile epithets, the nuns become extraordinary, their virtues setting them apart from the rest. They somehow lose their female humanity in the text and become perfect according to the religious model of the time, whose standard was masculine, in accordance with the misogynistic values of Aristotelian philosophical traditions continued in the doctrines and practices of the Catholic Church. Still, drawing on the historicized model of dialogic feminism proposed by Laurie Finke, we find women authors in the convent employing discourses created by the oppressor in order to actively challenge patriarchal domination. When taking up the pen in the cloister, women demonstrated resistance by creating spaces of contestation, borrowing the language and style of these three genres that were in constant dialogue.

The Apuntes of Corpus Christi: The Original Version

The religious practices and notion of spirituality adopted by the indigenous population after Spaniards invaded their territory have been the main topics of an important body of academic investigation.[12] These studies yield a cache of interpretive possibilities regarding the impact of Catholic religion and missionary proselytizing on the indigenous population. Several key variables shape this phenomenon, particularly cultural differences between ethnic groups and missionary orders, as well as the age, gender, class, and region of those indoctrinated. When missions were first established in the Americas, mendicant orders baptized first generations of natives in mass numbers without much indoctrination, but by the eighteenth century Catholicism had become an entrenched aspect of Indian ethnic identity.[13]

Jorge Klor de Alva proposes that by the seventeenth century, Christian teachings brought from Spain to Mexico had been completely "Nahuatized" by the Indians, "who considered themselves genuine Christians even as they worshiped many spiritual beings, disregarded the significance of the teachings on salvation, and continued to make this-worldly ends the legitimate object of their religious devotion" (174). Many terms have been applied to the complexity of the religious-spiritual spectrum in colonial Mexico: acculturation, adaptation, syncretism, resistance, or even Nahuatization. The broad variety of terms reveals that no single conceptual paradigm describes the full dimensionality of the colonial religious experience under conquest and colonization.

The concept of "local religion," coined by William Christian Jr. in his book on sixteenth-century Spain, and used later by Martin Austin Nesvig to refer to colonial Mexico, yields a fruitful methodological approach to the problem of analyzing diverse religious practices on an equally diverse stage. The religious practices of Catholicism develop local and popular traditions that diverge from the norm but do not necessarily contradict official doctrine; rather, they overlap and on occasion are "officially tolerated, other times officially ignored, still other times formally prosecuted" (Nesvig xix). The notion of local religion developed to analyze peninsular Spain functions as a useful tool to understand the interactions established between indigenous groups and representatives of the Catholic Church in Mexico heading into the eighteenth century.

The convents founded exclusively for noble indigenous women were an adaptation of a traditional institution that existed for European women. Indigenous women were not allowed into the same convents established for criollas in New Spain, but instead, cloisters were founded exclusively for noble Indian women and restricted to a certain class. Thus, the indigenous monastic experience unfolded as the singular articulation of one particular community. On the other hand, the women who took part in this experience found themselves united by ethnic consciousness and the class prestige their families had enjoyed for centuries; a sense of nation set them apart from the other nuns living in the convents of New Spain. Even so, why would indigenous women enter the convent if to do so apparently meant accepting the imposition of the hegemonic colonial culture?

The question resists simple answers. Surviving documents suggest some possible motivations why these women chose religious life, what moved their parents to support them in this decision, and what led other indigenous people to accept the convent as positive. Studies of convents for indigenous women in colonial Mexico indicate that the cloister served as an affirmation of the colonial status of the women who inhabited it. Ultimately, it represented an instrument of control. For instance, Asunción Lavrin notes that indigenous women adopted certain values and behaviors of Spanish society but still maintained their own identity; nevertheless, she asserts that the convent represented a defeat for indigenous women because they accepted the religion of the conqueror (*Latin American Women* 14). Susan Schroeder suggests that the delay in opening a convent for indigenous women in part can be explained by their resistance to the imposition of religion on them (9). An issue that remains unacknowledged by Lavrin and Schroeder is that by the eighteenth century, the indigenous noble class considered conventual life a privilege that affirmed indigenous ethnic authority in the colonial scheme.

Closer examination of the Corpus Christi convent records in light of these theoretical perspectives prompts further questions. Did the indigenous nun's religious devotion parallel or differ from that of the Spanish nun? Was the Spanish desire to maintain supervision inside the convent due to a fear that the Indian women would use the Nahuatl language or that they would maintain certain ethnic characteristics that, although not interfering directly with an orthodox Catholicism, were viewed as suspicious? Although there are no means to answer these questions fully, I propose that what actually distinguished these convents was their designation as an indigenous space, endorsed by colonial authorities but maintained and defended by the nuns themselves.

Until recently, there was only one known biographical manuscript concerning seven of the convent's indigenous nuns and one of the criolla founders of the Convent of Corpus Christi. Josefina Muriel published this manuscript in 1963 with the title *Las indias caciques de Corpus Christi* (The

Indian Noblewomen of Corpus Christi).[14] The manuscript is composed in the third person, and even though no author's signature appears, it was evidently written by a priest and not by one of the nuns, as Josefina Muriel concluded. Through archival research I was able to locate one further manuscript composed by the indigenous nuns which parallels the narratives included in the *Las indias caciques* manuscript.[15] Entitled *Apuntes de algunas vidas de nuestras hermanas difuntas* (Notes on Some of Our Deceased Sisters), it consists of eight biographical narratives that re-create everyday language and quotidian activities within the convent while blending hagiographic aspects in a characteristic oral style (fig. 4).[16] While the priest's narration is highly structured and formulaic, the women's narratives are full of what Arenal and Schlau called "domesticated religious jargon and spiritualized household terms" ("Stratagems" 33).

The *Las indias caciques* manuscript includes the hagiographic biographies of Sor Petra de San Francisco, first abbess and criolla founder, Sor Antonia de los Santos, Sor Rosa, Sor Rosa de Loreto, Sor Apolonia de la Santísima Trinidad, Sor Gertrudis del Señor San José, Sor Magdalena de Jesús, and Sor María Felipa de Jesús. Not all the narratives are of the same length, nor do they have the same structure. The last two particularly are longer, and the life of Sor María Felipa is so formally presented that it gives the impression of having been prepared for publication, perhaps even as a work separate from the others.

These published narratives share certain characteristics with hagiographic biographies. For example, each story starts with the nun's childhood, when she is taught good behavior by her parents or witnesses her parents as virtuous role models. Nevertheless, in some cases, the parents' names are not revealed, only references to "don" and "doña." All the nuns described in the narratives display the model hagiographic virtues of humility, mortification, penance, fasting, and poverty. Finally, all die of a long illness that weakened their health but did not interfere with their work or keep them from being examples for the community; they happily bear their cross until the day they die. They also share a strong devotion to the Virgin Mary.

An important detail about the hagiographic biographies in *Las indias caciques* is that information is missing from some sections, specifically the dates. For example, if the story recounts a nun taking her vows, it only states that "she took her vows on . . ." followed by a blank space, or, for example, "she died on . . ." It is possible that the manuscript published by Josefina Muriel was an early version of a later, more complete manuscript or that the writer intended to fill in those blank spaces with reliable information

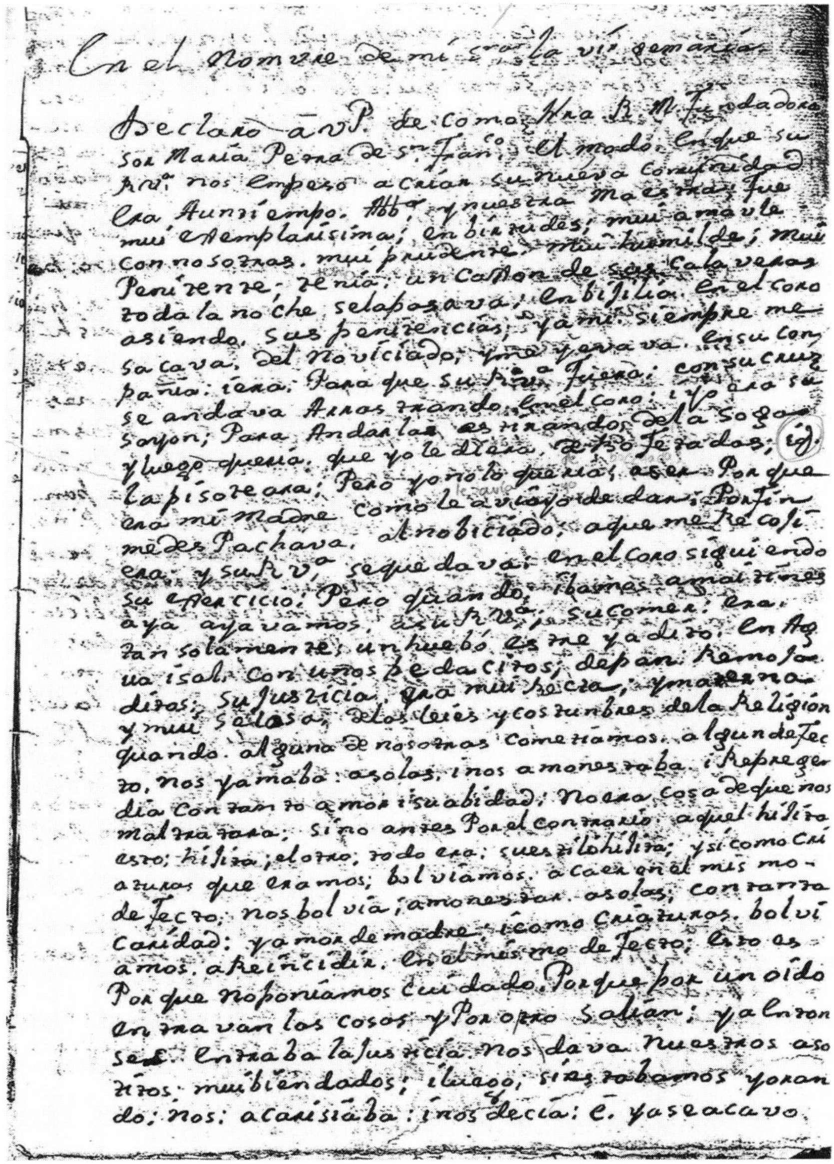

Figure 4. The first page of *Apuntes de algunas vidas de nuestras hermanas difuntas*. (Courtesy of the Monasterio Autónomo de Clarisas de Corpus Christi, n.d.)

provided by the convent nuns or from the registry and information book, a task that was never completed.

In the *Las indias caciques* version, the biographer recounts that Sor Antonia de los Santos was one of the first noble Indian women to take the habit and that after her novitiate, she was accepted by the other nuns.[17] The text also states that she constantly sang the "Tota Pulchra" (a song to the Virgin Mary, most common in Franciscan communities) and played the *vihuela*, a kind of guitar. The narrative emphasizes her obedient nature. For instance, "nunca le vieron acostada en su cama, sino que en un petatito" ("They never saw her lying in her bed, but rather on a little straw floor mat.") The diminutive use of the word "petate" is a common indigenous usage. The male writer repeatedly employs metaphors, a stylistic trait associated with the male narrative composition of this era.[18] For example, regarding the mystery of Jesus's birth, "Engolfábase tanto en la consideración de este misterio, que forcejeando la fuerza del espíritu hacia lo exterior rompía los muros de la gravedad y modestia que estaba tan acostumbrada en su porte" ("She would be plunged so deeply into the consideration of this mystery that the strength of her spirit, making its way outward, would break through the walls of solemnity and modesty that were so much a part of her bearing"; 125).

In clear contrast to the published hagiographic biographies, the female-composed manuscript housed in the archives of the Convent of Corpus Christi, the *Apuntes*, also relates the life of Sor Antonia. The female writer of the biography offers a few anecdotes from Sor Antonia's life relating how she picked through food that had been tossed out, and instead of eating what the other women ate in the refectory, she would eat the onion stalks she found in the trash (*Apuntes* 11, *Las indias caciques* 117). But the style and language of the female-authored and male-authored versions differ greatly. In a section recounting how Sor Antonia would sing the "Tota Pulchra," the female biographer describes her as "bailadora y tocadora" (dancer and musician), and when describing her death, she relates that "se fue quedando como dormidita nana Antonia" ("Sister Antonia gradually faded away as if she were just getting sleepy"; 13). The language used in the biography written by a woman does not employ complex metaphors, and although the narrative includes some common hagiographical elements—such as the subject's bodily mortifications with a cilice (hairshirt) and her humility, shown by her using a little stick in place of a spoon—the female author's writing style is relatively informal and lacks the priest's artifice.

The nun writer without a doubt knew how to follow the hagiographic model but avoids the commonly used language of male-authored hagiographic biographies. The tone this female biographer employs in the *Apuntes* differs greatly from the male writer's in *Las indias caciques*, making the narrative seem more first-hand and thus more credible, although hagiographic conventions can still be identified. The female writer affirms the authenticity of her biographical narration: "De todo esto que he dicho es mucha verdad de que doy fe y hago mi signo" ("All that I have said here is very true, as I do swear and sign with my mark"; 13). Her "mark" is the cross, commonly used in lieu of a signature by the illiterate.[19] The nun who signs with her mark the biography of Sor Antonia dictated this narration to a scribe, yet by adding her signature, the biographer was inscribing herself in the narrative of her deceased sister (Donahue 238).

According to the hagiographic biography of Sor Rosa in *Las indias caciques*, she was one of the first Indian women to take the habit, just like Sor Antonia. Similar to the other life stories, the biography of Sor Rosa narrates that she fasted, and even when she was suffering, she appeared to be happy. It emphasizes her patience and her serving as the "sacristana" (the person in charge of the sacristy). Much like Sor Antonia, Rosa suffered from a gangrenous lesion that eventually led to her death.

The hagiographic biography of Sor Rosa included in the published version recounts that she was taught good behavior by her parents, that she was born in Capuluac, and that she and her sister were donadas, or community servants, in the Convent de la Concepción. One of the linguistic marks that allows me to assert once again that the composition was written by a priest is present in the following passage that refers to what the women learned while they were donadas: " . . . mezclando las de devoción con otras, propias de su sexo" ("mixing [the lessons] of devotion with others, proper to their sex"; 163). A nun would most likely not have referred to the female sex as *their* sex.

To illustrate how humble Sor Rosa was, the *Apuntes* version of her life narrates that she would gather up "las andalias" (a phonetic spelling of "sandals") of all the nuns and wash them, and that she would visit the sick nuns at four in the morning. The narrator recounts one particular instance about Sor Rosa on her deathbed: sisters requested Sor Rosa not to die during the night because it would frighten nuns in the convent, a request she honored by dying at eight in the morning. This particular life story exemplifies the orality in the nun's writing in clear contrast to the textualiy of the priest's version: "Cada vez y siempre que la encontraba iba andando con sus pasitos de gato y con los ojos cerrados y le decíamos 'nanita ya te vas durmiendo' y los abría tantito." (Every time I ran into her, she would be shuffling along quiet as a cat and with her eyes closed, and we would tell her, 'sister you're falling asleep,' and she would open them a little; 18).

Figure 5. A portrait of an indigenous Clarisa
nun, Sor María Joaquina del Señor San Rafael.
(Anonymous, nineteenth century; courtesy of the
Museo Nacional del Virreinato—INAH; Fototeca
del Museo Nacional del Virreinato)

A passage in the *Apuntes* narrating Sor Rosa's illness invites comparison with the style and intent of the male compiler-editor of the hagiographic biographies of the *Las indias caciques*. In *Las indias caciques* we read: "Por una temporada padeció un carbunclo que le salió en el cerebro y que le debilitó tanto que andaba testereándose con las paredes sin que se observase en alguna ocasión desabrida, ni se le oyese desahogar su dolor con alguna queja" ("For a time she suffered from a carbuncle on her brain which weakened her so much that she would go about bumping into the walls, yet without ever looking cross, nor did anyone ever hear her complain about her pain"; 193).[20] By contrast, the *Apuntes* relates " . . . que le salió un carbunco. En el cerebro: cuya enfermedad sufrió con tanta paciencia, pero que con tanto purgar le desflaqueció el cerebro; y andaba trastabillando a modo de loquita" (" . . . that she developed a lesion on the brain; and she suffered that illness with such patience, but also with so much purging that it weakened her brain; and she would reel around like a crazy woman"; 19). The two versions clearly use different styles and language to illustrate their different purposes. A narrative aspiring to set an example would not describe the nun to be like a "crazy woman." In the *Las indias caciques*, the editing and modifications of the earlier text are evident.

The colloquial style of the narratives apparently written by indigenous nuns springs from a tradition imitated not just from female-authored religious texts but also from a linguistic practice deeply rooted in their culture. Through their writing, the noble Indian women combined the oral tradition of recovering their indigenous past with the narrative stratagems common to female conventual writing. One of the impositions that the Spaniards brought to American territory was the use of the written word. Walter Mignolo in *The Darker Side of the Renaissance* studies the alternate forms of historicity and literature used by indigenous groups. The word *tlatollótl*, "devoted to conceptualizing discursive configurations and discursive types," illustrates the methods Nahua groups used to record their histories (142). From the Western point of view, oral genres as well as pictographic and ideographic writing were given far less cultural value than alphabetic textual production in certain prestigious forms. As Mignolo observes, during the sixteenth century only that which was recorded in a written genre and was part of the historical discursive configuration was considered history (142). Although the religious practices of confession and the actual task of writing a hagiographic biography influenced the way in which these women recorded their histories and constructed their own subjectivity, oral tradition continued to permeate their discursive practices.

The *Las indias caciques* version states that Sor Apolonia de la Santísima Trinidad was the seventh nun to take her vows in the Convent of Corpus Christi. Drawing on the same hagiographic descriptive elements in the biographies of other nuns, it relates the anguishes Sor Apolonia had suffered and describes her as a hard worker. It also recounts how she had always maintained silence, and it narrates the story of the illness that led to her death. With regard to Sor Gertrudis del Señor San José, the *Las indias caciques* version states that she was robust and healthy, a description that had already been used with Salvadora de los Santos in chapter 3, and that she was still in the Convent of San Juan de la Penitencia when she was introduced to Sor Petra de San Francisco, who advised her to learn to read and write in order to be admitted into the Corpus Christi convent. Identified as one of two indigenous nuns alleged to be descendants of Juan Diego, Sor Gertrudis is said to have come from the town of Nuestra Señora de Guadalupe.[21] She is presented as a visionary: "En una ocasión advirtieron el que solamente hablaba y no sabiendo con quién, le preguntaron que qué plática era aquella y con quién. Y ella sencillamente satisfizo diciéndoles: 'Ha estado aquí el Esposo vestido de pastor y me dijo que iba a ver a sus ovejas y que a las cuatro vendría por mí para llevarme'" ("On one occasion, they say, she was all alone, talking, and having no idea whom she was talking to, they asked her what she was talking about and with whom. And she easily answered them with: 'The [Divine] Bridegroom has been here, dressed as a shepherd, and He told me that He was going to tend his sheep and that at four o'clock he would come to take me away'"; 239). Such visions and voices recur as significant elements in some of the hagiographic biographies included in *Las indias caciques*.

The life story of the "Venerable Mother" Magdalena de Jesús in *Las indias caciques* relates that she had come from Guadalajara and had been a servant in a convent, the Convent of Santa María de Gracia, according to the *Apuntes* version. The male narrator suggests, through a description of the retinue that accompanied the nun on her journey, that she came from a wealthy family: "Asalarió una competente comitiva de indios mecos, mansos, que armados de arco y flecha, hacían escolta para la defensa" ("She hired a capable entourage of traditional and compliant Indians armed with bows and arrows, who formed a defense convoy"; 257). The image of Indians with bows and arrows, which is picturesque at best and does not appear in the original version of the biography, might be considered poetic license on the part of the editor of the hagiographic biographies. The narrative indicates that along the way, they almost landed in a ravine, but a man appeared to show them the correct path. The *Apuntes* also recounts this anecdote, adding in a later passage that "y cuando ya estaba acá dentro, luego que vido a Nuestro Señor Crucificado que estaba en el coro, luego lo conoció a su magestad y dijo que aquel señor era el que le había salido en el encuentro, en el camino" ("And once she had arrived here in the convent, as soon as she saw [the image of] Our Lord Crucified in the upper choir, she recognized His Majesty, and she said that man was the one who had appeared to her on the road"; 14).

Sor Magdalena's apparitions are recounted in both versions, which means that her visions met with the approval of her confessor, mentioned in the *Apuntes* as Fray Miguel Lozano, at that time the convent chaplain. The edited biography and the *Apuntes* recount that when Sor Magdalena saw Jesus in the upper choir, the other sisters told her to be more humble, or she could have problems with the Inquisition (*Apuntes* 14; *Las indias caciques* 287). Sor Magdalena's life narration illustrates what Arenal and Schlau have identified as key characteristics of nuns' writings: "They include both explorations of inner religiosity (visions, ecstasies, theological interpretations of personal and mystical experiences) and descriptions of active lives" ("Stratagems" 27). The nun writer responsible for recounting Sor Magdalena's life story includes her sister's religious experiences in her narrative but at the same time places her within the community of nuns, including their voices and opinions on everyday matters.

Both versions take into account Sor Magdalena's virtues, but the *Apuntes* emphasizes that she was "pobrísima" (extremely poor). It also notes that she wore cilices and was very obedient. However, *Las indias caciques* stresses (as do all the other hagiographic biographies) her devotion to the Virgin Mary, her fasting, discipline, and constant prayer. A significant detail in *Las indias caciques* is its reference to the existence of the nun's writings: " . . . pero no se sabe con individualidad cosa alguna, aunque pudieran saberse muchas si la desgracia no hubiera perdido los papeles de apuntes que hicieron sus confesores" ("But no single detail is known with absolute certainty, although we could have known many had those papers, with notes written by her confessors, not been lost through misfortune"; 273). This confirmation that annotations written by her confessors once existed immediately suggests the possibility that Sor Magdalena could have written down her religious experiences and thoughts in the form of an examination of conscience for her confessor. Nevertheless, neither the original notes nor those of the confessor have been found, leaving only the possibility that the writing practice that existed in convents for criollas and Spaniards existed among indigenous nuns alike.

The hagiographic biography of Sor María Felipa de Jesús in *Las indias caciques* is the longest of all the biographies in the collection, and yet it remained incomplete. In this text, we can distinguish an attempt to be more formal and meticulously detailed in the description of her life, perhaps because she was the first indigenous nun who held the post of prioress in the Convent of Corpus Christi. Her life story begins, like many others, with the good behavior taught her by her parents, and it stresses her "entendimiento claro" (lucid intelligence), her many virtues, and her devotion to the Virgin Mary. Still, her life story is much more closely related to the hagiographic model and structured using formulae commonly found in hagiographies, like her practice of reading books of devotion and retreating into the desert.

The narrative recounts the anecdote of the day a priest arrived in the village where María Felipa lived. In the confessional, when she showed an interest in the religious life, the priest mentioned the possibility of becoming a nun because a convent for indigenous women had opened up in Mexico City. Because of her father's opposition to her desire, the priest helped Felipa run away from home to Mexico City. For two years, she was examined and the *informaciones* were compiled to determine if she was right for conventual life; finally, she was accepted into the Convent of Corpus Christi. As part of the construction of her "saintly" life, María Felipa heard divine voices: " . . . oyó clara y distintamente voces que salían del mismo simulacro y que le decían: 'Felipa hasta cuando te has de dar toda mía'" ("She heard very clearly and distinctly voices that came from her delusions, voices that said: 'Felipa, when will you devote yourself to me completely'"; 303). She also had visions, such as one in which she witnessed a statue of Jesus of Nazareth move its lips (350).

Another of Felipa's religious experiences occurred when she turned herself into a child again: " . . . de repente se sintió como transformada en una niña como de cuatro o cinco años, no daba crédito a novedad tan extraña" ("Suddenly, she felt as if she had been changed into a little girl of about four or five years old, but she could hardly understand such a strange occurrence"; 341). The narrator of the biography explains that Felipa turned herself into a little girl because Jesus Christ said that we should be small and childlike in order to be worthy of salvation (345). Here we have yet again a case of supernatural experiences endorsed by a priest. In a manner similar to what Kathleen Myers recounts of the "rescripting" of María de San José's life by her biographer, Santander y Torres, the biographer of the indigenous nuns, carefully edits and manipulates information in order to create an ideal subject (*Neither Saints* 84). He reformulates the original information to present a narration of trial for the *perfecta religiosa* that required many tests be passed to attain perfection in this life and the aftermath.[22]

The last life story in the *Apuntes* concerns Sor María Francisca and is especially significant because it does not appear in the published version of *Las indias caciques*. In the title of the story, the nun biographer includes the possessive pronoun "mi" (mine) in front of the subject's name, which had not been used in any of the other biographies. This particular life story is very short and cannot be considered biographical because of the minimal information it provides. It narrates that Sor María Francisca, originally from a town in Oaxaca, was a very poor orphan, and the main point of the narrative sketch recounts the miracle she experienced. As the narrator tells us, when Sor María Francisca was on her journey from her hometown to the Convent of Corpus Christi, she stopped to spend the night in a cave that was the haunt of lions and foxes. But on that night, the animals never showed up, and in this way "quiso Jesús haberles amanecido con bien" ("Jesus assured that they would be safe when they awoke"; 16). She was in danger on several occasions, but Jesus protected her so that she could arrive safely at her destination and take the habit.

From a comparative analysis of the two sets of biographical narratives, we can conclude that the priest who wrote the manuscript published as *Las indias caciques* did not simply base his written work on the manuscript written by the indigenous nun from Corpus Christi but had a clear purpose in mind with the editing and reworking of the *Apuntes*. When placed in the context of the debate about the suitability of Indian women for religious life, the manuscript of *Las indias caciques* reveals many additions tied to arguments in the testimonials analyzed in chapter 2 and presented by the priests in favor of the convent for Indian women. That is to say, the rewriting and editing of the original indigenous writing could have been planned for publication as a means of defending the indigenous women as capable of not only living in a community but also leading an exemplary and, in some cases, even saintly life. The supporting argument in favor of the indigenous nuns focuses on the following points, which are repeated in all the hagiographic biographies: their good behavior taught them by their parents, their ability to read and write, their maintenance of the vow of chastity, and, finally, their practice of mental prayer.[23]

The hagiographic biographies recount, for example: "Desde que Rosa entró en la religión tomó con mucho empeño el ejercicio de la oración mental a la que le daba muchas horas del día y de la noche" ("From the moment Rosa entered religious life she threw herself with great determination into the exercise of mental prayer, devoting many hours each day and night to it"; 148–149). Of Sor Rosa de Loreto: "Aplicóse a la frecuencia de los santos sacramentos, e impuesta en el modo de tener oración mental, abrazó ésta con exquisito ardor" ("She dedicated herself to taking the holy sacraments frequently, and once initiated into a routine of mental prayer, embraced it with exquisite ardor"; 163). Of Sor Magdalena of Jesus: "Impulsóla ésta (la madre Cierva) en el modo de tener oración mental, ejercicio que tomó Magdalena con mucho empeño" ("Sister Cierva initiated her into a routine of mental prayer, an exercise Magdalena employed with great dedication"; 249). There is even a clear reference to something Teresa of Ávila ponders in *The Interior Castle*; the writer says of Magdelena: "De suerte que siendo tanta dada a la oración, se podía dudar de si era más apta para los ejercicios de Marta, que para los de María, porque solamente cuando estaba en el coro la hallaban desocupada" ("Being by good fortune so well disposed to prayer, one could wonder if she was more suited to the exercises of Martha than to those of Mary, because only when she was in the upper choir did they find her unoccupied"; 267).[24]

The issue of mental prayer practiced by indigenous people was especially controversial, given that it had been used as an argument *against* opening the cloister for indigenous women. The Jesuit Joseph María Guevara of the Colegio de San Gregorio argued in a written testimonial opposing a monastery for Indian women: "Uno de estos Pobres Naturales merece más y agrada más a Dios nuestro Señor poniéndole flores a un santo, encendiéndole sus velas, echándole su saumerio, que si gastara muchas horas en el ejercicio tan santo de la Oración mental, en la cual, sin duda, gastará el tiempo sin provecho" ("One of these Poor Natives is more worthy, and pleases Our Lord God more, by placing flowers before a saint, lighting candles to them, cleansing them with aromatic incense, than if they were to spend many hours in an exercise as holy as mental prayer, in which, without doubt, the time would be wasted and with no benefit"; AGN, Hist., vol. 109, exp. 2, fol. 30). Joseph María Guevara tries to present an image of the Indians as simple, childlike souls, but what he does is debase them to a level inferior to the Spaniards and affirm that they cannot understand the complexities of the faith. In response to this, the group of hagiographic biographies included in *Las indias caciques* are offered as proof not only that the indigenous women could become nuns but also that they had the ability to penetrate the mysteries of the faith by practicing mental prayer and by experiencing the visions, voices, and other "mystical gifts" that marked the path of perfection they had chosen to follow.

In addition to enumerating the religious virtues the indigenous nuns possessed, the writer of *Las indias caciques* showed awareness of the criticism of the founding of a convent for Indians by noting in the hagiographic biography of Sor María Felipa de Jesús that she had reflected on the happiness that had come to her as a result of the conquest of these lands. And she would say to herself: "Yo soy Cristiana por la gracia de Dios y hará trescientos años ¿qué eran mis abuelos, mis ascendientes? ¡Ay de lo que me libró Dios!" ("I am a Christian by the grace of God and three hundred years ago, what were my grandparents, my ancestors? Oh, what God has freed me from!"; 357).

Possibly, this monologue was included to support more indigenous foundations and to demonstrate the true Christian faith of these nuns. The priest faced a contradiction when writing about the nuns as "Indian," since the discursive construction had to distance the indigenous perfecta religiosa from her native religion while at the same time emphasizing her ethnicity, which explained her humility, obedience, and submissiveness, for example: "Quedó el devoto padre gozosamente admirado, de haber encontrado en aquel miserable pueblo, a una pobre indita en quien Dios había derramado tan superabundantemente los tesoros de su gracia" ("The devout priest was joyfully admired for having found, in that miserable village, a poor little Indian woman into whom God had poured so many of the superabundant treasures of his grace"; 311). The use of the diminutive *indita* could be considered pejorative, but in the context of ecclesiastical discourse, it presents indigenous women as childlike and justifies the priests' protection and control. The image of the indita resonates with the Jesuit José María Guevara's discourse, but in the case of the biographical hagiography, the smallest (the meek) end up as the greatest (who inherit the earth), as the Bible suggests.

I have left for last an analysis of the first of the life stories that appear in both *Las indias caciques* and the *Apuntes*. Here the active participation of the writer nun in the convent's ethnic conflicts opens up the discussion of indigenous women's active engagement in defending this conventual space for the women of their "race."

This first narrative contains vignettes from the life of Sor Petra of San Francisco, one of the founding criolla nuns of Corpus Christi and its first abbess.[25] From the beginning of Sor Petra's biographical narration, we can appreciate the differences between the texts composed by the priest and the nun, not only in narrative style but also in quantity of information and details included in their respective versions. The initial difference between the texts is that the biographies authored by the indigenous nun are written at the request of her confessor, following the model established by Teresa of Ávila.[26] The text in the *Apuntes* begins: "Declaro a Vuestra Paternidad de cómo nuestra Reverenda Madre Fundadora Sor Petra de San Francisco. El modo en que su Reverencia nos empezó a criar en su nueva comunidad"

("I declare to you, Father, the manner in which our Reverend Founding Mother Sister Petra of Saint Francis began to nurture us in her new community"; 7). Yet the text composed by a priest and published by Josefina Muriel dives directly into the subject matter of the biographical narration: "La reverenda madre Sor Petra de San Francisco, pasó del convento de San Juan de la Penitencia, a éste de Corpus Christi en calidad de abadesa . . . " ("The Reverend Mother Sister Petra of San Francisco came from the Convent of San Juan of the Penitence to this one, Corpus Christi, in the role of abbess . . ."; 75).

We also find clear linguistic marks through which the writer of the *Apuntes* includes herself as a member in the convent community: "Fue muy ejemplarísima en virtudes, muy amable con *nosotras*, muy prudente, muy humilde, muy penitente" ("She was the very highest model of virtue, very kind to *us*, very prudent, very humble, very penitent"; 7).[27] Although the female biographer also makes use of hagiographical elements, her style is more colloquial and much less rhetorical than that of the male writer. She recounts that women who wished to enter the Convent of Corpus Christi used to visit Sor Petra in her previous convent, where she taught them to read Latin and the prayers of the Divine Office, demonstrating that the indigenous nuns possessed the same degree of religious culture as the Spaniards and criollas at the time of profession.

The female narrator of the *Apuntes* offers the following portrayal of Sor Petra: "Nos daba nuestros azotitos bien dados y luego si estábamos llorando nos acariciaba y nos decía: Esto ya se acabó hijitas. Más azotaron a nuestro esposo y peores cosas hicieron con su majestad" ("She would give us our good little lashes and then if we were crying, she would caress us and she would tell us: This is over, my daughters. They gave more lashes to our Bridegroom and did worse things to His Majesty"; 7–8). According to the writer, Sor Petra wanted to teach her conventual sisters that their suffering could not be worse than that of Jesus. The depiction of suffering as an essential element of spirituality, which always appears in the genre of the vida, is clearly present in Sor Petra's teachings.

Once the biographer concludes her version of the life of Sor Petra, she continues writing about the conflicts created by the entrance of the four Mothers ("cuatro madres") from the Convent of San Juan whom, she says, Fray Pedro de Navarrete imposed upon us ("nos echó encima") after Sor Petra closed her eyes ("cerró el ojo")(8). Fray Pedro Navarrete was one of the instigators of the conflicts not only in the Convent of Corpus Christi but later in the Convent of Cosamaloapan in Valladolid, where he again allowed criolla women in the convents founded exclusively for indigenous women.

The writer of the *Apuntes*, taking advantage of the strong likelihood that her account will be read by an ecclesiastical authority, offers her version of the situation in the convent. Although the Convent of Corpus Christi had been conceived as an indigenous institution, the nuns who served as founders were all women of Spanish descent from the Convent of San Juan de la Penitencia. The original plan proposed that as soon as indigenous nuns had the ability to govern their own convent, the criolla women would leave the noble indigenous women in their cloister. But who should decide if the indigenous women had the capacity to govern themselves, and when?

Thus, the indigenous writer, who claimed to be offering a biographical narration, did not limit herself to hagiographical formulae but included in her discourse a denunciation of the conflictive situation that had developed in the convent as a result of having allowed Spanish women to enter:

> ¡Qué guerra! Lo más mínimo que hacíamos solo nos estaban atisbando para acusarnos nuestro Padre Navarrete. Cuando menos nos percatábamos ya estaba allí, ya nos venía a despotar [sic] y a penitenciarnos y a quitarnos los velos, y a pleito querían también que votáramos a fuerza a las novicias españolas para que profesaran. No queríamos porque la mente del patrón fue que sólo para las indias. (9)

> (What a battle! They [the criollas] were constantly watching us for even the smallest thing that we did, so they could accuse us of wrongdoing before Father Navarrete. When we were least expecting it, he was already there, acting as a despot, punishing us and taking away our veils. He wanted to force us to vote for the Spanish novices so they could profess in the convent. We did not want that because our patron's idea was that the convent be only for Indian women.)

The writer uses rhetorical devices and strategies familiar to female religious writers. She follows the model usually found in spiritual autobiographies and in conventual foundation narratives in which the conflicts between nuns or with ecclesiastical authorities function as obstacles to the achievement of the ultimate spiritual goal. At the same time she clarifies the political and social impediments that kept the indigenous women from having an exclusively indigenous space.

The indigenous writer candidly recreates Sor Petra's voice in the same oral style of the other life stories in the *Apuntes*, allowing the reader to "listen" to the advice the community of women received from the criolla abbess: "Miren hijitas, no sean bobas, procuren el no ser tan muertas, es fuerza que vayan poniendo mucho cuidado en todas las cosas; vayan mirando, cuiden muy bien porque ustedes son las que se han de quedar solitas en su conventito porque Nuestra Santa Regla y Constituciones así nos lo manda; por eso lo hago con mis hijitas" ("Look, little daughters, don't be foolish, [and] try to not be so uninterested. You must put more effort into everything that you do. Keep a close watch. Be very careful, because you are the ones who are going to remain in your little convent all by yourselves, because our Holy Rule and Constitutions requires it. That is why I do this with my little daughters"; 8).

The indigenous writer could have been drawing on the "tricks of the weak" when she decided to include the abbess's comment about remaining by themselves in their convent, especially her use of the diminutive form "solitas" (by themselves) in their "conventito" (little convent). Josefina Ludmer in her discussion of rhetorical "tricks of the weak" calls attention to the positionality of the writing subject, subordinated and marginalized by her realm of social relationships (87). The writer, by reporting Sor Petra's speech, urges the community of nuns not to be foolish and to strive in everything they do, for any day now they could be left alone in their convent. Since the main interlocutor of the writing nun was a male reader of superior rank, her textual remarks are not gratuitous. They should be read as a clear objection to the inclusion and permanence of criolla nuns in the convent for Indians.

The indigenous writer ends her narration with the strange anecdote that opens chapter 3 in which the father of a Spanish novice accepted into the Convent of Corpus Christi tries to kill the indigenous nuns living in the convent. The writer glosses the anecdote by lamenting how much she and her fellow indigenous nuns suffered while Spanish nuns and novices lived among them in the convent: "Y fue mucho, mucho lo que padecimos" ("And it was a lot, a lot what we endured"; 10). Again, although the anecdote of the butchering lacks details, such as the names of the novice or her father, it functions allegorically to exemplify the extreme obstacles they had to overcome in order to obtain the ethnic exclusivity of their cloister.

In ecclesiastical colonial discourse, the indigenous nuns discovered the means to defend the ethnic authority of the space granted to them. They employed the suffering of the "poor" Indian women in their own discourse to create alliances inside and outside the walls of Corpus Christi and the other cloisters founded exclusively for indigenous women. Nevertheless, most of the information included in Sor Petra's life story was erased or modified in the *Las indias caciques* version. Yet despite the control exercised by the Church in an attempt to mold the identities of Indian nuns into the image of Spanish women, we can see that these indigenous women forged a space that scrutinized patriarchal and imperialistic colonial instruction, and affirmed their ethnic identity. Eventually, the Spanish nuns and novices were expelled from the Convent of Corpus Christi and left the Indian women with a convent of their own.

Panegyric Sermons

Dialogic Spaces and Examples of Virtue

The study of sacred rhetoric, that is, of public preaching, became an important part of intellectual life during the Renaissance. Humanism conferred great value on the study of language in Spain and across Europe. As part of this interest, humanists revived the study of classical rhetoric, particularly Cicero's *De inventione*, in which eloquence plays a fundamental role. According to Cicero, discourse, reason, and eloquence civilized men who lived in barbarous conditions (Abbott 7). Part of the colonial agenda was the Indian's transformation into a civilized people of reason and faith through religious discourse and rhetoric.[1] Rhetorical treatises concerning religious preaching in Spain responded to the reforms of the Council of Trent, such as the *Retórica Eclesiástica* (1576) by Fray Luis de Granada, which assigns great importance to the art of persuasion in order to intensify Christian faith. These treatises on the rhetorical arts, composed in the light of the Counter-Reformation as guides that would reinforce the practice of preaching, made their way to the Americas from Europe.

A particular kind of sermon, the funeral panegyric, frequently provides detailed information about a particular nun or, in some instances, a community. These sermons are easily found in print now because, as Hilary Smith notes, they were ordered and paid for by the deceased nun's family, who made sure the sermon would be printed as a *pliego suelto* (separate sheet) and distributed among their friends (21). Sermons have been studied as much for their rhetorical composition as for their effect in the religious arena, since it is a genre that can be considered both a performed event and a text.[2] A sermon has the advantage of being a written genre when printed and an oral genre—or, as Mikhail Bakhtin asserts, a speech genre—when preached.[3]

Panegyric sermons functioned as discursive spaces where an idealized subject was constructed that in turn became an authorized model of religious conformity. Yet this construction also implied a multilevel dialogue in which the voices of society—the Church, the priest, and the nuns themselves—could be heard. Through these sermons, therefore, priests provided nuns, lay religious, and all sectors of society with models of spirituality and social conformity sanctioned by the Roman Catholic Church.

Las indias caciques de Corpus Christi includes the hagiographic biographies of several nuns who lived in the convent, among them Sor Petra de San Francisco, one of the founding nuns and its first abbess. Sor Petra lived most of her life in the Convent of San Juan de la Penitencia in Mexico City, but she left in order to establish the Convent of Corpus Christi, where she died three years later. The same year of her death, 1727, a sermon honoring Sor Petra, preached by Fray Joseph López at her funeral, was published. The life story of Sor Petra narrated in *Las indias caciques* is consistent for the most part with the life detailed by López in his sermon, clearly illustrating the dialogism sustained by colonial texts. It also suggests that the interactions among men and women inside the microcosm of the convent, as well as with those who lived extramurally, produced written discourses that were not only of spiritual or religious intent.

Several more sermons concerning the convents for indigenous women survived. A founding sermon for the Convent of Nuestra Señora de Cosamaloapan in Valladolid, preached by the Jesuit Juan Uvaldo de Anguita in 1737, advances an argument of earlier texts supporting indigenous foundations that evoked the indigenous nobility's quick religious conversion and willingness to accept the new faith. In 1773 a panegyric sermon from the Convent of Corpus Christi was dedicated to Sor María Teresa de San José, another of the founding criolla nuns. This sermon is particularly interesting because her life narrative is not included as one of the hagiographic biographies in *Las indias caciques de Corpus Christi*, and only through this funeral sermon do we glean bits of information about Sor María Teresa's life. She took the habit in the Convent of San Juan de la Penitencia and later, at nineteen years of age, left with Sor Petra to found the Convent of Corpus Christi, where she was abbess four times.[4] Only in 1799, twenty-six years after the preaching of the sermon dedicated to Sor María Teresa, did Joseph Victoriano Baños preach the first funerary eulogy dedicated to an Indian nun, Sor María Teodora de San Agustín, founder and abbess of the Convent of Santa María de los Ángeles in the city of Antequera.

Panegyric sermons, like other colonial texts, allow us to appreciate the religious ideology and language that supported imperial power. The two funeral sermons dedicated to the founding nuns of the Convent of Corpus Christi and the sermon dedicated to the Indian nun who founded the convent for indigenous women in Antequera offer an alternative and idealized construction of the identities of Sor Petra, Sor María Teresa, Sor María Teodora, and, occasionally, other nuns in these convents. The identities of the female subjects of these three sermons are created following the conventions of the hagiographic biography: even when included, biographical details do not correspond to a biographical genre but inscribe themselves rather in religious discourse. The nuns' depiction is intrinsically related to the genre chosen. Nevertheless, the sermons dedicated to the criolla nuns differ from that dedicated to Sor María Teodora, which lacks any biographical details. The two sermons about the founding women of Corpus Christi include the rest of the noble Indian women in the convent, and it is easy to see the manner in which they are rhetorically incorporated in the sermon's ideology of difference. A study of these specific funeral sermons reveals the construction of subjects by means of metaphors and their symbolic equivalencies that modeled the virtues of the perfecta religiosa within the mysticism of the conventual space.

The Sermon and Its Dialogue with Other Genres

The sermon as a genre takes part in two different kinds of dialogues. The first one involves the open dialogue established among the distinct types of texts that participated and shaped what is known as colonial discourse. Hybridity has been identified as one of the main characteristics of this discursive production from the first years of contact.[5] As Mignolo and other scholars have noted there is no clear difference between one colonial genre and another; therefore, an analysis of rhetoric is useful to understand a text's composition and the author's rationale. Studies of colonial works have discovered that their compositional models were similar texts that borrowed characteristics from other genres, making them open discourses susceptible to dialogue. The discourses produced once the colony and its institutions were established reveal a similar phenomenon. Although generic differentiation is useful, it is evident that a dialogue of genres and signifiers, rhetoric and style, was taking place. Kathleen Ross observes that with religious writings (convent chronicles, spiritual vidas, hagiographies, sermons, and letters), a generic approach is only partially satisfactory because "the categories run over and into one another" (153).

The second kind of dialogue in which sermons participate involves the social act of transmission and the reception of the message. Hilary Smith notes that "the context of a sermon and the precise circumstances under which it is preached are an essential part of the sermon, and they cannot be ignored without seriously affecting its meaning" (11). The priests charged with the task of composing sermons took into account the historical and cultural circumstances in which they were eulogizing the two criolla women living in a convent for indigenous women, as did the priest charged with eulogizing Sor María Teodora, the first indigenous abbess in New Spain. Contextual conditions are important here: the broadest being the Counter-Reformation ideology transplanted in New Spain by Spanish humanists, the most immediate being the debated ideas that emerged with the opening of a convent for indigenous women, a controversial proposal that met with the disapproval of some and the approbation of others.[6] The sermon is a social dialogue that includes various implicit voices: those of a society undecided about the indigenous women's capacities; of priests who supported the idea of the convent but who depended on the criolla nuns to construct an environment of peace and harmony therein; and of the nuns who considered themselves privileged to have a convent exclusively for Indians.

The clearest objective of the Counter-Reformation was to establish order from the apparent political and social chaos that prevailed. Mary Elizabeth Perry notes that women were thought to need protection from not only external influences but also their own weaknesses, and the "natural" reclusion of the convent was the ideal place for them (175). The mindset of the Counter-Reformation had an immediate effect on gender relations. The number of convents increased substantially during this period, as did the rigidity of many conventual rules. In the case of the Convent of Corpus Christi, a hierarchical social and political order was recreated. Once indigenous women got a convent exclusively for their community, they were not allowed to govern themselves. In the microcosm of the convent, there prevailed a hegemonic power represented by the criolla nuns and the priests who supported them. The ultimate purpose of the founding nuns' funeral eulogies was to report to and, at the same time, assure society and ecclesiastical authorities that order prevailed in the convent because of the presence of the criolla nuns.[7]

Yet the reality was quite different. We know there were disputes between Spanish and Indian nuns, which supports the affirmation of Anne J. Cruz and Mary Elizabeth Perry about the consequences of the Counter-Reformation's imposition of an almost feudal order on society. The authors assert that the incessant tensions between dominant groups and marginalized subaltern groups continually threatened to interrupt the social equilibrium (ix).[8] That equilibrium was maintained to a certain degree, and the indigenous nuns finally secured the right to govern the convent. But the contradictions and tensions were part of a long process that preceded an apparent pacification of the parties involved.

Catholicism underwent a profound transformation during the period of the Counter-Reformation, specifically during the Council of Trent (1545–1563), which directly affected the countries that remained Catholic and their colonies. In clear opposition to Protestant ideas, the post-Tridentine Church proposed the veneration of saints and at the same time imposed stricter rules on hagiographic production, limiting the number of canonizations (Rubial, "Espejo de virtudes" 97). Peter Burke affirms that there were only sixteen canonizations in the sixteenth century, increasing to twenty-four in the seventeenth century and twenty-nine in the eighteenth (46). Writing conventions as well as the spiritual and religious requirements for consideration for sainthood became common knowledge, given that printed books with hagiographic vidas and funeral sermons enjoyed ample circulation.

The Church in New Spain enjoyed immense political, economic, and social power, serving as a vehicle of control, together with the strong presence of the Inquisition. Hagiographic biographies, not of canonized saints but of idealized religious subjects, were very common in the colony. Sometimes they were autobiographical, such as the *Autobiografía Espiritual* of María de San José, and other times biographical, like *De los prodigios de la omnipotencia . . . en la vida de la venerable sierva de Dios Catharina de S. Joan*, written by Alonso Ramos.

As discussed in chapter 4, the spiritual autobiography stemmed from the relationship between a nun and her confessor and was usually written in response to priests' instructions that she record her religious life. Kathryn McKnight believes that through their vidas, women who wrote sought ways not so much to follow the ideology of the Counter-Reformation as to express a subversive creativity within the contradictions of their time (19). In contrast, biographical works were frequently written by priests in the hope that a fortunate nun or lay sister would be recognized, possibly even canonized, securing success as much for the subject of the narrative as for the biographer. At the very least, they were written with the purpose of showing society a model of a perfecta religiosa.

"Hagiographic biography" is the term used to describe this second type of religious literature with didactic and moralistic purposes. It is validly termed hagiographic because of the way the genre adopts hagiographic conventions. The hagiography, cultivated since the third century, used specific rhetorical and structural conventions such as highlighting an individual's life of isolation, humility, penance, sacrifice, and on occasion martyrdom, as well as prayer and the virtue of chastity. These hagiographical elements are easily recognizable in pre– and post–Counter-Reformation life narratives. There was also another more secular influence on these narratives, according to Antonio Rubial, who argues that the hagiographic narrative should be considered a literary genre because it took elements from the chivalric novel, and vice versa. He notes that the hagiography is replete with warriors of demonic forces, chosen by God to show the world, from infancy, the road each Christian should follow to reach heaven ("Espejo de virtudes" 90).

Because of its intertextuality, the panegyric sermon should be considered within the corpus of texts that treat monastic life. The hagiographic conventions on which the author clearly relied allow it to occupy an important place alongside the hagiographic biographies, since neither was written by the nuns themselves.[9] The sermon, unlike the biography, had the advantage of having not only an audience, since it was transmitted orally, but also having the capacity to be published and circulated in written form, thereby substantially increasing its reach. Gwendolyn Barnes-Karol asserts about colonial sermons: "One of the major outcomes of the Council of Trent was the (re)institutionalization of preaching as a means of (i) psychological manipulation and control, and (ii) dissemination of propaganda favorable to the continued survival of the traditional society of estates founded upon the pillars of Church, Monarchy and nobility" (53).

A sermon introduces verbal constructions of sonorous and theatrical grandiloquence in order to persuade the public to follow an exemplary lifestyle, as in the case of the panegyric. Another characteristic of the sermon affected by the Council of Trent is that it worked not only to persuade the public toward an exemplary life but also to create, manipulate, and disseminate images that would construct an aura of moral, theological, and socioeconomic homogeneity capable of implementing social order (Barnes-Karol 53). The images of sainthood and perfection in the colonial panegyric sermons had a broader intent than just holding up a model for living; they tried to affirm that order existed within the convent and its surrounding environs. According to Josefina Muriel, the purpose of these sermons was to highlight for a select audience who attended funerary honors, and who were able to read, the life of a Christian woman who could serve as an example for others (*Cultura femenina* 32). Clearly, the characteristics of panegyric sermons coincided with the political agenda at work in the Spanish colonies.

The Art of Preaching

Saint Augustine in *De doctrina Christiana* was the first to adapt classical rhetoric for use in the pulpit, shaping the subsequent type of preaching by the Church Fathers and what we now know as the homily (Luján 289). The first three books of *De doctrina Christiana* focus on the interpretation of Scripture, and the fourth book is an argument in favor of the use of *eloquentia* or elegant, persuasive public speech in Christian oratory. Since 1200, these treatises promoted an analytical spirit and a sermon composed with a specific structure: prologue, division, proof, and conclusion; or anathema (introduction to the theme), prayer, theme, division, and conclusion.

These latter sections are based on the five canons of the classical rhetorical model established by Cicero: *inventio, dispositio, elocutio, memoria, pronuntiatio*. According to the Roman orator, the inventio is the discovery of truths and likelihoods that make a cause probable; the dispositio, the ordered distribution of those ideas; the elocutio, the use of the appropriate words; memoria, the firm grasp of thoughts relevant to the events; the pronuntiatio, the control of voice and body in keeping with the dignity of the event (Luján 84). The characteristics employed by early preachers were maintained up to the Renaissance and enriched by a series of treatises written during the Middle Ages intended to emphasize the differences between pagan and Christian preaching. Although the treatises of Saint Augustine and Pope Gregory VII continued to be influential, the Renaissance sermon focused on inspiring admiration, gratitude, and a desire to imitate; basically, it aimed to teach by means of persuasion. The ethos and pathos of Aristotelian rhetoric were clearly present, as was the Ciceronian *actio* (O'Malley 240).

Fray Luis de Granada's contribution to the development of the sermon, the *Retórica eclesiástica*, evolved as a response to Tridentine reform to revitalize Catholicism in the face of Protestantism. Don Paul Abbott explains that Fray Luis de Granada based his work on the Ciceronian model but changed it according to his goals as a Christian preacher. One of the characteristics of Granada's rhetoric, transported to the New World, was an appeal to the noble emotions of his audience (13). Granada believed that the integrity of the preacher was important and that it was necessary for the intentions of his preaching to be widely known. The author exhorts preachers to forget their own honor and human comforts and to concentrate exclusively on the salvation of souls; with this principle in mind, they could begin preaching:

A quienes Dios encomienda el cuidado de resucitar las almas muertas en el pecado, con el báculo de la severidad divina, y virtud de las palabras evangélicas, deben con tantas veras entregarse a la importancia de este ministerio, que olvidados de todo respeto humano, en esto sólo piensen, en esto mediten los días, y las noches; ni por dependencia alguna de este mundo se abstengan de esta ocupación; para que a la grandeza del ministerio corresponda el cuidado, y diligencia del ministro. (23)

(Those to whom God entrusts the care of resuscitating souls deadened by sin, with the support of Divine severity, and the virtue of evangelical words, should give themselves up to the importance of this ministry with great fervor, and forgetting all mundane concerns, should think only of this, meditate day and night on this; for no earthly reason should they abstain from their task; so that the greatness of the ministry is reflected in the care and diligence of the minister.)

In 1579, a few years after Fray Luis de Granada published *Retórica eclesiástica*, *Retórica Cristiana* was published in Perugia, Italy, by Fray Diego Valadés, the first mestizo born in New Spain to publish a book in Europe. The son of a Tlaxcalteca Indian woman and the conquistador Diego Valadés, he was born in 1533 and was a student of Pedro de Gante. He was ordained a priest of the Franciscan order despite his mestizo origins and worked in the indigenous missions as he had command of the Nahuatl, Otomí, and Tarascan languages. In 1581 he traveled to Europe, where he wrote his *Retórica*. He remained there for ten years, and it is believed he died there in 1592. Unlike Granada, whose objective was to form skilled sacred orators, Valadés combined "Old World erudition and New World anthropology" (Abbott 41). In other words, Valadés merged his mastery of classical rhetoric with his knowledge of the missionary endeavor in the Americas. He drafted his *Retórica* in Latin to reach the widest possible audience in Europe. It was not translated into Spanish until 1989.

One of the most noted elements of his book is the inclusion of twenty-six copper engravings, some of which are clearly European in theme (e.g., the seven liberal arts), while others are evidently American, such as the engraving that describes the pre-Hispanic world and illustrates native vegetation like the maguey, the cactus fruit, and the guava. The *Retórica Cristiana* is particularly significant as it constitutes a text dedicated to preaching newly converted peoples in the context of the Spanish colony in America. The book includes a defense of "the sincere Christianity of the Indians," which is relevant in the debate that would centuries later bring about the proposal to found the Convent of Corpus Christi. Valadés states:

No pretendo colocar a los indios entre los santos, lo cual sería en todo caso, oficio propio de la Iglesia y del Sumo Pontífice, sino que trato de refutar, con razones, aquello de que han sido vituperados; puesto que yo fui testigo no de oídas sino de vista, y no sólo estuve presente sino que aun los tuve a mi cargo. Han abrazado la religión cristiana de muy diversa manera que los moros; pues, en primer lugar estos indios fueron instruidos con mayor cuidado, y por ministros que sabían hablar con grande expedición su lengua nativa. En segundo lugar, los indios son de natural más tratable, más mansos, más pacíficos y de trato más fácil [. . .] además abandonaron el culto de sus templos al darse cuenta de la inhumanidad y fealdad de su idolatría. (427)

(I do not pretend to place the Indians among the saints, which in any case would be the official charge of the Church and the High Pontiff, rather I try to refute, with reasoning, that for which they have long been vilified; given that I was an eyewitness, not to hearsay but rather present among them, and I was in charge of some of them. They have embraced the Christian religion in a different manner than the Moors; in the first place, these Indians were taught with greater care, and by ministers who knew how to speak their native language with great efficiency. In the second place, the Indians are by nature more tractable, meeker, calmer and easier to deal with . . . moreover they abandoned the cult of their temples when they realized how inhumane and ugly their idolatry was.)

Valadés's comparison of the indigenous people to the Moors indicates that his discourse was directed to the Iberian public. He stands for the importance of missionaries in the colonizing enterprise and describes the Indians, once again, as "meek," an epithet intended to confer a positive and paternalistic distinction, and portray the Indians as subjects in need of the missionaries' protection. Valadés's *Retórica* is an excellent example of a manual that combines classical rhetoric with an understanding of the most recent political and ideological events the Church and empire were confronting. This ideological position persisted, as we have seen, in the textual production surrounding the convents for indigenous women. The priests who faced the tasks of preaching the founding and funeral sermons in these convents echoed the same language and rhetoric employed by Valadés.

Structure and Images of the Sermon

Sermons varied in length, but the funerary panegyric sermons were usually short (about eighteen printed pages), written to be preached and then published, and to inspire the public to follow the Christian path of good deeds.[10] When published, a sermon also included a *dedicatoria* and an *aprobación* (dedication and validation) in which priests, generally important ecclesiastical authorities, gave their point of view and commented on the content of the sermon on various pages, followed by one or a number of *pareceres* in which they once again judged the content or shared some opinion about the deceased subject. On occasion, they also included a *sentir*, which was much like the previous sections.

The funerary panegyric sermon itself was structured in two or three sections. The first centers on a description of the grief brought on by the death of the nun, along with an account of her greatest quality and an image used as the principal metaphor to illustrate her virtues throughout the sermon ("a lily among thorns" or "the new Ruth").[11] After the first section, an Ave Maria was usually prayed. If the sermon had only two sections, the first dealt with the life of the nun, according to the hagiographic conventions, and the second referred to the sadness and desolation shared by her friends left behind to grieve. If the sermon had more sections or chapters, it usually divided the nun's life into more than one chapter.[12]

The language of the sermons of colonial Spanish America, according to Mariano Picón Salas, is hyperbolic and superlative, as it incorporated two highly complex language traditions: the baroque and the religious (124). Classical and biblical images were used in large part to convey the setting of the sermon and gave rise to subsequent references to the great virtue of the nun. It was common in colonial panegyric sermons to praise the subject to the point of rendering invisible her human traits and emphasizing her achievement of celestial perfection; in this way, the preacher could show his mastery of rhetoric as well as his own humility. The poetic language and the use of stylistic elements with religious meanings are two of the unique elements of these three funerary sermons. For example, Sor Petra de San Francisco was born on the eve of the feast of San Pedro (Saint Peter), which is why she was baptized with the name Petra, and in the sermon, the priest plays with the meaning of their names, both originating in the word "piedra" (rock), as well as the image of Saint Peter and his position as the cornerstone (*piedra fundacional*) of the Catholic Church.

The first reference to this central metaphor appears in the aprobación: "piedra durísima por su constancia, y por eso escogida para primera y fundamental Piedra de este Religioso Edificio" ("hardest of rocks for your constancy, and for that reason chosen as the first and cornerstone of this religious building"; n. pag.). Subsequent references include "piedra tan limpia por su pobreza," "piedra como la del desierto" ("stone cleansed by its poverty," "like a desert stone"). The preacher elaborates the image of the stone in relation to Sor Petra de San Francisco throughout the sermon. In the margins of the printed text, we find a reference to a bible verse from the Book of Isaiah reworked by the priest in the body of the homily. His use of the verse alludes to the mystical cornerstone, "founded in the foundation" (Isa. 28:16). This is an important reference because Isaiah was guided by the light of God and his mission was to see to the fall of all pagan villages.

The author of the first parecer also refers to her "rocklike" steadfast-ness: "Bautizada con el nombre de Petra, el cielo quería que fuese piedra, y piedra muy preciosa" ("Baptized with the name of Petra, heaven had decreed that she be a stone and a very precious stone"; n. pag.). Nicolás Quiñones, vicar of the convent, refers to Petra in the second parecer as a foundational stone of the mystic Zion (a reference to the convent) and establishes her relation with other important figures considered rocks in the history of the Church: Christ and Saint Peter. He then pronounces her a cornerstone. Finally, the sermon by Fray Joseph López depicts Petra as "esta racional Piedra" ("this rational rock"; 6). It is especially significant that all the priests who included their comments and opinions in the pub-lished sermon considered Petra the foundation of the religion that the "new" Indian nuns would lead.

It is important to note that some ecclesiastical officials used the same symbolic images to define the Spanish abbesses and to refer to the rest of the indigenous nuns. Thus the rock's symbolism is used to portray other women living in the convent, although not in the same manner. Fray Juan Antonio de Oviedo, chaplain of the cloister and author of the first parecer in Sor Petra's funerary sermon, notes that the Indian women gathered in the convent appeared to be like rocks. Yet he proceeds to disassociate the exemplary meaning that rock conveyed in the person of Petra from the new meaning it acquires with the Indian nuns, who seem to be rocks because coarseness and roughness are their natural traits, making them less suited for a life of perfection in the cloister. Nevertheless, he is quick to add that contrary to this opinion, there appears to be abundant perfection in the convent.

By defining the indigenous nuns as rocks along with the founding abbess, they became part of the sermon's rhetorical play. Fray Joseph López, preacher of the funeral eulogy for Sor Petra, refers to "tantas piedras en tantas doncellas Indias nobles, e hijas de caciques" ("so many stones found among so many noble Indian maidens, daughters of caciques") and "piedras bien labradas" ("well-carved rocks"). Fray López also indicates that they were formerly "coarse" rocks, but after having received the education needed from Sor Petra in the Convent of San Juan de la Penitencia, they became "piedras labradas."

The images chosen to represent Sor María Teresa in the second sermon are the olive and the olive tree. According to the *Diccionario de autoridades*, the olive was a symbol of peace. Father Miguel de Guevara refers to Sor María Teresa as "una Oliva grande tan hermosa como fértil" ("a large olive as beautiful as she is fruitful"), a phrase repeated later on. He adds that she embodied another property of the olive, "la fertilidad, ó fecundidad" ("fertility or fecundity"), given that she took part in the founding of the Convent of Nuestra Señora de Cosamaloapan in Valladolid, a convent he refers to as a "vergel" (orchard; 12).[13]

One of Guevara's most revealing descriptions of Sor María Teresa evokes the qualities of the olive, as she is affected by neither the rigors of winter nor the ice and snow, with a tolerant and majestic character, which the priest describes as "una Señora Religiosa informada de Dios con espíritu varonil, que en nombre del Señor rigió, gobernó y trabajó" ("a religious woman infused by God with a virile spirit, who in the name of God guided, governed, and worked"; 5). The masculine qualifier "virile" is especially significant because it undermines the widely held image of the weakness of the feminine spirit, reflecting the discursive conventions of the era. If we draw a parallel between the description of Sor María Teresa and the equally masculine characteristics with which Sor Petra is defined, we can conclude that the founding ideals, set by the nuns who were to have the power and the authority, were based on virtues attributed to men; they had to be *mujeres varoniles*.[14] The exaltation of a religious woman's virile nature was typical in hagiographic narratives as well.

Fray Miguel de Guevara also includes the Indian nuns as part of the rhetorical construction of his sermon. He elaborates the image of the olive tree into a complex construction where the hearts of the Indian nuns are seen as fertile land in which solid piety puts down deep roots; nevertheless, they need to be tended with the sort of diligence that new olive trees demand. The preacher then refers to the way Sor María Teresa treated the nuns in the convent: "Haciéndose India con ellas, a todas las volvió Españolas en el modo de proceder, trato y orden de vida igualmente regalada que labrada" ("By becoming an Indian with them, she converted them all into Spanish women in the manner of their behavior, mien, and orderly life as spiritually favored as filled with work"; *Oración fúnebre* 12). The idea that perfection had to emanate from a Spanish model and could not possibly begin in the indigenous women is recurrent. According to Guevara, nuns only reached the state of being perfecta religiosa by becoming more like the *españolas*.

In the sermon dedicated to Sor María Teodora, the priest does not use the kind of image employed by preachers to define the criolla nuns but compares her instead to the biblical figure Judith, a comparison that focuses on the nun's character:

> Aplicad en hora buena a la insigne Teodora el mismo elogio de la heroína de Betulia: Ninguno otro a mi juicio, puede ofreceros idea mas cabal de su carácter. ¿Os acordais que el retiro del mundo, el cilicio, el ayuno y el Santo Temor de Dios hicieron tan famosa la ínclita Hebrea? Pues en eso mismo, ¿Qué otra cosa habeis sino el modelo de que es vivo retrato, copia muy natural nuestra esclarecida Americana? (Castañeda Guzmán 84)

> (Apply in good time to the renowned Teodora the same praise as the heroine of Bethulia: None other, in my judgment, can offer a truer sense of her character. Do you recall how isolation from the world, the cilice, fasting, and the holy fear of God made the illustrious Jewess famous? Well, in that very line, what else do you have here but the model of which she is a living portrait, a very natural copy of our own illustrious woman of the Americas?)

Judith represents one of the women renowned for her utmost steadfastness and courage in sacred stories of the Bible. Left a widow, she was very rich and beautiful, but after her husband died, she always wore mourning clothes and feared God in an exemplary manner. Her faith allowed her to save her village, Bethulia, by killing Holofernes. Father Joseph Victoriano Baños compares Judith to Sor María Teodora, highlighting both women's righteousness.[15] However, Judith has certain virtues the priest does not include in his praise of the nun, like her beauty and bravery, and most important, he omits the violence entailed in the act of killing Holofernes.[16]

Many of the sermon's images illustrate the dialogism discussed earlier, as they deal with images taken from other texts, particularly the Bible, or refer to historical context. For instance, the concept of the convent as Paradise is derived from biblical tradition, but at this point in colonial times, it also appears as an immediate referent to the *Paraíso occidental* by Sigüenza y Góngora. The metaphors describing the convent always connote perfection and order, an ideal that was not always met.

The language and structure of the funeral panegyric sermons confirm the complexity of the genre's constitution. Behind the religious and baroque, we glimpse the image of a flesh-and-blood woman, but her life story is transformed into a fictitious narration with a moralizing purpose. The result is a hybrid genre, a product of the culture of the baroque and of the political and social tensions of the time. Mabel Moraña notes the many contradictions and controversies attributed to the colonial era, commenting on the contrasts between authority and subalternity, faith and reason, scholasticism and humanism, centrality and marginality (*Viaje* 264). The sermons considered in this chapter emerged from these contrasts, a context that allows for many and diverse readings of the same discourses.

The First Abbess

The funeral panegyric sermon dedicated upon the death of Sor Petra was preached by Fray Joseph López, an instructor of theology and advisor to the Holy Office. Fray Joseph, who structures his sermon around the metaphor of the cornerstone, indicates which parts of Sor Petra's life he is going to praise. The standard hagiographic conventions appear from the beginning of the sermon: the statement that she was sent from heaven and chosen by God. Sor Petra was born April 28, 1663, and both the manuscript published in *Las indias caciques de Corpus Christi* and the sermon mention that her parents were Sebastiana de Luna and Pedro de Alvarado, a descendant of the famous conquistador. Her family's economic situation was precarious, but Petra learned to read and write when she was a child, along with other "exercises appropriate for women" like embroidery. Yet in keeping with hagiographic predestination, she searched for someone to guide her on the spiritual path from a young age. The sermon then offers this passage about Petra's life with her sister and about her honor:

> La tribulación que más rigorosa afligía su espíritu era tener, con una madre pobre, una hermana singularmente hermosa: y como la hermosura, según dijo un discreto, es una pared blanca, en donde cualquier necio quiere echar su borrón; por no ver manchada la limpieza de su noble prosapia; o, lo que fuera más sensible, denigrado el candor espiritual de su hermana, con el borrón de alguna flaqueza, a que suele deslizar, en quien menos piensa, una hermosura necesitada: para evitarlo se aplicó diligente a maestra de niñas, enseñándoles a copiar en el alma del lienzo las labores, y en el lienzo del alma las virtudes. (López 7)

> (The tribulation that was the greatest spiritual affliction to her, was to have, along with a poor mother, a singularly beautiful sister: and that beauty, as a wit once said, is a white wall on which any fool would want to leave his mark. In order not to see the purity of her noble lineage stained, or, more hurtful, her sister's spiritual integrity eroded by the mark of any character flaws, such as the need to be beautiful, which can cause even in one whom we least expect it, to backslide; to

avoid just that, she concentrated diligently on being a role model for young girls, teaching them to copy good works and the virtues onto the canvas of their soul.)

Comparing this passage in the sermon with the one in the *Las indias caciques* version reveals the preacher's didactic and moralistic purpose in contrast with the biographer's goal. The biographer mentions neither her "spiritual affliction" nor her sister's "beauty," and he omits the final word play on souls and virtues. This does not mean that the manuscript was more faithful to the hagiographic biography of Sor Petra, but in comparing them, we can easily identify some differences between the rhetoric of the sermon and that of the hagiographic biography. Still, the biographer of the Corpus Christi manuscript follows and maintains certain conventions in all the vidas he relates, such as the rhetorical devices used to describe the nuns' virtues: "Cuando vino a la religión venía ya bien ejercitada en ayunos, cilicios y disciplinas y otras austeridades que inventaba su fervoroso espíritu y hallándose en ella, crecieron tanto sus ansias de padecer que las austeridades comunes del instituto, satisfacían poco a sus deseos. Ayunaba todos los días a pan y agua" ("When she joined the religious life, she arrived already well-versed in fasting, the use of cilices and disciplines, and other austerities that her fervent spirit invented; and following religious life, her eagerness to suffer grew so strong that the common austerities of the convent were insufficient to satisfy her desire. She fasted every day, having only bread and water"; Muriel, *Las indias caciques* 187).

These elements commonly used to describe Christian perfection are also mentioned throughout the sermon, fulfilling the text's didactic purpose of inspiring the community: "Tuvieron ocasión oportuna para leer, en la palidez de su rostro, lo mancerado de su cuerpo con ayunos, vigilias, silicios, disciplinas, y otras muchas, asperas mortificaciones" ("They had ample opportunity to read, in the paleness of her face, the body wounded by her fasting, vigils, cilices, disciplines, and many other intense mortifications"; López 15).[17] The sermon recounts that when young Petra became gravely ill, her parents placed on her an image of Saint Francis, which led to her miraculous recovery; therefore, she chose San Francisco for her religious name. Even though Petra wanted to follow religious life, her lack of dowry prevented her from entering a convent. The preacher offers this as further illustration of the divine obstacles she had to overcome to achieve the ultimate goal of dedicating her life to God.[18]

Fray Joseph López elaborates on the prolonged trials she underwent to be able to enter the convent. The nuns at San Juan de la Penitencia finally promised to accept her, even without a dowry, as long as she learned music to help in the choir. She took her vows on July 13, 1692, the feast of Saint Anthony of Padua, when she was 29 years old. The preacher stresses the symbolic importance of this date because of the legendary 1692 riot in which a shortage of maize occurred in New Spain. This situation was aggravated by the colonial officials' poor management of popular unrest that escalated into a *tumulto* (riot): "Año memorable para esta ciudad, por el estrago del tumulto, y por el ingresso de N. V. M. [Nuestra Venerable Madre] en el convento. Porque es de meditar con reflexión, que, cuando amotinados los Naturales arruinaron el edificio del Palacio, y otras casas, comenzase Dios a labrar en la penitencia la primera Piedra para esta casa de Señoras, Caciques Naturales" ("A memorable year for this city, because of the damage caused by the riot, and the entry of Our Venerable Mother into the convent. Because we must meditate and reflect on the fact that, when the Natives were instigated to destroy the Palace building, and other houses, only then did God begin to sculpt through her penances, the first cornerstone of this house for indigenous noblewomen"; 10).[19]

Douglas Cope has incisively observed that the official version, forged for the most part by Carlos de Sigüenza y Góngora in his letter to Admiral Pez, transformed an apparent act of resistance incited by the lower classes' precarious conditions into a treacherous Indian plot against the colonial order. Elite Spanish and criollos blamed the Indian population's unrestrained intake of pulque. In his sermon, Fray Joseph López describes the riot in these latter terms, as a revolt of the Indians, and not of the castas who had developed bonds of solidarity with those oppressed by the elite. Quick to benefit from the "official" version of the story, colonial officials banned pulque and restricted Indians to their own barrios.[20] Fray Joseph argues that the convent for indigenous noblewomen was a place of Christian perfection, where indigenous women worked within the cloister to help secure the salvation of the indigenous population *extramuros*. Although Sor Petra was not Indian, it was her mission to mold those "imperfect" spirits until they became cornerstones as precious as she was. Fray Joseph's sermon thus effectively sustained the colonial ideology of ethnic differences and imperial order within the discourse of religious conformity.

The panegyric sermon refers to Sor Petra with unending praise, stating that she was always "pronta a la obediencia, sola en el retiro, fervorosa en la oración, continua en los ayunos, áspera en el vestuario, rigurosa en la penitencia, frecuente en el coro, afable en el trato, suave para las demás monjas y estricta con ella misma" ("quick to obey, alone in her retreat, fervent in her prayers, constant in her fasting, severe in dress, rigorous in penance, frequently appearing in the choir, friendly in manner, gentle with the other nuns and strict with herself"). It also describes her chastity as "pura, candida y tan indefectible" ("pure, guileless and so unfailing"). Sor Petra lived in the convent of San Juan de la Penitencia for thirty-one years before her presence was requested as the founder of the new convent for noble Indian women. Clearly, her humility and Christian perfection were considered ideal for guiding the new indigenous nuns. Petra lived just two years, eight months, and eighteen days in the new Convent of Corpus Christi. She died when she was 74 years old.

Ten years after the death of the first abbess of the Convent of Corpus Christi, the renowned Jesuit Juan Uvaldo de Anguita preached a sermon on the occasion of the opening of a second convent for Indian noblewomen, the Convent of Nuestra Señora de Cosamaloapan, in Valladolid on March 25, 1737 (fig. 6). In *El divino verbo*, Anguita followed an argumentative line similar to the one his Jesuit predecessor, Castorena y Ursúa, had developed in the founding sermon of the Convent of Corpus Christi (chap. 3). Asunción Lavrin calls this approach a "syncretic line" established mainly by preachers in the sixteenth century (*Brides of Christ* 271). Two centuries later, the syncretic line still resonated with colonial preachers who identified a symbolic link between pre-Hispanic religious beliefs and Christian ones, not necessarily supporting Christianity among the Indians *avant la lettre*, as suggested by Fernando de Alva Ixtlilxóchitl, but rather by demonstrating their readiness to accept the truths of the new faith.[21]

Contextualizing his sermon with local events, Anguita refers to Tarascan history and the arrival in Michoacán of Cristóbal de Olid, who brought the "true religion." Anguita recounts the immediate conversion and baptism of King Calzonzin, who was given the Christian name Francisco. Indian noblewomen are referred to as lilies that grew from the soil where the seed of religious faith was sown. The sermon presents an image of the harvest of the Incarnate Word as the cultivation of old and new fruit, Spanish and Indian nuns, respectively. The phrase "newly converted" in reference to the cacicas appears numerous times throughout the sermon.

Anguita's references to the writings of Juan de Torquemada and Carlos de Sigüenza y Góngora exemplify the dialogism of his sermon. He illustrates what both these authors had recorded about the seemingly "conventual" practices that pre-Hispanic noblewomen observed:

> Llamó a las vírgenes con el nombre *zihuatamatztle*, y a las ancianas venerables que puso a su cuidado con el de *ichopatlatoque* y a un sacerdote superior, que con el *tecoacuili* fuese como vicario y superintendente de este recogimiento y cuidase de la observancia más exacta de los vanos ejercicios y supersticiosas leyes a que estaban obligadas. (19)

EL DIVINO VERBO GRANO,

QUE SEMBRADO EN LA TIERRA

VIRGEN DE MARIA

SANTISSIMA NUESTRA SEÑORA

DA POR FRUCTO UNA COSECHA

DE VIRGENES.

SERMON PANEGYRICO,

QUE EN EL SOLEMNE INGRESSO
de las Religiofas Indias Caziqnès de la primera Regla
de SANTA CLARA, en el nuevo Convento de N. Sra.

DE COZAMALUAPAN,

el dia 25. de Marzo del año paffado de 1737. en que
fe celebró el Sacro-fanto Myfterio de la Encarnacion

DEL VERBO DIVINO,

PATENTE EL AUGUSTISSIMO
SACRAMENTO DEL ALTAR.

PREDICÖ

EL Dr. Y Mrò. D. JUAN UVALDO DE ANGUITA
Sandoval, y Roxas, Cathedratico, que fue, en el Real, y
Pontificio Seminario de la Santa Iglefia Cathedral Metro
politana de Mexico, Canonigo Magiftral de la de Valladolid.
Examinador Synodal del Obifpado de Micheacan, Prefidente
de fus Synodos, y Vicario del Convento de Señoras
Religiofas de Sta. Catharina de Sena de dicha
Ciudad de Valladolid.

EN MEXICO: EN LA IMPRENTA REAL DEL SVPERIOR
Gobierno, y del Nuevo Rezado de Doña Maria de Rivera; en el
Empedradillo. Año de 1743.

Figure 6. The first page of *El divino verbo grano que sembrado en la tierra*.

(He called the virgins *zihuatamatztle*, and the venerable old women placed in his care were called *ichopatlatoque*, and one high-ranking priest, who with the *tecoacuili* would serve as vicar and superintendent of this *recogimiento* (house of retreat), and hold to the most exact observance of the vain exercises and superstitious laws to which they were obligated.)

The preacher applied here what Joseph Valadés suggested in *Retórica Cristiana* would appeal to an audience: classical rhetoric in the immediate colonial context. Anguita's skills as a preacher allow him to commend pre-Hispanic religious practices while disparaging the belief system that sustained it. He praises the noblewomen for their eagerness to join religious life and to follow the Spaniards' example. Although Anguita's use of local history is innovative, his argumentative line falls within established colonial religious discourse that continued to emphasize the ideology of difference.

The Second Abbess

We know few details about the life of the second abbess of the Convent of Corpus Christi, Sor María Teresa de San José. In the biographical section of his sermon, Fray Miguel Thadeo de Guevara, vicar of the convent, states that she was born in the city of Toluca, but he does not provide any information about her parents. He underscores the image of Sor María Teresa as a heavenly being but also refers on various occasions to her corporality; this is a clear difference from the sermon on Sor Petra, which, aside from references to her chastity and corporal sufferings, provides us with a vague image of the nun as a human being. When Sor María Teresa was fifteen years old, she took the veil in the Convent of San Juan de la Penitencia (no dates are specified), leaving there at nineteen to accompany Sor Petra de San Francisco in founding the Convent of Corpus Christi. Guevara justifies the selection of Sor María Teresa as a founder despite her tender age because of the "perfection of her Christian life." She served as abbess four times, governed for seventeen years, and lived in the Corpus Christi convent for forty-seven years until her death on December 26, 1772.

Reference is made to her pivotal role in establishing the Convent of Nuestra Señora de la Purísima Concepción de Cosamaloapan in Valladolid, as well as the convent of the Capuchin Indian noblewomen in the Villa de Nuestra Señora de Guadalupe in Mexico City.[22] Most of the sermon's plot centers on the role she played as a maternal and exemplary figure for the indigenous women during her years in the Convent of Corpus Christi. This depiction is disconcerting considering the complaints filed to the Council of the Indies in the convent's first years by the indigenous nuns who were dissatisfied with how poorly they were treated. The sermon refers to the beauty of the olive (the metaphor for Sor María), to her virtue, and to her perfection. One of the references to her corporality evoked not only the common virtue of chastity but also her aroma: "y una castidad muy pura, cuyo buen olor, y fragancia, se derivaba de ella como de cabeza a todos los miembros de su místico y venerable cuerpo" ("and such pure chastity, whose fine scent and fragrance radiates from her head to all parts of her mystical and venerable body"; 16).

Fray Miguel de Guevara was Sor María Teresa's confessor and spiritual director, which helps explain his describing the nun with sensory images that go beyond simple sight. His personal affection and admiration could have contributed to the verbal construction that shaped her persona. The sermon mentions similar deeds of perfection attributed to Sor Petra in the funeral sermon preached for her death: prayers, deprivations, use of the cilices, discipline, penitence, and austerity. As characteristics of her strength and ability to be founder of the convent, the sermon emphasizes "la pureza y Santidad de vida, la prudencia en el gobierno, la diligencia en el obrar, la rectitud en lo justo, y la ciencia para dirigir y enseñar" ("the purity and holiness of her life, her prudence in governing, her diligence in her work, her uprightness of judgment, and her knowledge to lead and teach"; 15). Moreover, he points out, in spite of her age, she fasted throughout the year, performed self-flagellation, and walked barefoot until the day she died.

Interesting similarities between the two funeral sermons, that of Sor Petra and the one for Sor María Teresa, are the references to the imperfection of the Indians and the beginning of their salvation embodied in these two criolla founding nuns, along with the symbolism used to describe the convent. Concerning the riot of 1692, Guevara indicates that the location on which the convent stood had previously been a still that produced pulque, adding that God was offended by the drunkenness and scandals occurring at this site of immorality and corruption. The sermon reinforces the stereotype of indigenous people who, according to colonial officials, were constantly getting drunk and causing turmoil. The convent would redeem the space by becoming a sacred place, and the Indian women would symbolically save the rest of the Indian "sinners" (9). The preacher refers to the olive branches that symbolically unite God and mankind in peace, the olive representing Sor María Teresa.

The textual construction of both nuns as literary subject and religious model throughout the panegyric sermons is much like that of hagiographic literature. The preachers use the founding nuns as examples of virtue for the community of indigenous women and for posterity in general, skillfully adopting the conventions of the sermon as a medium to inspire a desire for imitation. However, socio-ethnic subordination is present in the discourses produced by the Catholic Church, even when they allegedly supported the abilities of the indigenous women to take part in monastic life. The preachers of these panegyric sermons used the images of these two criolla women to model appropriate behavior that the indigenous nuns needed to follow. In their opinion, these two women embodied superior social and religious qualities.

Through their preaching, Guevara and López delineate a social hierarchy, situating the two criolla nuns at the pinnacle of religious perfection. The anonymous male writer of the hagiographic biographies included in *Las indias caciques de Corpus Christi*, addressed in chapter 4, also reinforced the social hierarchy of New Spain. He praises the cacica nuns because of their nobility and purity of blood, thus granting them a more privileged position than the rest of the indigenous population. According to Ruth Hill, "viceregal Spanish American societies had a norm of *inequality*: a written and unwritten hierarchy that ostensibly mirrored nature and its laws but was in fact a social construct" (197). Society, then, was based on differences not necessarily entrenched in genetic heritage but rather rooted in privileges conceded in relation to religious practices and nobility status. Therefore, Amerindians were defined as *pobres* and *miserables* not because of their skin color but because they were considered newly converted peoples in the Catholic faith. Ironically, there were still reservations about noble Indian women participating fully in religion well into the eighteenth century. Ultimately, the women's nobility and ability to prove *limpieza* (purity) granted them the status required to enter one of the religious institutions reserved only for Spanish and criollas in colonial Spanish America.

The Third Abbess

Not until 1799 did a preacher make an indigenous nun the subject of praise in the same way that the criolla nuns had been remembered upon their death. The indigenous founder and abbess for life of the Convent of Santa María de los Ángeles in Antequera was Sor María Teodora de San Agustín. There, as in Valladolid, the need for a convent for indigenous women was imperative, given the large indigenous population and the native leaders' initiative in negotiating spaces where their daughters could take the veil. Sor María Teodora left the Convent of Corpus Christi after twenty-seven years to found the convent in Antequera, where she lived for another sixteen years. She took the veil in 1755 and fulfilled various roles in the Convent of Corpus Christi, such as mistress of novices, vicar, and abbess. She lived to be sixty-two. Joseph Victoriano Baños preached her eulogy on May 10, 1799.

Sor María Teodora's eulogist directed his reflections toward the community of indigenous nuns: "No lo dudeis Religiosísimas vírgenes: y aunque protesteis que no es la muerte sino la falta irreparable de una Madre la que habeis llorado hasta ahora aun así, las esperanzas que su dichosa muerte os da su vida religiosa y ejemplar, deberá ser desde hoy vuestro paño de lágrimas" ("Do not doubt, most religious virgins: and although you may protest that up until now it is not her death, but rather the irreparable lack of a mother you have been lamenting, even so, the hopes that her fortunate death gives you, her religious and exemplary life, shall be from this moment on, your cloth to absorb your tears"; Castañeda Guzmán 83). In these very first phrases dedicated to the nuns in the convent, Baños establishes the virtue that will be most salient in Teodora: having lived an exemplary life as a role model for the community of nuns in her charge. Although this was expected of any criolla nun, in an Indian nun, it was considered a wonder.

The priest clarifies that the life of Teodora was not extraordinary because she did not experience visions, revelations, or raptures; rather, her virtue resided in commanding obedience through the powerful model of her own example (Castañeda Guzmán 85). He explains that Sor María Teodora did nothing that was not ordered by Holy Law. Throughout the sermon, the preacher constructs an image of Teodora based on her Indian identity. The eulogy dedicated to Teodora, then, did not depend solely on her exemplarity as a virtuous nun but also on her status as an indigenous nun. One epithet Baños uses to describe her is *americana*, and although a criolla woman born in New Spain could also be called americana, in this case it emphasizes her Indian descent.

Baños also refers to her as an "india santa" (holy Indian), "nobilísima india cacique" (most noble Indian cacica) and "pobre india" (poor Indian).[23] The preacher clearly uses the same ambivalent constructions employed in the founding sermon for the Convent of Corpus Christi preached by Castorena y Ursúa in 1724 (chap. 3). On the one hand, Baños recognizes that Sor María Teodora is worthy of a funeral eulogy and that the Indians have made sufficient advances in their religious practices to be considered equal to the Spanish. On the other hand, he repeatedly expresses wonder at the fact that the Indian women in the convent lived such exemplary lives. This ambivalence becomes most evident in the preacher's *defensa*:

Todas las almas son iguales en lo físico, y en lo moral, á los ojos de Dios . . . sea Español, sea Indio, sea Mulato, sea Mestizo, o de cualesquiera casta; ¡Dios Inmortal! Cuánto me temo, al considerar las bellas disposiciones naturales que por lo común se notan en los Indios para las virtudes cristianas y máximas del Evangelio, que si son limitados los progresos que hacen en la virtud, somos nosotros la causa principalísima, si no total, de que no adelanten; Instruyéramoslos con las patéticas eficacísimas lecciones del buen ejemplo, y se verían á cada paso Indios muy Santos. (95)

(All beings are physically and morally equal, in God's eyes . . . be they Spanish, Indian, Mulatto, Mestizo, or of any caste; Immortal God, how I tremble to consider the beautiful, natural talent for Christian virtue and principles of the Gospels that are commonly found in the Indian people; that even if the progress they make toward virtue is limited, it is we who are the most principal cause, if not the entire reason, why they do not progress. Let us instruct them with the moving and most efficient lessons of good examples, and they will at every turn be seen as very Holy Indians.)

This passage advances two arguments, the first being the equality of all colonial subjects in spiritual matters. Although Baños declares this to be so in his sermon, he contradicts himself by the very fact that he *defends* the existence of an Indian woman who lived religious life in accordance with the orthodoxy of the Church. His second argument has its origins in the Franciscan missionary discourse of separating the indigenous population from the Spaniards to preserve the childlike state in which the missionaries found them and thereby avoid "contamination" from Spaniard vices.[24] Baños argues that the Indians are naturally inclined to virtue, and the Spaniards are to blame if they have failed to advance further in matters of faith. This position, although it defends the natural goodness and virtue of the indigenous women, also conveys a paternalistic tone suggesting the "noble savage," a depiction of primitive beings who, without outside corruption, are good by their very nature.

The ambivalent discursive construction of the Indian subject is exacerbated when Baños imparts a comment made by another priest, Father Arzola, who, hearing Sor María Teodora speak, had been fooled into thinking they had sent him not an Indian woman, but a Spanish one, and one of the finest (89). Praising an Indian woman for being as refined as a Spanish woman continued to be the norm; social discrimination still reigned on the eve of the nineteenth century. Joseph Victoriano Baños gives little biographical information about Sor María Teodora, neither the date and place of her birth nor the identity of her parents. He also fails to include any anecdotes about his relationship with her, or her relationship with other nuns in the convent, as in the case of Sor Petra's funeral sermon, or her relationship with her confessor, as in the case of Sor María Teresa.

Some details offered as praise include, for example, that Sor María Teodora lived in extreme poverty, to the point that she did not even have her own cell in the convent. The eulogist also mentions that she suffered through an illness without any nourishment. Yet he repeats throughout the sermon that her greatest virtue was "el haber ella formádose un sistema de virtud tan común, tan ordinaria, tan ajena de toda singularidad y ostentación" ("having created for herself a system of virtue that made her so common, so ordinary, so removed from individuality and ostentation"; 88). According to Baños, and possibly the rest of the non-Indian population, Sor María Teodora was an example of virtue not because she had done anything particularly virtuous but because she lived like a Spanish nun in spite of being Indian. The funeral eulogy elevated her to heights of unattainable virtue never before reached by an Indian woman: "Nobilísima India Cacique, que tiene el particularísimo honor de ser la primera en su Nación que por su virtud se haya hecho acreedora al de un Elogio fúnebre" ("The most noble Indian cacica, who has the very special honor of being the first of her nation who, because of her virtue, has made herself worthy of a funeral eulogy"; 94). According to the preacher, being ordinary and disciplined in following her monastic rule constituted her highest virtues.

This third panegyric sermon does not follow the model of the two previously analyzed because it does not conform to the hagiographic style. For example, it does not give particular *exempla*, nor does it exaggerate her virtues to a supernatural degree.[25] Although constructed around the model of an exemplary life, the parameter by which her virtue is measured is significantly different than that used for the criolla nuns. That is, even though the honor of a funeral eulogy is finally bestowed on an indigenous nun, the subject's life is not embellished in the same ways that idealize a Spanish nun. There are two reasons for this: in the social hierarchy of the colonial order, the Indians were still placed in the lowest position; and the religious reforms introduced by the Bourbons during the eighteenth century promoted a less baroque style of preaching.[26]

This eulogy for Sor María Teodora de San Agustín makes it clear that the ideology of difference continued to prevail in conventual relationships and writings during the eighteenth century and was epitomized in religious colonial discourse. The eulogy dedicated to Sor María Teodora did not highlight the virtues she had displayed in her life; rather, it focused on how admirable it was that an indigenous woman could lead an exemplary religious life. Ethnic politics had changed between 1724, when the first convent for Indian women opened, and 1799, when this sermon was preached, but it is clear that little measurable improvement had taken place; the secular and religious perceptions of differences between indigenous and Spanish women were still pronounced.[27]

Through the analytical reading of the funeral sermons, we can appreciate the paternalistic attitude that emerged from the rhetorical constructions crafted by preachers. This became problematic when they tried to fashion themselves as defenders of the conquered nation, since they could not distance themselves from the same language that sustained the colonial ideology of difference. The pale portrait painted by the preachers' words about the Indian nuns and the two Spanish abbesses is more a reflection of colonial ideology and of the era's religious and social conformity than of the lives and virtues of real women. These sermons in particular and others still unpublished permit us to understand the ways in which religious discourse aided the colonial system, buttressing the ideology of discrimination and emphasizing difference. This more enlightened understanding allows us to begin dismantling the mechanisms of colonial power.

Letters from the Convent

Struggles through the Written Word

The epistolary genre was the most common vehicle of communication available to writers of both sexes during the Early Modern period. This was especially the case for women, both in and outside the convent. Letters can be analyzed for their rhetoric and content, and because letter-writing was a widely accessible genre, it became an important medium of expression for colonial subjects to articulate their affirmation of and resistance to the hegemonic system.

In the conventual spaces of New Spain, letters also functioned as a hybrid genre that revealed the same dialogism we have seen in other colonial discursive genres. Often conventual letters shared rhetorical conventions and language similar to those of the vida, the hagiographic biography, the sermon, and, even in some instances, the legal defense.[1] The significance of these letters resides not only in the nuns' mastery of classical rhetoric in epistolary composition but in their combining it with other religious and cultural elements that could be considered part of colonial spiritual rhetoric. In the specific case of the Convent of Nuestra Señora de Cosamaloapan in Valladolid, the Indian nuns who had access to and cultivated the epistolary genre skillfully manipulated rhetorical language to defend the ethnic autonomy of their cloister. Their use of colonial constructions of difference in their writings can be termed the rhetoric of "Indianness."

Letters written by nuns have been classified into two basic categories, those concerning material life and those dealing with spiritual issues (Lavrin, "De su puño y letra" 44). Other scholars have identified nuns' letters as "quotidian" or "confessional" (Araya, Azúa, and Ivernizzi 271). The quotidian type focuses on issues of finance and the economic life of the convent. The confessional type involves those the nuns wrote to a confessor or spiritual director. These have also been called *relaciones* or *cuentas de conciencia* and have been studied within the conventions of spiritual life or vidas.[2] Sor Sebastiana Josefa de la Santísima Trinidad, the criolla nun who entered the Convent of Corpus Christi during the initial years of the convent's life (chap. 3), wrote sixty letters to her spiritual father Fray Miguel Lozano, epistles that later served as a basis for the composition of her hagiographical biography authored by Joseph Eugenio Valdés in 1765.[3]

Yet there also exists a body of letters written by nuns that do not necessarily fall into either of these two categories, although they may share similar characteristics. The epistolary corpus deals directly with personal issues and conflicts within a conventual community, such as problems with a nun or confessor. These letters do not usually delve into spiritual insights or correspond to the administrative formal letter required of many nuns in posts of governance. These letters may contain details of everyday life, and less frequently, spiritual matters, depending on the addressee of the letter.[4]

In the convents for indigenous nuns, the largest number of letters originated from Nuestra Señora de la Purísima Concepción de Cosamaloapan in Valladolid; some are addressed to the commissary general in New Spain, Fray Pedro Navarrete, and others to Fray Juan Fogueras, the next commissary general, and other ecclesiastical authorities. This correspondence substantiates the social and political dynamic established with the nuns in the convent, as well as the way in which they maintained written relationships with ecclesiastical authorities.

These letters also contain an informative element especially relevant to the study of the ethnic conflict that developed in the convent. Throughout the letters written by various nuns in the Convent of Cosamaloapan between September 1743 and May 1745, there are repeated references to the strife between the criolla and indigenous nuns in the cloister. As in the case of the Corpus Christi convent, Commissary General Navarrete considered it "necessary" to allow Spanish nuns to enter the cloister. Although there are no descriptions of the specific mistreatment the indigenous women suffered, it is possible to identify in these epistolary writings the tone in which these conflicts are related, the manner in which the argument is constructed, the differing loyalties that were established, and the ethnic and gender power relations that were prevalent. Most important, the letters authored by Indian nuns use the rhetoric of Indianness to reassert their ethnic identity in order to defend their autonomous space.[5]

In order to set the stage for the subsequent epistolary grievances of indigenous authorship, the epistolary corpus considered herein includes a selection of the epistolary language and rhetoric that the first two criolla abbesses used. Through their use of the written word, indigenous nuns exercised agency with an authority denied to secular and *macehualli* indigenous women. They appealed to an ethnic memory that stemmed from the historical preservation of their noble lineage and from the privileged place they occupied as nobles in the eyes of the Church and the colonial state. Even as male ecclesiastical discourse elevated the Spanish model of perfection in sermons and hagiographical biographies that considered the Indian nuns their subject, the nuns themselves drew from the earliest constructions of their identities and recreated their Indianness to defend their space in the colonial religious arena. First, a look at the epistle as a colonial discursive genre is in order before delving into an analysis of the letters produced in the Convent of Nuestra Señora de Cosamaloapan that discuss the ethnic autonomy of the cloister.

The Epistolary Genre

Similar to the arts of oratory and preaching, epistolary rhetoric occupied an important place in humanism and religious education. Rhetorical strategies were essential to "proper" letter-writing, and detailed manuals with organizational systems and language usages were composed and published. The earliest treatises on epistolography adapted the general principles of oratory, but more detailed manuals developed through the centuries (Thompson 92). The epistle is, without doubt, the most popular genre cultivated by the writers studied here, since it carried neither gender nor social restrictions.[6] The letters produced in the colonial context are valuable documents for their historical content, but they are also part of the hybrid discourses of secular and religious colonialism. In this light, letters become spaces for contesting identities and for power struggles. Moreover, the historical value of the letters does not reside exclusively in the recovery of events that permit us to understand the past but also in the clear documentation of the manner in which the stories of this era were told. As Margarita Zamora suggests, in order to examine colonial texts, we must study the way in which authors and readers make use of the text, under what circumstances, and with what consequences.[7]

During the Classical era, Cicero made a distinction between two kinds of letters: the official (*libelli* or *codicilli*) and the private (*litterae*). The first refers to business letters; the second, to letters of personal exchange between friends. This same distinction may also be applied to the body of letters composed by nuns in eighteenth-century New Spain. Among conventual letters, one finds epistles directed to the current viceroy informing him about new convent foundations and nuns who had professed, seeking financial support for some project, or wishing him a Merry Christmas or Easter. These could be considered letters from material life in Asunción Lavrin's categorization, although they do not always address convent finances ("De su puño y letra" 44). According to Cicero's classification, these epistles would be official letters. On the other hand, the letters composed by nuns to their confessor, to another priest, or to sister nuns can be classified as private epistles. At times, these letters address conflicts within the convent and, on occasion, possess a more spiritual character.[8]

In the Middle Ages the structure of the letter followed the sequence of classic oratory that included the *exordium, narratio, argumentatio, conclusio* and, sometimes, the *salutatio* (Trueba 36). The Renaissance epistle holds a fundamental place in humanistic studies because epistolary rhetoric was part of the curriculum. In addition, manuals were written as guides for the correct writing and classification of letters. One of the best-known manuals was *De Ratione Conscribendi Epistolas Liber* by Erasmus. It included a guide to the proper usage of epistolary structure, along with a compendium of different examples of letters classified according to their subject. Familiar letters, for example, concerned quotidian matters such as congratulations or private requests. The sequence of their arrangement resembled the classical model, but the narration was followed by the proposition, confirmation, conjuration, and peroration (Thompson 92).

Another important manual was Nicolás Perotto's *Rudimenta grammatices*, which specifically mentioned in its classificatory system the epistles of religious subject matter such as those by Seneca, Aurelius Augustine, Jerome, Ambrose, and Cipriano, among others (Trueba 51). Up to this point, the development of the letter and the sermon coincided. During the Renaissance, however, a break with medieval scholastic tradition occurred as authors began to place greater importance on content than on form. Perotto's interest in classifying letters according to their subject matter, similar to Erasmus's manual, illustrates a heightened concern with epistolary content.

Donald W. Bleznick in "Epistolography in Golden Age Spain" asserts that the most important manuals on the theory and practice of epistolary writing became available during the Spanish Golden Age. He considers *De conscribendis epistolis* by Juan Luis Vives, published in 1536, and Erasmus's *Liber utilissimus de conscribendis epistolis*, which appeared in 1522, the most transcendent epistolographic treatises in Spain and other European countries in the sixteenth and seventeenth centuries. Introduced by Erasmus, the familiar letter, which allowed the writer greater liberty of expression, would be perfected later by Antonio de Guevara in Spain (13). Another useful resource for writers included sample letters. The first to consider them in the Castilian language was *Cosa nueva, este es el estilo de escrevir cartas mensajeras*, published in 1547 by Gaspar de Tejada. In 1553 he expanded his tract and included a new title: *Cosa nueva, primero libro de cartas mensajeras en estilo cortesano para diversos fines y propósitos con los estados*. This expanded edition included some four hundred letters that, according to Bleznick, "cover the entire range of the epistolary genre, beginning with letters to the Pope and cardinals and ending with 'algunas cartas graciosas, amorosas y de burlas para descansar el trabajo de las versa que dejamos atrás'" (15).

Although manuals of classical rhetoric and the more practical guides like Tejada's continued to be widely used by those who had access to an education, the use of epistolary rhetoric evolved. For example, the manuals were no longer composed in Latin, and the forms of epistolary composition grew more relaxed, even prosaic, which broadened their public reach. The general public could recognize rhetoric not necessarily because they were familiar with the manuals written in Latin but, rather, because they had read sample letters.[9]

Although the majority of women did not formally study rhetoric, evidence exists of their ability to reproduce it.[10] Jamile Trueba Lawand has analyzed the letters of Teresa of Ávila and identified in them a more humble style than the rhetorical mode that characterized contemporary letters by male writers. Nevertheless, Trueba distinguishes in Teresa's letters the use of classical rhetoric, particularly in the appropriation of the *captatio benevolentiae* (112).[11] Although no in-depth study has been done on Teresa's epistolary style, it is possible that she used similar strategies to those she employed in her other writings to establish her authority.[12] The "spiritual rhetoric" in many of Teresa's letters is evident in the letters written by the nuns in the Convent of Cosamaloapan.[13]

According to Enrique Ballón, the letter can be defined as a writing of private character that implies a pact of privacy and confidence between the writer and the reader (43). This definition describes the relevance of letters in the private space, but in the epistles defending the ethnic character of the Convent of Cosamaloapan, we can also identify a subject matter that belonged to the public sphere. Although the correspondence of individuals supposes that its private character and the confidence of both parties will be maintained, in reality, the letters addressed an issue that was as much a part of the consciousness of the conventual community as of the confessor and other ecclesiastical authorities. Elizabeth Cook has identified this dual nature of the conventual letter: "The letter became an emblem of the private; while keeping its actual function as an agent of the public exchange of knowledge" (6).

An important function of the epistle, aside from its communicational purpose, was to establish control. Communication between the nuns and their confessors, or with priests in higher positions of authority in the Church's power hierarchy, was mandatory. The abbess was supposed to report the conditions of her convent and any extraordinary occurrences, material or spiritual. This function of the letter was not limited to the conventual space nor to colonial era epistles. Walter Mignolo notes that letter writing, in addition to being a vehicle of communication for fifteenth-century humanists, had become an essential instrument of administrative and governmental control by the sixteenth century (*The Darker Side* 172). This function is readily apparent in the letters and accounts the first explorers wrote of their adventures in the Americas.[14] The explorers' acts of communicating their experiences in a "different world" and their implicit requests for economic assistance in exchange for loyalty and riches meant that, even from a distance, governmental control was being exercised. This structure of control is similar to the relationship between nuns and priests, one of loyalty and subordination.

The rhetoric of conventual letters varies from that of other epistles. Conventual letters constitute a subgenre within the epistolary genre that employs both classical and spiritual rhetoric. Teresa of Ávila and other European religious women served as models for nuns in New Spain. In "Subversive Obedience: Confessional Letters by Eighteenth-Century Mexican Colonial Nuns," Sarah Owens identifies specific techniques used by colonial nuns in their letters: *"imitatio christi*, holy anorexia, visions, and *captatio benevolentiae"* (115). In letters from the Convent of Cosamaloapan, we notice the recurrent use of the imitatio christi and the captatio benevolentiae, and in the case of the indigenous nuns, the appeal to their Indianness with all the connotations their native identity evoked in religious and secular arenas.

Sor Juana Inés de la Cruz makes exemplary use of classical rhetoric in her *Carta atenagórica* and *Respuesta a Sor Filotea*. In both narratives, we can discern classical epistolary divisions: exordium, narrative, confirmation, and peroration. Rosa Perelmuter Pérez, in her revealing study on the rhetorical structure of the *Respuesta*, notes that it was rhetoric in general and forensic discourse in particular that provided Sor Juana with a model to present her ideas and defend them in a coherent style (158).[15] Yet even though the captatio benevolentiae is an element from classical rhetoric, Sor Juana's use of the device is possibly derived from Teresa of Ávila's model, which Perelmuter Pérez refers to as "the formula of affected modesty." The rhetorical manuals suggest this formula, but according to Perelmuter, Sor Juana's treatment of modesty is pushed to the limits; it is "hyperbolic" (153).[16] If this affected modesty is considered in the colonial context of religious literature, Sor Juana may have simply been following the ideological canons of religious writing that dictated greater humility for women writers because their status in the Church hierarchy was subordinate to that of their male readers.[17]

Carole Slade asserts that Teresa of Ávila's manipulation of the written genre was her principal means of representing herself as innocent before Inquisitorial scrutiny (4). This claim implies that the writer possessed knowledge of rhetoric and intentionally adapted it to a given genre, be it a spiritual autobiography or a letter, to appeal to her audience. The manipulation of a discursive genre, in this case the letter, is evident in the writing practices of the nuns in the convent of Nuestra Señora de Cosamaloapan. Their writing derived not from the random manipulation of genres but from the inherent malleability of the colonial genres they had at hand, despite the rigid patriarchal context in which the writing nuns found themselves.

Kathleen Myers notes that by the seventeenth century, the epistolary genre was highly structured and that it could serve "as a public or private document and as a legal or spiritual aid" (*Neither Saints* 17).[18] This is a key element in the relationship established between a nun and a priest; given their superior positions, clerics had the power to transform a private document into a public one. Nuns, however, would also manipulate the rhetoric of the discursive genre to obtain their epistolary objectives.

Occasionally, letters written by nuns would be addressed to a nun in another convent, but most frequently, the letters that survived were addressed to a male reader. The most common addressees for indigenous nuns were the commissary general and other important Church authorities whose assistance the nuns sought. The subordination of the female author to the male reader here is similar to the relationship of the author and reader of vidas. María Dolores Bravo Arriaga has studied some of the letters written by Bishop Manuel Fernández de Santa Cruz addressed to other nuns, documents that reveal a discourse of power "with the implacable verticality that supplies the superior-subordinate relationship" (107). Despite the unequal relationship between sender and receiver, and the clear use of conventions that impede the free expression of the female writer, the letters function as a space in which women negotiated their identities and expressed themselves within the precepts established by the Church. As Asunción Lavrin asserts, letters written by nuns reveal the protagonism of the female subjects in an authentic and indisputable way (59). Thus, through the strategic use of classical and spiritual rhetoric, the nuns employ epistolary writing to lodge their complaints, make their petitions, and communicate their needs—all while maintaining the hierarchical relationship that existed between them and the recipients of their letters. By rhetorically sustaining that implicit contract of subordination, they assured that their complaints would be heard.

Conflict in the Cloister

The Convent of Nuestra Señora de la Purísima Concepción de Cosamaloapan, founded in 1737 in what is now Morelia, was the second cloister established exclusively for noble Indian women. However, just as in the Convent of Corpus Christi, the commissary general of the Franciscan Order in New Spain, Fray Pedro de Navarrete, allowed the admission of criolla women other than those who arrived in Valladolid to be founders of the convent. Immediately, a series of conflicts broke out between the criolla and indigenous women, and between some women and the convent's vicar and chaplain, difficulties documented in the body of letters that have been preserved. Unfortunately, the sequence of events lacks a discernible linear order, as there were several hands authoring different letters during the same period of time. For the most part, the letters were addressed to Fray Pedro de Navarrete, who does not appear to have interceded for the nuns, thereby allowing the conflicts to continue for years. The latest letters were addressed to Fray Juan Fogueras, who replaced Navarrete as commissary general of the Franciscan Order.[19]

The problems these letters describe appeared to center on the socio-ethnic division within the community of nuns. Some of the criolla founders requested they be sent back to their original convents, claiming the environment in this new convent was unbearable. The indigenous nuns defended the original Indian character of the foundation and stressed their fear that accepting more Spanish novices would eventually make the convent just another religious institution that subordinated Indians.

This body of letters allows us to appreciate the manner in which the writing nuns made use of classical and spiritual rhetoric to appeal to the recipient of their letters with narratives that conveyed a complaint, petition, or confession. Sor María Gregoria Cayetana de Jesús Nazareno and Sor María Josefa de San Nicolás, the first two abbesses of the convent, produced most of the letters. Yet, it is the few writings authored by indigenous nuns in an appeal to oust the Spanish nuns and to maintain the cloister exclusively for indigenous nuns that provide a richer understanding of the strife in the cloister.

The correspondence from the convent begins in 1743 with the letters written by Sor María Gregoria Cayetana, the first abbess of the convent, who composed her letters after having recently vacated her position as abbess. Her rhetoric derives from this role as another nun in the convent without any particular authority over the governance of the cloister. She appeals to her reader by making use of the captatio benevolentiae, which corresponds to traditional religious feminine discourse: "Aunque yo soy tan mala, tengo un gran temor al juicio tremendo de Jesús y si es una gravísima maldad inquietar una comunidad sólo por una forma, o de forma propia, bien sabe Vuestra Reverendísima que desde que vine empecé a padecer y a ser mandada y a obedecer a Vuestra Reverendísima y a mis compañeras" ("Although I am so bad, I do greatly fear Jesus's tremendous judgment, and if it is a very grave evil to stir up an entire community in just one way, or because of one's own manner, Your Reverence knows well that since I came here I began to suffer and to be commanded by and obey Your Reverence and my fellow sisters"; AINAH, FF, vol. 100, fol. 135).

Sor Gregoria immediately claims to be "bad" for having stirred up her community (an accusation she does not deny), and this first part of her letter also makes clear her obedience to the masculine figure, as well as her suffering, all elements that present her as a model nun. Sor Gregoria explains that when she had been abbess, she had wanted to impose the Rule in the same way as the Convent of Corpus Christi, a decision the community did not accept, and for that reason the other nuns "corrieron con Vuestra Reverendísima diciendo era de mala condición y que quería milagros" ("ran to Your Most Reverend, saying that I was wrong and expecting miracles [from them]"; AINAH, FF, vol. 100, fol. 135). The nun relates the nightmares and suffering she endured all this time, always exempting herself from blame. In closing her letter, she asks the prelate for his advice, requesting that he believe she had done everything she could to keep peace in the convent and that he not think ill of or lose confidence in her.

Five months later, Sor Gregoria wrote again to the commissary general of New Spain. This letter is more specific about the identities of the women involved in the conflicts: "Ya sabe Vuestra Reverendísima que la barberena y la indita han sido mis enemigas y que me han difamado repetidas veces y otras tantas las he perdonado" ("As you already know, Most Venerable Reverend, the *barberena* and the *indita* have been my enemies, and they have defamed me repeatedly and each time I have forgiven them"; AINAH, FF, vol. 100, fol. 150). When Sor Gregoria refers to "la barberena," she is speaking of Sor María Josefa de Jesús de Barbarena, one of the nuns who had asked to be transferred to the Convent of Santa Isabel de México (AINAH, FF, vol. 100, fol. 151). In her brief letter, Sor Gregoria appears to be facing serious difficulties in the convent, since her petition asks that she be allowed to continue wearing the habit she had worn for twenty years and tries to persuade the priest by referring to how good a nun she has been (AINAH, FF, vol. 100, fol. 150). In her letter writing, Sor Gregoria presents herself as even more exemplary by claiming that her strength of will does not emanate from inside her own being but was received, rather, as a divine gift, a direct declaration of God's approval of her alleged good conduct.

Both Sor Gregoria and Sor María Josefa de San Nicolás, the next abbess and also a cofounder of the convent, were seriously challenged in their efforts to maintain order in the convent. Asunción Lavrin asserts that the many letters Sor María Josefa addressed to the commissary, Fray Juan Fogueras, reveal the degree to which she was unable to resolve internal confrontations ("De su puño" 52).[20] Her first letters were written when she began her tenure as abbess in the Convent of Cosamaloapan in 1743.

She begins one of her communications to Fray Pedro de Navarrete in a tone similar to Sor Gregoria's: "Mi muy amado y querido Reverendo y venerado prelado" ("My very dear and much loved Reverend and Venerated Prelate"; AINAH, FF, vol. 100, fol. 138). A characteristic element of Sor María Josefa's style, also present in the letters of other nuns, is the use of the term "padrecito" (dear padre). The diminutive form of the word "Father" (priest) represents one of those instances in which nuns reproduced speech in written form; the formula of respect and gratitude would also "protect its subversive undertones" (Arenal and Schlau, "Stratagems" 27). In this letter, Sor María Josefa reminds Fray Pedro de Navarrete that he had promised to visit the convent and stresses that his presence is much needed because of conflicts that only he can help solve. This letter and Sor Gregoria's first epistle date from April 1743; Sor Gregoria's second, in which she incriminates the "barberena" and the "indita," and the three letters I address below date from September of that same year. It is highly significant that just when the other nuns of the community were writing their version of events, Sor Gregoria wrote a letter to defend her position when she was abbess and again later as just another member of the community.

On September 2, 1743, Sor María Josefa de Jesús de Barbarena writes to Pedro de Navarrete, six years after she entered the Convent of the Purísima Concepción in Cosamaloapan. This period of time, according to her, "ha sido un puro padecer sin faltar día de tanta discordia" ("has been pure suffering without a day's respite from such discord"; AINAH, FF, vol. 100, fol. 151). "La Barbarena" also refers to Navarrete as "padrecito" in her letter, creating a tone of entreaty from a loving daughter to her father and setting the stage to put forward her request. As Arenal and Schlau indicate, formulas of respect and gratitude signified more than conformity (27). Sor María Josefa de Barbarena's problems are not limited solely to her conventual relationships in the community of nuns but also extend to her connection with the priests. She mentions experiencing difficulties with the vicar and the chaplain, both of whom refuse to give her communion.

She makes her main request in the final part of the letter as a way of closing the missive: "Por María Santísima que no me mande Vuestra Reverencia confesar con los Padres de acá, vicario y capellán que son muy sencillos por Jesús que me de Vuestra Reverencia el consuelo del confesor que tengo" ("In Blessed Mary's name, Your Reverence, please do not send me to confess with the priests from here, the vicar and chaplain are very simple. In Jesus's name, Your Reverence, allow me the comfort of the confessor I now have"; AINAH, FF, vol. 100, fol. 152). "La Barbarena" adds that because one of those priests is the abbess's confessor, she does not want to confess her sins to him. This letter also indicates her desire to return to the Convent of Santa Isabel, but given her emphasis on the letter's final petition, her main complaint appears to be her problem with the chaplain and the vicar.

Just seven days later, Sor María Jesús del Santísimo Sacramento, an Indian nun in the convent, also wrote a letter addressed to Pedro de Navarrete. Sor María Jesús demonstrates the same command of spiritual and classical rhetoric as the criolla nuns. For example, she employs the stratagems of self-deprecation, presenting herself as small and insignificant before her masculine reader, just as the criolla nuns do. She also includes an element of orality that resemblances the confessional act in her letter. Sor María Jesús writes: "Que le confieso la verdad como si estuviera a los pies de vu[e]s[tr]a paternidad de que me hallo indigna . . . no había yo de tener semejante atrevimiento de coger la pluma" ("I confess the truth to you as if I were at your feet, My Father, for I am unworthy . . . I should not have dared to take up the pen"; AINAH, FF, vol. 100, fol. 167).

Sor María Jesús's allusion to taking up the pen as "daring" does not necessarily stem just from the rhetoric of Indianness but also from the rhetoric of humility, particularly as the content of her writing will contribute to continued turmoil in the convent. Aside from the historical value of the letter's content, we should note that this is a "confession" written by an indigenous woman to an important authority figure in the religious sphere. Sor María Jesús writes:

> Le digo a Vues[tr]a Paternidad Reverenda para descargo de mi conciencia quienes son la causa de que acá no haiga paz que son las tres Reverendas Madres fuera de nuestra Reverenda Madre [Abadesa] y esto es sin pasión porque con estas tres señoras acá esta esto hecho un infierno fuera de a que, Padre nuestro estara hecho una gloria porque la Madre Sor María Magdalena es la que hace la división de nosotras las cacicas con las españolas que no debe ser eso. (AINAH, FF, vol. 100, fol. 167)

> (I will tell you, Most Reverend Father, to clear my conscience, who the three Reverend Mothers are, aside from our own Reverend Mother [Abbess] who are the cause of the lack of peace here, and I say this without anger because with these three women here things have turned into hell when otherwise, it would be a glory, for our Father, because Mother Sor María Magdalena is the one who creates a division between us, the cacicas, and the Spanish women, which should not be so.)

Sor María Jesús adds that the Spanish women are all "saints," except for the three women who cause problems and whose names she does not mention. She describes the company of the Spanish women as lovely and amiable, and contends that they, the indigenous nuns, are not worthy of it (AINAH, FF, vol. 100, fol. 167). We can be certain that Sor María Jesús is a noble Indian. She asserts her identity as such when she writes *"nosotras las cacicas"* ("we, the cacicas").

This passage in Sor María Jesús's letter reveals the way loyalties played out in the convent. For instance, the case presented by this particular Indian nun illustrates that not all indigenous nuns shared an exclusive bond of solidarity due to their ethnic difference. She makes a distinction between her and the other indigenous women, emphasizing her noble lineage and referring to the nuns as cacicas and not *Indians*. From the beginning of the letter, Sor María Jesús tries to disassociate herself from Sor María Magdalena, an indigenous nun whom Sor María Jesús openly blames for creating discord between the two groups. These two communities, although identified clearly by their ethnic quality, do not necessarily reject all the nuns of the other group. Sor María Jesús is quick to clarify that if her name has appeared on any group letter, it is because someone has signed for her without her consent.

Sor María Marta de Jesús, another nun in the convent, wrote a letter the same day Sor María de Jesús composed hers. Notably, both letters identify Sor María Magdalena and the three Spanish women who came as founders as the agents of discord between the two groups of nuns, and Sor María Marta also clarifies that not all of the Spanish women cause problems. She writes: " . . . y será esta casa un cielo en la tierra a bien que con esta carta de la Madre Magdalena verá Vuestra Reverendísima cómo ésta es la que perturba a las cacicas que viendose estas tres que son las que las fomentan estas cederán, que no son todas, serán seis o siete las aliadas" (". . . and this house would be heaven on earth if after this letter from Mother Magdalena, Your Most Holy Reverend will see that she is the one who stirs up the cacicas, that in seeing that these three are the ones who encourage them to rebel, and that they will yield, for it is not all the women but only six or seven who are allied in this"; AINAH, FF, vol. 100, fol. 161).

It is safe to assert on the basis of the document's information that one incomplete letter lacking the author's signature was authored by the renowned indigenous nun Sor María Magdalena, mentioned in other nuns' missives.[21] The first part of the letter states that she is a native of Oaxaca ("de Oaxaca de donde soy criolla") and that she took the holy habit in Mexico City in the Convent of Corpus Christi, from which she set out for Valladolid as a founder of Cosamaloapan.[22] As in the writing of Sor María Jesús, Sor María Magdalena's use of the epithet "criolla," which demonstrates a clear sense of ethnic identity, makes an important distinction between nobles and the rest of the indigenous population.

In the archives of the Convent of Corpus Christi, there are two *informaciones históricas* (historical reports), one of which is about the establishment of the Convent of Nuestra Señora de la Concepción de Cosamaloapan. It lists the names of the five nuns who left Corpus Christi to found the convent: "Reverend Mother Sor María Gregoria Manuela de Jesús Nazareno, Reverend Mother Sor Josepha Gertrudis de San Nicolás, Reverend Mothers Sor Josepha Eligia de Santa Coleta, a black veiled cacica Indian nun in this convent for 5 years and 9 months, and Sor María Magdalena Coleta de Jesús Nazareno, a black veiled cacica Indian nun in this convent for 3 years and 7 months and 22 days, and Sor María Estefanía, a Spanish novice for 22 days" (ACC, Informaciones n. pag.).[23] This report helps us match the name of the founder with information in the letter. The comments of other nuns in their letters also aid in solving the puzzle of the enigmatic authorship of the incomplete letter. In addition, this letter differs from the others in that it is addressed to Father Juan de Altamirano and not to Fray Pedro

Navarrete. From what Sor María Marta de Jesús wrote, we can assume that Sor María Magdalena also wrote a letter to Commissary General Fray Pedro de Navarrete, but we have no other evidence.

In her letter, Sor María Magdalena shows a clear understanding of the conflicts between regular and secular priests over jurisdiction of the convents. Given that Franciscan officials contravened the royal decree ordering the ethnic exclusivity of the convents of Corpus Christi and Cosamaloapan, she supports the secularization of the convent and rejects being under the jurisdiction of the Provincia del Santo Evangelio.[24]

Her rhetorical style follows the same formulas found in the corpus of letters composed by nuns in the convent: She refers to her recipient as "Mi Señor" and "Padrecito" to appeal to his benevolence. Sor María Magdalena also frames her epistle narrative as a confession, which she specifies must remain a secret. The purpose of her letter is to request that Father Altamirano compose a letter in the name of all the convent's nuns to send to the king of Spain, asking that "they leave us alone in our convent" ("nos dejen solas en nuestro convento"; AINAH, FF, vol. 100, fol. 165). She recounts that as the convent's secretary, she had access to the documents in the conventual archive and realized that the king of Spain thinks that "todas somos indias y que no hay españolas y ya Vuestra Merced ve que no es así porque los prelados hacen lo que quieren" ("all of us are Indian and that there are no Spanish women, and Your Excellency already sees that it is not that way because the prelates do as they please").

Sor Magdalena recounts in her letter to Altamirano that Fray Navarrete had admitted three Spanish women to her former Convent of Corpus Christi, despite the existence of a papal bull that should have prevented it. She asks that Altamirano, once his letter is written, send it to her so that all the nuns can sign it, and they will then return it to him to be sent to Spain. In addition to the royal decree she was seeking for the convent of Cosamaloapan, she asks that he help them negotiate a papal bull in order to have sufficient documentation to maintain the native autonomy of the cloister. Sor Magdalena writes:

> Le suplico la procure con todos aquellos requisitos y expresiones que caben, de tal suerte ponga Usted la cosa que venga en ella que si en algún tiempo quisieran forzarnos los Prelados Regulares a que entren españolas, tengamos nosotras la libertad para responder que queremos pasarnos al gobierno de los señores obispos para que así nos podamos librar porque son muchas las razones de los prelados a fuerza quieren que recibamos a cualquiera en admitiéndola sus paternidades. (AINAH, FF, vol. 100, fol. 166)

(I beseech you to make this happen by following all the appropriate and necessary requirements and expressions. Include everything in [your] letter in such a way that, if at any time the Regular Prelates should want to force us to admit Spanish women, we will have the liberty to respond that we wish to be governed by the bishops so that we can be free, because there are many reasons the prelates want to force us to receive any woman the fathers wish us to admit.)

The argument that Sor María Magdalena puts forth in her letter is much more sophisticated than that of other nuns, even the abbesses, who dedicated more lines to narrating their terrible sufferings than to presenting clear petitions to improve the situation of the cloister. Sor María Magdalena offers a solid understanding of religious governance, since she asks that the convents for Indian women (which at that time numbered only two) be moved from Franciscan jurisdiction to secular religious government. In addition, she supports her argument with evidence against the Franciscans, specifically Navarrete, whose actions threatened the purely indigenous character of the convents mandated by the Spanish king and created problems in those communities. Sor María Magdalena asks Altamirano for his intercession in removing the Spanish nuns the commissary general had approved, arguing that the Spanish women have numerous convents where they can serve the Lord but the "pobres indias" ("poor Indian women") have only two.

Sor María Magdalena is one of the indigenous nuns who, perhaps because she held a position of power within the convent, actively defended the native autonomy of the cloisters founded strictly for indigenous women. Throughout her letter, she employs the rhetoric of colonial discourse and Biblical images to define the identity of the indigenous women when she believes it useful to achieve her objective. To appeal to the priest, she claims that she has knowledge of his customary charity with the poor, and thus when she considered negotiating "alguna cosa para estas pobres" ("a little something for these poor people"), she thought immediately of Altamirano as the one who could secure this for her and her fellow sisters. In closing, she writes: "Le pido tenga y halle acogida esta pobrecita Comunidad ante los ojos de Vuestra Merced pues se halla afligida (y mucho) porque los lobos infernales no dejan de perseguirla" ("I ask that you keep and shelter this poor Community before Your Mercy's eyes because it has suffered [and a great deal] because the infernal wolves do not stop chasing it"; AINAH, FF, vol. 100, fol. 165). The epithet *pobre* (poor) in its diminutive form *pobrecita* implies knowledge of the language of social conformity that subordinates Indian women to the care of the communities of priests and Spanish women. As with the discourse of preaching (chap. 5) and testimonies of defense (chaps. 2 and 3), the use of the word "pobre" invokes biblical imagery, reinforced by the first images offered by the Franciscan missionaries and the renowned rhetoric of defense employed by Fray Bartolomé de las Casas in his *Brevísima relación*, but the term is also strategically deployed in their own discourses of negotiation to appeal to the ethnic exclusivity of the cloisters. The indigenous women resort to the image of pobrecitas to present their petition more efficiently and to conform to the colonial order imposed by the Church, but they also invoke it as active agents in the conservation of the tradition of ethnic consciousness and pride that the cacicazgos had made possible to maintain well into the eighteenth century.[25]

Two years later, when Fray Pedro Navarrete was no longer the commissary general, a largely indigenous group of nuns from the Convent of Nuestra Señora de Cosamaloapan wrote to the new commissary general, Fray Juan Fogueras, informing him of the problems and discord that existed in the convent:

> Discurrimos que se mortificará con nuestras impertinencias; pero qué hemos de hacer Reverendísimo Padre, los principios de esta sagrada fundación se erraron y si ahora que está en los principios todavía no se remedia tanto disturbio como hay; así se quedará y pobres de las que lo habitaren. (AINAH, FF, vol. 100, fol. 222)

> (We pondered whether you might be annoyed by our impertinences; but what should we do, Most Reverend Father, since the principles of this sacred establishment were misled, and if now that it is just beginning there is no resolution to all the upheaval that there is, thus it will remain and pity on those women who will live there.)

These women make use of the paradise image to which other letters allude: the nuns' belief that they were entering heaven when they entered the convent but, instead, found themselves in hell ("infierno"). One nun states that all the women who signed the letter are professed nuns and not novices, emphasizing their seniority and authority, and they ask for a solution to the situation because they are obligated to watch over their convent. Being professed nuns gave them the right to vote in conventual elections and on any decisions made in the cloister, prerogatives restricted by the abbess and the nuns aligned with her. They describe the community's division into two groups, one side made up of Indian women, twelve of the first ones to profess, pitted against the other side, consisting of the abbess, the vicaress, and eight more nuns, "y son todas las que tienen y pueden tener los oficios de vicaria, de maestra de novicias y todos los demás" ("And it is all those [nuns] who hold and may hold the offices of vicaress, mistress of novices and all the other positions"). They also indicate that the mistress of novices is just a young girl who does not command respect, that the vicaress does not know how to read, and that this group of nuns is not allowing them to cast their votes. Although this second group of nuns is believed to possess more skills for carrying out specific administrative responsibilities in the convent, they argue that the abbess selected young girls, possibly novices, whom they consider inadequate for these positions.

The women's complaints continue in the argument section of the letter, which states that they are persecuted and mistreated by the abbess, who should be the one to bring peace to the community and prevent gossip. The letter also claims that the nurse, assigned to her post by the abbess, takes more care in healing the women of her own inner circle ("séquito") and disdains the rest. Lastly, they ask the commissary general to assign them a mother abbess who is loving ("amorosa") with her daughters. It is possible that the nuns decided to write a letter as a group to strengthen their petition. Moreover, the nuns warn the commissary general that he may be confused by the abbess's efforts to impose her own opposing version of events: "La madre Abadesa le escribirá a Vuestra Reverencia muy contrario a lo que nosotras decimos y se sentirá aturdido . . . " ("The Mother Abbess will write to Your Reverence just the opposite of what we are saying and you will feel bewildered . . ."; AINAH, FF, vol. 100, fol. 222).

The nuns also state that they need an immediate solution to the strife because the other "parcialidad" (group) has been openly defiant since the conventual chaplain left. They indicate problems with their confessors, one of whom also serves as the abbess's confessor. When they confess to him, the abbess and her allies dismiss the concerns they revealed during confession as "cuentos" (gossip). They close by declaring that they are ill from so much grief but confident that the commissary general will be able to offer some consolation and resolution.

Significantly, Sor María Magdalena, whom we have seen previously as a clear protagonist in the convent's conflicts, is represented in this specific letter in a very different light. Its authors claim that they can speak neither good nor bad of her because she had done them no harm, but she is so cornered ("arrinconada") that her existence in the convent goes unnoticed. The letter later states that she has been punished for two years "por lo que Vuestra Reverencia tiene sabido (que todo es público)" ("for what Your Reverence already knows about (since everything is public)"; fol. 223).[26] Presumably, after Sor María Magdalena took into her own hands the issue of dealing with the convent's internal conflicts, and especially after she solicited the secular priests to remove the cloister from the control of the Province of the Santo Evangelio, she underwent some sort of official sanction.

Fray Pedro Navarrete no longer occupied the post of commissary general in 1745, yet the problems in the convent persisted, and this group of nuns participated actively in solving them by using written discourse to convey their discontent. Although the strife inside the convent was described by mirroring the *extramuros* hierarchical differentiation related to ethnicity, the nuns identified ecclesiastical officials they held accountable for conflicts in the cloister. Gender did not create strong bonds that would have presented a united front against the prelates, but even when some nuns were singled out in the correspondence, we can still identify the existence of a community of women whose solidarity allowed them to challenge the authority imposed by ecclesiastical authority.[27]

Mabel Moraña contends that the colonial confessor was a paternal protective figure who was equally tyrannical, an image of authority who represented faith and repression, salvation and condemnation ("Sor Juana y sus otros" 321). This fashioning of a dualistic clerical figure resonates with the image of the addressee in the nuns' letters. While we do not hear the voice of the priest in any of the letters, his prominence is undeniable, his authority implicit by virtue of his representing the potential fulfillment of their hopes. The use of the epistolary genre responds to the dynamic of control exercised within the ecclesiastical hierarchy, particularly in the conventual setting.

In sum, these conventual letters function as yet another dialogic discursive space, one that exhibits the same power relations documented in other genres of colonial religious discourse. The written discourse characteristic of the confessional letter reproduced an arena in which women, even as they found a voice, remained subordinate to the ecclesiastical and gender hierarchy. Power, as Foucault argues, "is not an institution, and not a structure; neither is it a certain strength we are endowed with; it is the name that one attributes to a complex strategical situation in a particular society" (*The History* 93). The strategies of power and control the prelates exerted are much more complex than we see at first glance, operating not in a relation of equality, nor in a limited binary, but in a network of exchanges with infinite possibilities. This body of letters has shown that the Church and patriarchal figures of authority are not the only ones present in epistolary dialogue; one must also listen for the voices of the abbess and other social groups who wished to govern. All involved in the conflict within the Convent of Cosamaloapan had in varying degrees the opportunity to produce discourses in an attempt to control the situation. The indigenous noble-women revealed themselves as active participants in the creation of spaces where they could practice religion in a privileged social position rather than in a subordinate situation as was the custom before 1724.

The exchange of letters between the nuns of the Cosamaloapan convent and the Franciscan prelates shows that noble Indian women participated actively in the defense of their convents. The "poor" Indian women, as they referred to themselves, knew how to create and manipulate alliances for their own purposes. In their discourse, they used stereotypes imposed on them by the Spanish religious colonial system, thereby participating in the construction of the ethnic identity in play during the years of colonial presence in New Spain. The Indian nuns understood Church politics and participated in a power struggle to uphold the indigenous character of their convents. Ultimately, noble Indians succeeded in securing a third and final convent for cacicas to be founded and governed by indigenous women from its inception, and throughout the later years it remained active.

Epilogue

One hot summer day in 1999, in front of the famed Tule Tree in Oaxaca outside the Templo de Santa María de la Asunción, I encountered a group of Franciscan nuns of the First Rule of Saint Claire selling *rompope* (punch) and cookies. I approached them and began chatting about my frustrated research for the now nonexistent archives of the Convent of Nuestra Señora de los Ángeles in Oaxaca City. They all seemed to know exactly what I was referring to, and one nun asked with great interest: "Oh, so you are looking for the convent of the indias caciques?" I was speechless. Here I was simply volunteering general information I thought would be of no particular interest to them, which actually in turn prompted their earnest question spe- cifically identifying the subject of my research, the indias caciques. I was even more surprised when they related their personal knowledge of the convent's history and the ethnic lineage maintained by its nuns. Furthermore, they all considered themselves descendants of the indias caciques who had lived there, just like their sisters in the Convent of Corpus Christi in Mexico City. According to Josefina Muriel, the convent no longer existed, but the Clarisa nuns at the Tule Tree reported that al- though the conventual archive had been destroyed, the convent, whose address and phone number they provided, remained. Because of their help- ful directions, I discovered that the convent does, indeed, still exist but is known today by the name of Monasterio Autónomo de Clarisas de Corpus Christi in Tacuba, Mexico City.[1]

This anecdote serves to illustrate the continuity, as much as the change, in the conceptualization of Indian identity. Through religion, Indian caciques and principales expressed community identity and autonomy. Matthew O'Hara presents a case in point with his study of the San Matías Ixtacalco parish in nineteenth-century Mexico. He demonstrates that even after the judicial category "Indian" no longer existed and parish use of that terminology was frowned upon, the community maintained its Indian identity well into the 1830s ("*Miserables* and Citizens" 25). Although "Indians" legally disappeared with the independence of Spain, the group had created a cohesive identity that persisted into the national period. It would be erroneous to contend that Indian identities have resisted change, and today there are perhaps even more competing discourses of what being Indian means. Still, we cannot deny the enduring influence of the colonial legacy. We cannot help but ponder, while hoping not to oversimplify, the complexities of identity-making and the multiplicity of meanings that the concept of Indian connotes. For example, how did an *indio* became a *campesino*? And how did the Clarisa nuns in 1999 become descendants of the cacicas of the eighteenth century?[2]

David Frye embarked on a difficult journey to elucidate how the Indian past of the town of Mexquitic informed its present identity. He found as much continuity in the inhabitants' discourses about being Indian as rupture, concluding that "the Indian presence in Mexquitic is denied precisely because the people of the town are forced to define their own identity in terms of a racial ideology that is ultimately colonial in origin" (5–6). Although today's political and media discourses that deal with indigenous women differ from those that developed in the colony, they still retain a colonizing tone, and their focus continues to be on *difference*. Certain communities of indigenous women have found support in grassroots and feminist groups, such as the Mayan women's social movements of political resistance. However, over time there has been no substantial improvement in indigenous women's quality of life or social recognition. Changes due to globalization have had the greatest impact on indigenous communities and created even heavier workloads for women. Difficult economic conditions have hindered the growth of their ethnic consciousness and the resistance they have engaged in since colonial times.[3]

Their story stands in contrast to that of the privileged native elites who were affixed the label of Indian (as well as the rest of the macehuales). They swiftly learned to operate in the system and with the rhetorical tools at hand.[4] As Yanna Yannakakis has revealed, native intermediaries found leverage for accommodation and resistance to colonialism within the state system and the Church, and within their own local Indian communities. Yannakakis argues that this maneuvering of native brokers continues to provide resources to the present day (225). The story of the native population of Mexico is one of plurality, and the related "Indian question" in the project of nation formation is an ambiguous one: on the one hand, they embrace multiethnicity, and on the other, homogenization through the policies proposed by *indigenismo*.[5] To this day, some communities convey a clear sense of ethnic identity derived from colonial times, while others reject identification as Indian precisely for its colonial import, as in the case of Mexquitic.

Focusing on how women, in this particular case, Indian women, adapted to colonialism and how it shaped their lives provides a focus for fruitful discussion (Jaffary 9). Noblewomen participated with their male counterparts in maintaining an indigenous historical memory, in transmitting the pride of belonging to a noble lineage, and in conserving particular meanings of being Indian.[6] Although native women's written script has never been considered together with the men's written corpus, I contend that the writings of Indian nuns, however limited in number, should have a place alongside the historiographical and literary texts that recover and recreate the Indian past, forging a new colonial identity. As Frances Karttunen proposes, it is through discursive written forms that indigenous peoples articulated the change and continuity of their ethnic identities. These discourses have taken different shapes, from traditional and more European forms to hybrid and other not-yet-defined genres.

Antonio de Nebrija published the first grammar of a modern European language in 1492. He dedicated his work to Queen Isabella and noted that "language has always been the companion of empire" (Abbott 6). We can attest to the impact of the Spanish language in the expansion of the Iberian empire and its consistent use as a mechanism of ideological control. The primary concern of this book has been the use and function of language, and although we have seen glimpses of historical individuals, the role they have played as cultural mediators in their writings has been this work's principal focus.

The discourses produced in relation to the convents for indigenous women in New Spain, particularly those produced within those very convents, must be appreciated in the immediate context of a colonial situation that affected not only their linguistic and referential configuration but also their very nature. Analytical readings of the various discursive genres in this study allow us to appreciate the complexity of the relations that colonial subjects established among themselves through the use of the written word.

One of the purposes of this book was to present a critical reading of the construction of the religious colonial discourses that emerged in the eighteenth century when cloisters exclusively devoted to the indigenous population were proposed. Ecclesiastical colonial power created discursive identities that the indigenous nuns with access to written discourse adapted, modified, and strategically employed—intricate discursive interaction that raises important questions about the ways in which the racialized and gendered Other is represented. Few texts authored by colonial indigenous women have survived, and the majority of documents analyzed in this book were produced by male representatives of the Church. Still, I attempt to listen to the sustained dialogue of the colonial subjects themselves in a situation of subalternity.

The active role of indigenous women is evident not just in their discursive production but also in their accomplishments demonstrating long-term resistance and, especially, negotiation.[7] Indigenous women were able to play significant roles in certain areas of society, such as those associated with the Catholic Church. The convents for indigenous women clearly were spaces in which they exercised agency, but there were other options outside of conventual life where this was also possible. Edward Osowski has described the participation of late eighteenth-century indigenous women in the gathering of donations to finance and restore chapels, churches, and religious images. These elite women were not just subjects the Church used for its own purposes. Empowered by the Christian education they had obtained from the Jesuits and bolstered by the support of the male indigenous elite, these women participated actively in society and enjoyed a certain mobility, which they used strategically to maintain cohesion and power within their communities (158).

We know that despite evidence of a certain acceptance of Hispanic cultural values, indigenous groups retained their ethnic consciousness and found strategies to maintain it within a system that sought to "de-Indianize" their communities even as it emphasized their difference from the colonizer.[8] During the colonial period, the Church established a mechanism of power that imposed its system of subjugation and control while, at the same time, opening spaces in which Indians and particularly women could exercise their own initiative.

Power relations between different genders and ethnic groups are considered in each chapter of this work, complex relations that cannot be simplified to binary relationships of domination and resistance. Power, then, is present at all levels and is inherent in discursive production; the nuns' discourse makes use of it as much as the priests' (Foucault, *The History* 95). The nuns' expression was restricted to some extent by the priests, who required writing in certain genres that followed well-delineated conventions. Even though they had to compose with an implicit male reader in mind, they were still allowed a certain freedom in their use of the rhetoric established by religious feminine models.[9]

We recognize an inherent ambiguity in the gendered and racial discursive constructions of the writings studied here. Priests and nuns made use of the language that had defined the Amerindians in legal and religious terms since the European's original conceptualization of the Americas. Discursive efforts to construct and define the colonial female subject became a field of rhetorical play that implemented several cultural categories according to the writing subject's wants and needs. The priests who sanctioned and defended the indigenous nuns did so with concepts generally related to the category of "Spanish" and not "Indian" woman. The malleability of the concepts remains evident, for example, in emphasizing chastity and not the lack of it; the first characteristic is tied to Spanish women, the second, to indigenous women. Similarly, in hagiographic biographies, indigenous women manipulated the discourse to stress those characteristics that make them more like Spanish woman in religious terms. Yet, socially they situated themselves within the privileged group of the caciques and principales who accepted Christianity quickly and helped evangelize the rest of the indigenous population. Evident in many of these writings is not just the struggle to defend the ethnic autonomy of space but also the shifting of apparently fixed concepts, thereby questioning the basis of the established colonial socio-racial hierarchy.

This analysis of discursive production has focused on conflicts of ethnic identity, gender issues, and the use of the written word to create and convey power and resistance. The intricate relationships among all these variables are difficult to capture in a single reading like the one proposed here. It is evident, however, that indigenous women during this colonial era participated actively in the formation of their own identities, a project that persists and evolves to this day. This study is a step toward discerning the complexity of the relations established by discourses produced in a colonial context, but there is still much work to do.

Appendix A

*Selected Text from "Notes on
Some of Our Deceased Sisters"*

Spanish Text

1. Archivo del convento de Corpus Christi. Apuntes de algunas vidas
   · de nuestras hermanas difuntas. Primeramente N. M. R. M. Fundadora
   Sor Ma. Petra de San Francisco, anónimo, sin fecha.

En el nombre de mi señora la Virgen María.

  Declaro a vuestra Paternidad de cómo nuestra Reverenda Madre Fundadora Sor María Petra de San Francisco, el modo en que su Reverencia nos empezó a criar su nueva comunidad. Era a un tiempo Abadesa y nuestra maestra. Fue muy ejemplarísima en virtudes, muy amable con nosotras, muy prudente, muy humilde, muy penitente; tenía un cajón de sus calaveras. Toda la noche se la pasaba en vigilia en el coro haciendo sus penitencias y a mí siempre me sacaba del noviciado y me llevaba en su compañía y era para que su Reverencia fuera con su cruz. Se andaba arrastrando en el coro y yo era su sayón para andarla estirando de la soga y luego quería que yo le diera de bofetadas y la pisoteara, pero yo no lo quería hacer porque era mi Madre ¿cómo le había yo de dar? Por fin me despachaba al noviciado a que me recogiera y su Reverencia se quedaba en el coro siguiendo su ejercicio. Pero cuando íbamos a maitines, allá hallábamos a su Reverencia. Su comer era tan solamente un huevo estrelladito en agua y sal, con unos pedacitos de pan remojaditos. Su justicia era muy recta y materna y muy celosa de las leyes y costumbres de la religión. Cuando alguna de nosotras cometíamos algún defecto nos llamaba a solas y nos amonestaba y reprendía con tanto amor y suavidad. No era cosa de que nos maltratara, sino antes por el contrario aquel "hijita esto," "hijita el otro," todo era su estilo hijita; y si como criaturas que éramos volvíamos a caer en el mismo defecto, nos volvía a amonestar a solas con tanta caridad y amor de madre y como criaturas volvíamos a reincidir en el mismo defecto, esto es porque no poníamos cuidado. Porque por un oído entraban las cosas y por otro salían, ya entonces entraba la justicia. Nos daba nuestros azotitos muy bien dados y luego si estábamos llorando nos acariciaba y nos decía: "Esto ya se acabó hijitas. Más azotaron a nuestro esposo y peores cosas hicieron con su Majestad." Por nuestro amor nos ponía presente su Pasión Santísima para consolarnos, y con eso se nos quitaba el pesar de los azotes. Pero luego nos decía: Miren hijitas no sean bobas, procuren el no ser tan muertas, es fuerza que vayan poniendo mucho cuidado en todas las cosas; vayan mirando, cuiden muy bien porque ustedes son las que se han de quedar solitas en su conventito porque Nuestra Santa Regla y Constituciones así nos lo manda; por eso lo hago con mis hijitas. Y dice así que si la primera vez cometiéramos algún defecto sea a solas amonestada la dicha, y si volviere a caer en la misma culpa, hasta la tercera vez entra la justicia de sus azotitos. Y se sigue comer en tierra, pan y agua en el refectorio y de ese modo, nuestro padre, nos fue intimando las cosas de la religión. Tenía espíritu profético y murió en opinión de santa.

Mi madre de mi alma a mí siendo novicia me sacaba del noviciado. Íbamos las dos a cuidar a los operarios de la obra, y como un día estuvimos con los que apagaban la cal se encaló su Reverencia y le dio tabardillo cual fue la causa de su muerte. Una noche me espantaron sus calaveras porque estaban haciendo un ruido en su cajón y en su manguita andaba trayendo su mordaza. Y a donde oía rumor de hablar recio allá iba a dar con la que estaba quebrantando el santo silencio, y le decía hijita abre la boca y le metía la mordaza. Andaba todo el día por todas partes con su mordaza. Todo esto me parece a mí que no era por temeridad sino por nutrirnos la religión por lo propio que nos estábamos criando nosotros y empezando a criar religión. Cuando éramos pretendientas estaba su Reverencia en San Juan y hasta allá íbamos todos los días a ver a Nuestra Madre y su Reverencia nos enseñaba a leer en latín y a rezar el oficio divino. Nos llevaba a la iglesia allá solitas y nos hacía poner a dos coros paradas para el oficio divino para imponernos en las ceremonias. Con eso, cuando entramos ya hacíamos nuestras canturrias, y nuestras madres eran las hebdómanas [sic]. Había acá una cruz grande con sus argollas adonde se crucificaban, y nuestra Madre Gregoria por una hora. Nosotros éramos los judíos que les ayudábamos a subir y en las argollas metían las manos y nos estaban esperando para bajarlas. Yo de todo en lo que conocí y manejé a mi madre le doy razón a Vuestra Paternidad, porque de todas las grandes que viven ni madre ninguna conoció a nuestra Madre Petra. Y así, nuestro Padre, aunque digan que nos daban guerra nuestras madres fundadoras, no, no es así pues antes, cuando mi madre se murió, luego que cerró el ojo, nuestro Padre Navarrete nos echó encima otras cuatro madres del convento de San Juan y otras tres novicias pero sólo estas dos señoras de San Juan eran las que nos daban tanta guerra. Y esas mismas le dijo el Padre Margil que no convenía que las trajera de fundadoras porque no llevaban a la nación. Y así sucedió, ¡qué guerra! Lo más mínimo que hacíamos sólo nos estaban atisbando para acusarnos nos nuestro Padre Navarrete. Cuando menos nos percatábamos ya estaba allí, ya nos venía a despotar [sic] y a penitenciarnos y a quitarnos los velos, y a pleito querían también que votáramos a fuerza a las novicias españolas para que profesaran. No queríamos porque la mente del patrón fue que sólo para las indias. Hasta que quiso Dios que viniera la cédula del Rey Nuestro Señor y el Breve de Su Santidad para que salieran del convento las Madres y las novicias. Pero nuestra Madre Isabel era una santa, la Madre Antonia era una santa, las novicitas eran tan humanitas [sic] y tan santas como lo manifiesta en su vida la Madre Sebastiana de San Juan. Tanto que padecimos, nuestro Padre, en defensa de nuestro convento, hasta nos quería matar su padre de una novicia, y la noche que había puesto ya la escalera para escalar la tapia para venir a hacer la matanza, esa noche lo mataron a él en la vinatería y con una máquina de hombres venía prevenido y los mismos convidados lo mataron a él esa propia noche que venía a hacer la carnicería. En fin hasta que se segó Nuestro Padre Navarrete, y fue mucho, mucho lo que padecimos.

2. Archivo del convento de Corpus Christi, anónimo, sin fecha.

En el nombre de la Santísima Trinidad J. M. J.
Comienzan los puntos de las vidas y dichosas muertes de mis hermanas que fueron mis compañeras y es como siguen.

La vida de mi hermana Sor Antonia de Cristo, poblana, fue muy abstinente en la comida, muy mortificado su apetito, no comía ni fruta ni dulce, ni apetitos, continuamente sus silicios puestos, su trabajo continuamente atendiendo en todas las cosas de las ordenaciones, con tanta alegría sufriendo las mortificaciones y contratiempos que en aquellos primeros tiempos se ofrecieron. Muy pobre, que andaba continuamente pepenando las cosas que se tiraban y sólo con eso se mantenía, como era recoger los rabos de cebolla para aprovecharlos, los mendruguitos nomás comía que no se desperdiciaban. Las sandalias nunca estrenaba nuevas sino recogía las desechadas y las componía y esas usaba hasta que se gastaban de total, hasta que ya andaba sólo con los pies en el suelo. El petate de delante de la cama sólo era de una vara, en cuanto sólo le cabían las dos rodillas que ni aun se acostaba derecha en su cama, sino en cuclillas como quien está en vigilia, esperando, y luego, en cayendo la campana para maitines, la primerita que estaba ya en el coro, y de esto cantando y rezando con tal espíritu y fervor como si no padeciera una enfermedad tan grande como era de una llaga gangrenosa que tenía debajo del brazo y le cundió todo el brazo. No comía con cuchara sino sólo con un palito, cualquiera tarjanimalito [sic] con que topaba en el suelo y esto por la Santa Pobreza. Muy humilde, sufrió una disciplina porque Dios quiso que la mortificaran, pero quedaba tal cosa tan serena y tan sosegada en su interior que ni la más leve mutación se le apercibía.

. . . .

obediente, caritativa, las dos caridades le asistían la personal y la del prójimo, alegrísima, continuamente andaba cantando la 'tota pulcra', bailadora, toca- dora. La Noche Buena no dormía, sino que con la escalera grande se ponía a tocar con su arpita o con su guitarrita que se hacía [rajas] y nuestra Madre Petra le decía: "Sor Antonia, tú eres como nuestro Padre San Francisco el loquito de Belén". Esta fiesta era delante de la Santa Imagen de mi Señora de Belén que está en la escalera. Un sufrimiento y tolerancia, tenía en el padecer de su llaga de cangro [sic]. A las cuatro de la mañana ya estaba en el coro, en oración o de maitines. Ya no volvía a la cama sino que se que- daba. Y al fin de toda su vida un día un día [sic] empezó a decir: "que me lla- men a la 'tamalona'", que lo decía de cariño, "que venga la 'tamalona'". María Gertrudis vino y díjole: "¿qué quiere Sor Antonia?". Se empezó a quejar que le habían quebrado su jarrito, conque le dijo: "pues no se apure su caridad, voy a traerle otro". Fue a traerle otro de Guadalajara, muy bonito y oloroso, conque lo cogió y lo que hizo con eso fue estarse dando de porrazos a la llaga con el propio jarrito y le decíamos: "Sor Antonia, que estás loca, no hagas eso que se te inflama más la llaga", y le daba a la llaga con él y le decía: "toma, toma huele toma huélelo". Y así que acabó de darse con él empezó a cantar la 'tota pulcra' y nos decía: "¿ven a los ángeles, oyen como están cantando la 'tota pulcra'?", le decíamos: "no, no lo vemos",—"pues ahí está mi Señora y su niñito". Y que se fue quedando como dormidita y luego que expiró, ni los padres la vieron cuando vinieron a cantarle el credo. Ya estaba muerta y venían las vecinas, las mandaderas, nana Antonia, su tía de Nues- tra Madre María Teresa a preguntar al torno que qué recreación tenían y les decían que ninguna, que antes Sor Antonia estaba acabando y ya se había muerto, decían los de fuera: "pues madres, que música tan buena hemos estado oyendo". Y yo antes de que muriera estaba lavando y oí que ya estaban cantando el credo, dejé de lavar y me fui a ver a la enferma y la hallé muy cantando la 'tota pulcra', entonces me empezó a dar muy buenos consejos como hermanas que éramos y siempre me los andaba dando ojalá mi padre, y de todo me hubiera yo aprovechado. De todo esto que he dicho es mucha verdad de que doy fe y hago mi signo.

Translation

1. Convent of Corpus Christi Archive. Notes on Some of Our Deceased Sisters. Firstly Our Most Reverend Founding Mother Sister Maria Petra of Saint Francis, anonymous, undated.

In the name of my Lady the Virgin Mary.

I declare to You, Father, the manner in which our Reverend Founding Mother Sister Petra of Saint Francis began to nurture us in her new community. She was the Abbess and our teacher at the same time. She was the very highest model of virtue, very kind to us, very prudent, very humble, and very penitent; she had a drawer for her skulls. She would keep vigil all night in the choir doing penance, and she would always pull me from the novitiate quarters and would take me with her so that the most Reverend Mother could carry her cross. She would haul it around the choir, and I was her enforcer, pulling her along by a rope and then she would want me to slap her and humiliate her, but I did not want to do that because she was my Mother. How was I going to hit her? Finally she would send me back to the novitiate to rest, and the Reverend Mother would remain in the choir to continue with her exercise. But when we would go to matins, there we would find her Reverence. She would eat only one fried egg in water and salt, with a few pieces of moistened bread. Her sense of justice was fair and maternal, and held closely to the laws and customs of religion. When one of us would err, she would summon us alone and admonish us, and reprimand us with such love and gentleness. She never mistreated us, on the contrary, she would say "my daughter this," "my daughter that," it was the way she was with us, calling us "daughters;" and if like the children we were we would err again, she would admonish us again alone, with such kindness and motherly love, and like children we would commit the same misdeed yet again, because we did not pay attention. Because things would go in one ear and go out the other, justice was then needed. She would give us our good little lashes and then if we were crying, she would caress us and she would tell us: "This is over, my daughters. They gave more lashes to our Bridegroom and did worse things to His Majesty. Because he loved us he sent his most holy passion to comfort us;" and with that we no longer felt the weight of the whip. But later she would tell us: Look, little daughters, don't be foolish, [and] try to not be so uninterested. You must put more effort into everything that you do. Keep a close watch. Be very careful, because you are the ones who are going to remain in your little convent all by yourselves, because our Holy Rule and Constitutions requires it. That is why I do this with my little daughters. And it says this, that if the first time we commit some error we should be happy to be admonished in private, and if we again fall and commit the same fault, it is not until the third time that you must face the justice of those little lashes. Followed by eating on the ground, bread and water in the refectory, and in this way, our Father, she went about instilling in us the matters of religion. She had a prophetic spirit and died in a state of holiness.

My dearest Mother would take me out from the novitiate. We would go together to care for the workers, and one day when we were with those who slaked the lime, the Revered Mother became covered in lime and she contracted a burning fever, which was the cause of her death. One night her skulls frightened me because they were making so much noise in her drawer, and in her sleeve she was holding her gag. And wherever she would hear the murmur of loud talking she would go there to whoever was disturbing the holy silence, and she would say, little daughter open your mouth, and she would insert the gag. All day long, she went everywhere with her gag. It seems to me that all this was not to frighten us, but rather because she wished to instill in us a sense of religion for the very reason that we were beginning to nurture ourselves in it. When we were candidates, our Reverend Mother was in San Juan, and we would go there every day to see our Mother, and she would teach us to read in Latin and to pray the Divine Office. She would take us to church there by ourselves and would have us form two standing choruses for the Divine Office so that we would get used to the ceremonies. With this, once we entered the convent, we already could do our singing, and our mothers were the weekly choir mistresses. There was a large cross here with rings from which one could be crucified, and our Mother Gregoria would do so for one hour. We would act as the Jews, helping them up onto the cross, and they would put their hands through the rings and then wait for us to help them down. I declare to you Father, of everything that I knew and experienced with my Mother, because of all the elder ones who live here, no one else knew our Mother Petra. And so, our Father, although it has been said that our founding mothers were at war with us, no, it is not that way because before, when my Mother died, after she had closed her eyes, our Father Navarrete imposed upon us four more mothers from the Convent of San Juan and another three novices, but it was only those two women from San Juan who gave us such war. And Father Margil told him that it was not a good idea to send those very women as founders because they would not be able to lead the nation. And that is what happened. What a battle! They (the criollas) were constantly watching us for even the smallest thing that we did, so they accuse us of wrongdoing before Father Navarrete. When we were least expecting it, he was already there, acting as a despot, punishing us and taking away our veils. He wanted to force us to vote for the Spanish novices so they could profess in the convent. We did not want that because our patron's idea was that the convent be only for Indian women. Until finally, God saw fit that by a royal decree of the king our lord and of a Papal brief of his Holiness, the Mother and the novices had to leave the convent. But our Mother Isabel was a saint, Mother Antonia was a saint, the little novices were so humane [sic] and so holy, just as Mother Sebastiana of San Juan illustrated in her Vida. We endured so much, our Father, in defense of our convent. The father of one of the novices even planned to kill us; but instead the night he had set up a ladder to climb the garden wall and begin the killing, he was killed in the winery by the very men he had invited along to help him do the butchering. In short, until our Father Navarrete stopped, it was a lot, a lot what we endured.

2. Convent of Corpus Christi Archive, anonymous, undated.

In the name of the Most Holy Trinity J. M. J.
The details of the lives and blessed deaths of my sisters who were my companions begin herein and it is as follows.

The life of my sister Sor Antonia de Cristo, from Puebla, was marked by abstinence from food, she mortified her appetite, she did not eat fruit or sweets, always wore her cilice. She continually worked to carefully follow all things having to do with the order's Rule, suffering with such happiness the mortifications and setbacks that were present in those early times. She was very poor and constantly went around scavenging for things that had been thrown out, and she survived on what she found, like picking up discarded onion stalks to make good use of them, and ate only crusts of bread so that they would not be wasted. She never wore new sandals but always picked up those that had been thrown out, and she would fix them and use them until they were completely worn out, until her bare feet were touching the ground. The straw sleeping mat was a single roll, such that only her two knees fit on it and she couldn't even sleep stretched out in the bed, but squatting like someone on a vigil, waiting, and then, when the bell would ring for matins, she was the very first to appear in the choir, singing and praying with such spirit and fervor as if she weren't suffering from an illness as serious as the gangrenous ulcer she had under her arm and that progressed along her entire arm. She did not eat with a spoon but only with a little stick any little insect she would find on the floor, and all this to live in holy poverty. Very humble, she suffered discipline because God wanted her to be punished, but she remained so serene and so calm at her core that not even the slightest change could be perceived.

. . . .

obedient, charitable. She was kind to all those who surrounded her, and always very happy. She sang the "Tota Pulchra" often; she enjoyed dancing and playing music. On Christmas Eve she would not sleep, but on the big staircase she would play her little harp or her little guitar with difficulty and our Mother Petra would tell her: "Sor Antonia, you are like our Father San Francisco, the little crazy man of Bethlehem." The Christmas Eve party would take place in front of the holy image of Our Lady of Bethlehem, in front of the staircase. She endured suffering and had to tolerate the pain of her ulcerous canker [sic]. At four in the morning she was already in the choir, in prayer or at matins. She would not go back to bed, but rather remained there. And at the end of her life, one day she began to say: "Call the *tamalona* for me," but she said it with affection, "Tell the tamalona to come here." María Gertrudis came and told her: "What do you want, Sor Antonia?" She began to complain that someone had broken her little jug, and Maria Gertrudis told her: "Don't worry about it; I'll bring you another one." So she went to Guadalajara to bring her another one, very pretty and fragrant, upon which she took it and began to hit the ulcer she had hard with the little jug, and we were telling her: "Sor Antonia, you are crazy, don't do that because the ulcer will get even more inflamed," and she kept hitting the ulcer with it and saying to it: "Here, here smell, here, smell it." And as soon as she stopped hitting herself with it she started to sing the "Tota Pulchra" and she would say: "Do you see the angels? Do you hear how they are singing the 'Tota Pulchra'?" We would say to her: "No, we don't see them"—"well there is My Lady and her Little Son." And then she appeared to have fallen asleep and later she expired, the priests didn't even see her when they came to sing her the Creed. She was already dead, and the neighbors came, the messengers, sister Antonia, the aunt of our Mother Maria Teresa, to ask about the kind of celebration there was, and they would tell them that we had none, that Sor Antonia had been declining and had died. The people from outside the convent said: "Well, Mothers, we have been hearing beautiful music." And I, before she died, was doing laundry, and I heard that they already were singing the Creed; and I stopped the washing and went to see how the sick Sor Antonia was doing; and I found her loudly singing the "Tota Pulchra." She then began to give me much good advice; as sisters that we were, she was always giving me advice. I wish Father that I had been able to benefit from all of it. Everything I have said is completely true; I bear witness and make my signature.

Appendix B

Selected Text from the Funeral Eulogy of Sor María Teodora de San Agustín

Elogio Fúnebre que en el aniversario de la M. R. M. Sor María Teodora de San Agustín fundadora y abadesa vitalicia del convento de Santa María de los Ángeles de Pobres Descalzas Indias de la ciudad de Antequera en el Valle de Oaxaca, dijo el día 10 de mayo de 1799 Don Joseph Victoriano Baños y Domínguez.

(Selección, primera parte)

¡Ea! Aplicad ya, si gustáis, aplicad en hora buena a la insigne Teodora el mismo elogio de la heroína de Betulia: Ninguno otro a mi juicio, puede ofreceros idea más cabal de su carácter. ¿Os acordáis que el retiro del mundo, el cilicio, el ayuno, y el santo temor de Dios hicieron tan famosa la ínclita hebrea? Pues en eso mismo, ¿Qué otra cosa habéis sino el modelo de que es vivo retrato, copia muy natural nuestra esclarecida americana? No bien conoce al mundo, cuando lo desprecia y abandona; y después de veintisiete años de estrecha clausura en el primitivo convento de Corpus Christi, conduce a Oaxaca esa apreciable colonial de vírgenes nacionales, se hace acreedora a que se le destina para primera piedra de este edificio por la notoria solidez de su virtud, y para que como principal arquitecta fabrique en esa religiosa clausura, el más seguro asilo a la inocencia India: *Fecit sibi secretum cubiculum, in quo cum puellis suis clausa morabiter.*

Si como advirtió Tertuliano, la vida del cristiano que vive conforme al Evangelio, más bien que vida, es verdadero martirio toleró Teodora prolongado y redoblado martirio por el largo espacio de cuarenta y cuatro años de religión, pues practicó con exacta puntualidad cuantos cilicios y ayunos, cuantas austeridades y mortificaciones prescribe y permite ese sagrado instituto, que no es en sí otra cosa que un maravilloso extracto y compendio de los preceptos, máximas y consejos del Evangelio: *Habens super lumbus suos cilicium, jejunabat ómnibus diebus vitae suae.*

Ella en fin, en el discurso de sesenta y dos años que contó de vida empleada todo en amar a Dios, temerlo y venerarlo, observó la Ley de Jesucristo en toda su extensión, según el pensamiento de San Bernardo. Si amó a Dios como a esposo, si lo veneró como a padre, temiéndole siempre como a dueño absoluto y señor soberano, manejó el arduo importante negocio de su eterna salud animada de aquel temor propio de un hijo que nada teme mas que ofender ingrato a su padre benemérito: de aquel temor casto que enriqueciéndola con las gracias, virtudes y prendas que eran conducentes a los designios del cielo, labró en ella una religiosa ejemplar, una prelada famosísima: *Erat in ómnibus famosissima, quoniam timerabat dominum valde.*

Sí, Señores, sí. Si me permitís servirme del apóstol en una monja ejemplar, en una abadesa acreedora a nuestros elogios, vais a ver ya a una India santa, y santa en todo, portentosa y extraordinaria. Pero ¿cómo y en qué? ¿En éxtasis? ¿En arrobamientos, en visiones, en revelaciones? ¿En otra cosa de esas que forman el ostentoso homenaje a la santidad? ¡Qué distantes estáis de mi modo de pensar! Nada de esto debéis esperar oír de mi boca. Santa, portentosa y extraordinaria fue nuestra cacique nobilísima, porque cultivó una piedra sólida, una virtud ejemplar, que nada tuvo de raro y singular. En ella solamente descubro yo una monja descalza, que como rosa de Dios, llevó siempre su propia cruz con honor y reputación: una pobre India tan observante de su instituto, que ni hace cosa que no le mande la Regla, ni omite una sola de cuantas ella permite. Y aquí en esto mismo (reduzco yo mis ideas para coordinar el discurso) he aquí una prelada famosa, porque supo el arte ingenioso de hacerse obedecer. Con el poderoso atractivo del ejemplo. Con el invencible aliciente de la suavidad y dulzura, que presentarán a vuestra atención el plan y economía de su Elogio. ¡Padre inmenso de las luces! Para que yo no profiera una sola palabra que no sea digna de mi Ministerio, y en todo conforme al oráculo, imploro vuestra asistencia, y en mis labios el sello de vuestra gracia. Pidámosla.

Ave María.

Translation

Funeral Eulogy on the anniversary of the Most Reverend Mother Sor
María Teodora de San Agustín, founder and abbess for life of the
Convent of Santa María de los Ángeles of Poor Discalced Indians in
the city of Antequera in the Valley of Oaxaca, preached on May 10, 1799
by Don Joseph Victoriano Baños y Domínguez.

(Selection, first part)

Apply now, if you will, apply on this felicitous occasion to the remark-
able Teodora the same eulogy as that of the heroine of Bethulia. None other,
in my opinion, can convey a more exact idea of her character. Do you recall
how famous the illustrious Jewess became due to her withdrawal from the
world, her use of the cilice, her fasting, and her holy fear of God? What
else do we have here but a model of which our eminent American is a living
portrait, a very natural copy? She did not know much of the world when
she rejected and abandoned it; and after twenty-seven years of strict cloister in the humble Convent of Corpus Christi, she leads to Oaxaca that significant group of indigenous virgins. She makes herself worthy of being
chosen to be cornerstone of this building for the well-known steadfastness
of her virtue, and so that as the principal architect she built in this religious
enclosure, the most secure sanctuary for the innocent Indian woman: *Fecit
sibi secretum cubiculum, in quo cum puellis suis clausa morabiter.*

If, as Tertulius warned, the life of the Christian who lives by the Gospels is more than mere life, it is true martyrdom, then Teodora tolerated
prolonged and repeated martyrdom during the long span of forty-four
years of religious life. She practiced with precise regularity as many cilices
and fastings, and austerities and penances prescribed and permitted by the
sacred religious institute, which is nothing less than a wonderful compila-
tion and compendium of the precepts, maxims and advice of the Gospels:
Habens super lumbus suos cilicium, jejunabat ómnibus diebus vitae suae.

In short, throughout the length of her seventy-two years she was
dedicated to loving God, fearing him and venerating him, she observed the
Law of Jesus Christ to the fullest, according to the beliefs of Saint Bernard.
If she loved God as a husband, if she venerated him as a father, fearing
him always as her absolute master and sovereign Lord, she handled the
arduous and important business of her eternal health inspired by that very
fear a child has who fears only offending his eminent father by being
ungrateful: of that honest fear that, enriching her with the graces, virtues
and pledges that were a path to heaven's plan, wrought in her a model

nun, a very famous abbess: *Erat in ómnibus famosissima, quoniam timerabat dominum valde.*

Yes, Gentlemen, yes. If you will allow me to call upon the apostle, in this exemplary nun, in an abbess worthy of our praises, you will see then a holy Indian woman, and holy in all things, prodigious and extraordinary. But, how and in what ways? In ecstasy, in raptures, in visions, in revelations? In those things that make up the ostentatious homage of saintliness? How distant that is from my way of thinking! Expect to hear none of that from my lips. Our highly noble daughter of caciques was indeed a saint, prodigious and extraordinary, because she cultivated a solid foundation, an exemplary virtue that was in no way rare or unique. All I find in her is a discalced nun, who as a rose of God always carried her own cross with honor and good repute: a poor Indian as observant of her convent who does nothing that is not ordered by the rule, nor omits any single thing it does permit. And herein lies the point (I abridge my ideas for the sake of the discourse); I have here a renowned abbess because she knew the ingenious art of making the nuns obey her through the powerful grace of example. Through the invincible allure of softness and sweetness, which offer up for your consideration the plan and economy of this eulogy. Great Father of lights! So that I not utter a single word unworthy of my Ministry, and that I act in all ways according to the oracle, I implore your assistance, and on my lips place the seal of your grace. For this let us pray.

Hail Mary.

Appendix C
Selected Letters

Spanish Text

1. Archivo Histórico del Instituto Nacional de Antropología e Historia, Fondo Franciscano, carta 2251, vol. 100, folio 165–166.

[Don Juan] de Altamirano J. M. J.

Muy Señor mío el todo poderoso le asista a vuestra Merced con su divina gracia y le comunique mucho de su amor.

Amado Padre y mi señor muchos días ha que deseo escribirle. Aunque cuando estuve en esa ciudad no tuve la dicha de conocer a Vuestra Merced para servirle, aunque muchos tiempos ha que tengo noticia de las relevantes prendas de Vuestra merced pues ha corrido su fama hasta la ciudad de Oaxaca de donde soy criolla, y tomé el Santo Hábito en la ciudad de México en el convento de Corpus Christi y con la ocasión de haber esta fundación quiso Nuestro Señor darme a este convento donde me hallo con el título de fundadora, queriéndolo así la Divina Majestad por sus altos juicios. Yo celebraré sea la salud de Vuestra Merced tan cabal como mi buen afecto desea, quedando la que gozo con muchos deseos de ejercitarse en cosas del servicio de Vuestra Merced que lo haré con mucho gusto.

Mi Señor y Padrecito, toda esta relación le hecho a Vuestra Merced porque tenga noticia de quien le escribe, y sabiendo yo y conociendo también por la experiencia la caridad que Vuestra Merced acostumbra con los pobres, no omito escribir a Vuestra Merced ésta, dándole noticia de nuestros trabajos para que según Dios se duela de ellos, y puede Vuestra Merced estar fijo que sólo inspirada de Dios puedo yo atreverme a hacerlo, porque aunque tengo personas como el Señor Obispo de esta ciudad y a otros, pero luego que se me propuso al pensamiento negociar alguna cosa para estas pobres, no me vino a otra persona tan al propósito sino sólo a Vuestra Merced, y así puesta a los pies de Vuestra Merced, con el rendimiento que puedo, le pido tenga y halle acogida esta pobrecita comunidad ante los ojos de Vuestra Merced pues se halla afligida (y mucho) porque los lobos infernales no dejan de perseguirla. Vuestra Merced amado Padre, ha de meter la mano en negocio de tanta importancia que nada menos es que celar la causa de Dios y la salvación de las almas y, conociendo yo de su gran caridad, tendrá efecto mi petición, paso hablándole con la llaneza y estilo que Vuestra Merced sabiendo yo ciertamente que todo quedará oculto en el archivo de su pecho y quedando juntamente esperanzada de conseguir mi deseo fiando Dios y el favor de Vuestra Merced. Pues Padrecito, dando principio a mi razonamiento, digo hallarnos todas muy afligidas. Ya Vuestra Merced sabrá que este convento lo hizo el Señor Don Marcos Muñoz de Sanabria canónigo de ésta Santa Iglesia, el instrumento principal fue Nuestra Madre Gregoria quien negoció fundaciones para las indias y dicho Señor vino en ello con mucho gusto luego que llegara desde entonces acá no ha sido más que batallar porque la contradicción que el demonio ha introducido con las señoras españolas y las religiosas les es sin tamaño la regular disciplina. Le puedo asegurar a Vuestra Merced que es por los "saelos" no por causa de las indias pero sí de las Madres que han sabido cultivar la regularidad y así vivimos inconsolables que lo que le suplico a Vuestra Merced, como a mi Padre, puesta a sus pies me haga el favor de recurrirnos a España pues tengo noticia de la mucha comunicación que Vuestra Merced tiene con los señores de allá por sus méritos y relevantes prendas. Le he de merecer por amor de Dios y de mi Señora la Virgen María me escriba una carta en nombre de todas las religiosas de este convento . . . digo pidiéndole a la Majestad algún alivio y que nos dejen solas en nuestro convento que aunque su Majestad piensa por los papeles que hay en el archivo de éste convento, y están en mi poder por hallarme con el oficio de secretaria he leído, y piensa el Rey Nuestro Señor que todas somos indias y que no hay españolas y ya Vuestra Merced ve que no es así porque los prelados hacen lo que quieren, yo mi convento de Corpus Cristi con mucha sinrazón ha metido el Padre Comisario 3 españolas aun habiendo 'Buleto' para que no entren y no siendo necesarias aquí discurra Vuestra Merced que harán estando esto tan recién plantado que quedan [sic] hacer y así nunca ha de haber paz por lo que le suplico a Vuestra Merced que de mi parte pido en dicha carta todo cuanto Vuestra Merced viere que es de alivio para estas pobres religiosas y escrita que sea dicha carta, si nos hace Vuestra Merced este favor como lo esperamos, nos la remitirá para firmarla todas con nuestros nombres y de ahí se la volveremos a Vuestra Merced para que allá Vuestra Merced nos la despache cuanto antes pueda, que espero en Dios que le dará oportunidad de que vaya su Majestad facilitará todas las dificultades que se puedan ofrezca para conseguirlo y también una Bula de su Santidad nos ha de negociarla para que así podamos sacar la cara cuando se ofrezcan semejantes lances, de otra manera es imposible poder hablar porque las Madres nos limitan tanto como lo estamos experimentando lo que queremos nosotras es lo mejor y más perfecto, que nos dejen solas y nos pondremos bien porque las madres como vienen de sus conventos las hechas a sus chiqueos en los demás conventos se cesan sin imperfección porque hay extensiones y más libertad que acá porque el instituto es muy estrecho, y lo que en otros conventos no es ni aun imperfección acá llegara a ser pecado y relajación. Nosotras por fin, como nos venimos a criar acá en lo estrecho nos hacemos con facilidad. Ya veo que todo esto parece vanidad mía pero sabe Dios que se lo digo sin más apego que el deseo de que todo este en su punto como Dios manda, que si Dios me permitiera poder ver a Vuestra Merced y hablarle acerca de las cosas viera que tengo razón y me sobra, y así fiada en Dios lo digo, deseando que en esto sea sólo su Majestad glorificado, y aunque nosotras seamos inútiles, que yo sola soy aquí, pero no ignoro que puede mucho la gracia en una resolución valiente. Sin Dios no puede la criatura hacer nada. Yo deseo que todo el mundo se salve y quiera que todos entraran en este convento a salvarse, pero vea Vuestra Merced: las españolas mis señoras tienen varios conventos donde poder servir al Señor pero las pobres indias sólo dos y ya se ve lo que sucede, que siempre vivimos con el recelo de si nos lo quitarán. En Vuestra Merced tengo fijas mis esperanzas de que nos ha de asegurar y por su intervención espero conseguir el consuelo deseado, que a bien que Dios es fiel pagador y sabe dar ciento por uno, como Vuestra Merced lo experimentará, y así le suplico no desprecie mis ruegos, sino poniéndose Vuestra Merced en Dios meta la mano que el brazo del altísimo le asistirá y en pago le dará y le llenará de aquellos consuelos que su Majestad sabe dar a los que hacen las cosas sólo por su amor y por el bien de las almas, y si Vuestra Merced me hace el gusto de negociarnos Bula de su Santidad le suplico la procure con todos aquellos requisitos y expresiones que caben, de tal suerte ponga Vuestra Merced la cosa que venga en ella que si en algún tiempo quisieren forzarnos los prelados y regulares a que entren españolas, tengamos nosotras libertad para responder que queremos pasarnos al gobierno de los señores obispos para que así nos podamos librar porque son muchas las sinrazones de los prelados, a fuerza quieren que recibamos a cualquiera, en admitiéndola sus paternidades a

Dios ya esta todo hecho sin mirar, como en otras partes se ven las pretendientas, se prueban, se mira si son para ello o no, si no que así que el prelado dio el sí a Dios ya está todo hecho que sea vieja la pretendienta, que sea débil, que sea o no para ello. Ello es que sea de [sic], porque sólo los respectos humanos son los que hoy en día se ven aun en el claustro, todo esto lo ve Dios. Y así de Vuestra Merced padrecito de mi corazón he de recibir yo todos estos.

. . . .

2. AINAH, Fondo Franciscano, carta 2252, vol. 100, folio 167, septiembre 9, 1723.

Nuestro Reverendísimo Padre Comisario General J. M. J.
Pedro Navarrete muy amado en el Señor.

La Divina Gracia del Espíritu Santo asista en el corazón de De [sic] Vuestra Paternidad reverenda y le dé mucho consuelo así espiritual como corporal. Padre Nuestro, me alegraré que al recibo de ésta se halle Vuestra Reverendísima con la salud muy perfecta, como mi fino amor se la desea en la amable compañía de toda esa santa y venerable comunidad que venero y deseo todo bien. Padre Nuestro, lo que me mueve solamente a escribirle a Vuestra Paternidad esta carta es sólo a satisfacerlo como a mi padre de mi corazón y crea Vuestra Paternidad, Padre Nuestro que le confieso la verdad como si estuviera a los pies de Vuestra Paternidad de que me hallo indigna. Crea Padre Nuestro que ni yo ni las las [sic] más digo que no he tenido parte en nada, porque no había yo de tener semejante atrevimiento de coger la pluma contra Vuestra Paternidad siendo mi padre que en eso sincero todo, aunque supe que en todos los escritos que han escrito me han firmado, pero es como si no hubiera sido porque mientras yo no supe nada, porque crea Vuestra Paternidad Reverenda que cuando lo supe me confundí grandemente de ver lo que había pasado. Ahora castigue Vuestra Paternidad que será muy bien hecho y si a mí también me quisiere Vuestra Paternidad Reverenda enviar castigo, nunca yo más dichosa que ese día que lo recibiré con mucho gusto. Padre Nuestro, lo que le sé decir es que las angelitas se están muy sosegadas pero quien las mueve a todo es la Madre Sor María Magdalena la fundadora que vino, y también le digo a Vuestra Paternidad Reverenda para descargo de mi conciencia quienes son la causa de que acá no haya paz, que son las tres Reverendas Madres fuera de Nuestra Reverenda Madre Abadesa, y esto es sin pasión porque con estas tres señoras acá está esto hecho un infierno fuera de a que, Padre Nuestro, estaba hecho una gloria porque la Madre Sor María Magdalena es la que hace la división de nosotras las cacicas con las españolas que no debe hacer eso porque le aseguro a Vuestra Paternidad Reverenda que la compañía de las señoras españolas es tan linda y tan afable que no la merecemos porque son unas santas que no sea Dios Padre Nuestro que tenemos una prelada que no la merecemos porque es cierto de verdad que no la merecemos porque es una santa y esto lo digo por indignas de tenerla por prelada. Unos padres que son también unos santos, un padre capellán Padre Nuestro, que si en toda la provincia con una no lo habían de hallar y así le doy a Vuestra Paternidad Reverenda miles agradecimientos de habérnoslo dejado y se lo vuelvo a pedir por las purísimas entrañas de mi amado Señor y señora a quien le pido con veras de mi corazón de los aciertos que le deseo con todas las felicidades que yo le deseo y Nuestro Señor lo haga un santo como quien se lo pido aunque mala, pesa más no pedir a Dios Nuestro Señor que me guarde la vida de vuestra Paternidad Reverendísima para consuelo de este convento de pobre descalzas de la purísima Concepción de Cosamaloapan y septiembre 9 de 1743 a B. S. M. N. P. V. Paternidad B.

Digna súbdita que en el Señor le ama Sor María del Santísimo Sacramento y reza. . . .

Translation

1. Historical Archive of the National Institute of Anthropology and History, Fondo Franciscano, letter 2251, vol. 100, folio 165–166.

[Don Juan] de Altamirano J. M. J.
My dear sire may the all powerful one assist you with his divine grace and communicate much of his love to you.

Beloved Father and my lord, it has been many days now since I have wanted to write to you. Although when I was in the city I did not have the good fortune to meet with Your Mercy and to be of service, I had heard news of your fame, for some time now which I heard in the city of Oaxaca from where I am native. I took the holy habit in Mexico City in the Convent of Corpus Christi and with the opportunity provided by this foundation, Our Lord wished to give me over to this convent, where I find myself with the title of founder, the Divine Majesty wishing it to be so according to his superior judgment. I celebrate the good health of Your Mercy with all the honesty of my good wishes, and I remain one who greatly desires to put into practice all things in the service of Your Mercy, which I will do with great joy.

My Lord and beloved Father, I have told you all of this so that you may know who is writing to you, and I, knowing, and also understanding by experience, the kindness with which Your Mercy always treats the poor, I do not hesitate to write this to Your Mercy, telling you about our struggles so that by God's mercy you would have pity on us. And Your Mercy can be certain that only inspired by God could I dare to do this, because although I have people like the Bishop of this city and others, I did not approach any other person to negotiate something for this poor community other than Your Mercy. And in this way, placed at your feet, with my complete devotion, I ask that you maintain and shelter this poor community before Your Mercy's eyes because it has suffered (and a great deal) because the infernal wolves do not stop chasing it. Your Mercy and beloved Father should get involved in a matter of such importance that is nothing less than watching over God's wishes and the salvation of souls, and knowing myself of your great kindness, I am certain that my petition will be heard. I dare to speak to you in this straightforward manner, knowing with certainty that all will remain hidden in the archive of Your Mercy's chest, and being likewise hopeful of obtaining my desire, having faith in God and the support of Your Mercy. Dear Father, to begin my argument, let me say that we are all very distressed. Your Mercy will already know that this convent was established by Don Marcos Muñoz de Sanabria, canon of this Holy Church; the main instrument was Our Mother Gregoria, who requested more foundations for Indian women, and the gentleman aforementioned got involved with great enthusiasm after he arrived. Since then there has been nothing but struggling because of the contradiction that the devil has introduced between the Spanish and the religious women; therefore, the discipline of the Rule is useless. I can assure Your Mercy that it is because of jealousy not because of the Indian women but because the Spanish Mothers who have enforced the Rule, and for this reason we are inconsolable. I beg Your Mercy, as my Father, placed at your feet, that you would do me the favor of giving us recourse to Spain, since I have heard of the frequent communication that Your Mercy has with the people from there because of your excellence and significant fame. May I be worthy, for the love of God and of My Lady the Virgin Mary, that you write a letter for me in the name of all the religious women of this convent . . . asking his Majesty for some relief and that they leave us alone in our convent, that although his Majesty thinks that, because of the papers housed in the archive of this convent, which are in my keeping because I hold the post of secretary and I have read them, and the King Our Lord thinks that all of us are Indian and that there are no Spanish women, and Your Mercy now sees that it is not that way because the prelates do as they please. In my Convent of Corpus Christi, the Father Commissary admitted three Spanish women for no good reason, despite the Papal Bull that forbids them admittance, nor are they needed. Reflect here, Your Mercy, what will they do, this being so newly implemented that they remain [sic] to do, and in this way there will never be peace. And for that reason I beg Your Mercy, that for my part I ask in that letter for all that Your Mercy consider necessary to achieve relief for these poor religious women. Once the letter be written, and that if Your Mercy does this favor for us as we hope, you would send it to us so that all of us can sign it with our names, and from there we will return it to Your Mercy so that you can send it as soon as you can. I hope in God that he will give his Majesty the opportunity to fix all the problems that might come up in order to achieve this, and also if he could negotiate a Bull from his Holiness so that we can defend ourselves when similar lances come along. Otherwise it would be impossible to speak because the Mothers limit us so much; we experience that every day. What we want is the best situation and the most perfect: that they leave us alone, and we will be fine. Because the Mothers, since they come from other convents and are used to the spoiled life of those other convents, they are satisfied with imperfection because they are more relaxed and have more freedom than here. Because our convent is very strict, and that which in other convents is not even close to imperfection here is considered sin and laxness. Given that we came to be raised here in strictness, we get on easily. I see that all this seems to be vanity, but God knows that I tell you this without any more intention than the desire that all this should happen as God demands, that if God allows me to see Your Mercy and to speak to you concerning these things, you will see that I have more than good reasons. And in this way, trusting God I say this, wishing only that in this matter his Majesty be glorified, and although we are useless, that I am here alone but I know that grace has great power in a brave resolution. Without God we can do nothing. I wish that the whole world be saved and that everyone would enter this convent to be saved, but see, Your Mercy: the Spanish women have several convents where they can serve the Lord, but the poor Indian women have only two, and see what happens, that we always live with fear that it will be taken away from us. I place my hopes firmly on Your Mercy that you will assure it for us, and through your intervention we will achieve the solace we seek. That for goodness God makes faithful payment and knows to give one hundred for one, as Your Mercy will discover, and thus I implore to you not to disregard my pleas; rather, that Your Mercy places his hand in God's so that the arm of the Almighty may assist you and in exchange will fill you with the advice that his Majesty knows to give those who do things only for his love and for the good of other people's souls. And if Your Mercy would grant me the favor of negotiating a Bull from his Holiness, I beseech you to make this happen by citing all the appropriate requirements and expressions, so that in this manner You can put things so that, if at any time the regular prelates should want to force us to admit Spanish women, we will have the liberty to respond that we wish to be governed by the bishops so that we can be free of this, because without any reason the prelates want to force us to receive any woman they want to admit. Then it is all done without looking, unlike other places, where you see the applicants, they are tested; it is seen if they are right for religious life or not. Whereas here, if the prelate says yes, it is all done; whether the candidate is too old, or weak, or that she is or is not right for this life. That is how things are now [sic], only human will is regarded today in the cloister, and God sees all of this. And thus of Your Mercy dear father of my heart I am to receive all of these.

. . . .

2. AINAH, Fondo Franciscano, letter 2252, vol. 100, folio 167, September 9, 1723.

Our Most Reverend Father Commissary General J. M. J.
Pedro Navarrete much loved by our Lord.

I ask the Divine Grace of the Holy Spirit to live in your heart, Reverend Father and give you much solace both spiritual and physical. Our Father, it would make me so happy if upon receiving this, your Extreme Reverence were in perfect health, just as my most sincere love wishes for you in the pleasing company of this entire holy and venerable community that I venerate and for which I wish all the best. Our Father, what moves me to write this letter to you is merely to satisfy you, dear Father of my own heart and believe, Reverend Father, Our Father, that I confess the truth as if I were at your feet, that I find myself unworthy. Believe, Our Father, that neither I nor the others, [sic] I say that I have not taken part in any of this, because I have had no reason to be so bold as to pick up the pen against our Reverend Father, being my father, that I am completely sincere. Although I knew that in all those writings that have been written they have signed my name, but it is as if it had not been because I knew nothing. My Reverend Father, you have to believe that when I found out I was greatly confused to see what had happened. Now you should send a punishment, Reverend Father, because it would be well done and if you would wish to punish me as well, never would I be more fortunate than on the day I receive that punishment with great pleasure. Our Father, what I do know is that the little angels are very tranquil but who moves them to action is Mother Sor María Magdalena, the founder who came here, and I am telling you, Reverend Father, in order to clear my conscience that it is the three Reverend

Mothers, aside from our own Reverend Mother [Abbess], who are to blame for the lack of peace in here, and I say this without anger because with these three women here things have turned into hell when otherwise, Father, it would be a glory, because Mother Sor María Magdalena is the one who creates the division between us, the cacicas, and the Spanish women, which she should not do because I assure Reverend Father that the company of the Spanish women is so lovely and so pleasant that we do not deserve it because they are saints. Thanks to God Our Father we have a prelate whom we do not deserve because it is certainly the truth that we do not deserve her because she is a saint, and I say this as one unworthy of having her as a prelate. Some priests are also saints, like the father chaplain, Our Father, another like him could not be found in all the province, and in this way I thank you greatly Reverend Father for having left him to us; and I ask again that by the most pure heart of my beloved Lord and Lady of whom I ask with truth from my heart that Our Lord make him a saint, I request this although I am unworthy. It is harder not to ask God Our Lord that he watches over your life, Most Reverend Father, as a comfort for this convent of poor discalced women of the Purísima Concepción of Cosamaloapan, September 9, 1743.

A worthy servant who loves you in our Lord, Sor María del Santísimo Sacramento prays. . . .

Notes

Introduction

1. Although I wanted to avoid the universalizing term "Indian" or "indigenous" when referring to the subjects in these book, the nuns themselves used these notions and not their individual ethnic identifications. The information about their family ancestry given at the moment of entering the cloister sheds light on the specific ethnic group to which they belonged, but once they took up the pen, they chose to identify themselves as "Indian" vis-à-vis the "Spaniards." We do not have the exact date of the letter's composition because the text is incomplete. The emphasis is mine.

2. According to Gayatri Spivak, the subaltern speaks but cannot be read or heard, particularly so in the case of indigenous women (308). However, several Latin Americanists, such as Fernando Coronil, Walter Mignolo, and José Rabasa, among others, have encouraged academics to listen and to speak to the subaltern (Coronil 649; Mignolo, "Colonial and Postcolonial" 130; Rabasa, "Of Zapatismo" 425).

3. According to Sherry Ortner, the term "agency" typically communicates power, which, as Foucault has argued convincingly, is present in all spectrums of domination and resistance. Ortner notes that dominated people possess certain capacities to exercise "some sort of influence over the ways in which events unfold" (78). These capacities will become apparent in the use of written discourses by Indian nuns to challenge the authority of male clerics in the conventual space.

4. I am borrowing the concept of reinvention from Karen Graubart's *With Our Labor and Sweat*. She refers to the participation of indigenous elites in the construction of themselves and their communities "juggling to produce legitimate succession both from the perspective of the Spanish regime and of their own subjects" (160).

5. These were based upon the bull *Alias Felices* of Leo X in 1521 and the *Omnimoda* of Adrian VI in 1522 (Ennis 66).

6. In *The Time of Liberty*, Peter Guardino identifies thirty-six cofradías in the city of Antequera by the eighteenth century (31). For the Virgin of Guadalupe and her significance, see David Brading, *Mexican Phoenix*.

7. Mendieta was a Franciscan friar who arrived in New Spain in 1554 and devoted his life to missionary work among the Indians.

8. For a detailed discussion, see Douglas Cope, *The Limits of Racial Domination*.

9. The figure of Felipe Guaman Poma de Ayala can provide a useful point of reference for understanding how Indian elites maneuvered within the new colonial order. See Rolena Adorno, *Guaman Poma*; Sara Castro-Klarén, "Historiography on the Ground: The Toledo Circle and Guamán Poma"; Raquel Chang-Rodríguez, *El discurso disidente: Ensayos de literatura colonial peruana*; and Rocío Quispe-Agnoli, *La fe andina en la escritura: Resistencia e identidad en la obra de Guaman Poma de Ayala*. Catherine Good notes that ethnographic research in present day Morelos, Mexico, shows that certain aspects of native social organization and values persist even in communities where Nahuatl language is no longer spoken (126). I would add that Indian identity does not reside exclusively in these cultural markers, however, for these communities generally practice Christian beliefs as well.

10. In reality, the *Ordenanza del Patronazgo* promulgated in 1574 intended to limit the parochial duties of the regular clergy, but this undertaking was not completely implemented during the sixteenth and seventeenth centuries.

11. See Konetzke, *Colección de documentos para la historia de la formación social*, vol. 3, 364–368.

12. For a discussion of the opening of seminaries for Indians, see Matthew O'Hara, *A Flock Divided: Race, Religion, and Politics in Mexico*, and Margarita Menegus, "El Colegio de San Carlos Borromeo."

13. María Concepción Amerlinck and Manuel Ramos Medina, *Conventos de monjas, fundaciones en el México virreinal*; Josefina Muriel, *Conventos de monjas*.

14. The first convent founded for women in New Spain was Nuestra Señora de la Concepción in 1540. It was conceived for Spanish women, although two daughters of Isabel de Moctezuma were admitted (Muriel, *Conventos* 32; Lavrin, *Brides of Christ* 247).

15. The Third Order was a "middle state" between the convent and the "world." It was conceived for people who wanted to follow St. Francis of Assisi's teachings but were married or had other impediments to entering the First or Second Order, which were cloistered. People of the Third Order are also called Tertiaries (*Catholic Encyclopedia*, http://www.newadvent.org/cathen/06217a.htm).

16. See Susan Migden Socolow, *The Women of Colonial Latin America* 90–111.

17. I use the term "españolas" or "Spanish" throughout the book, although ideologically problematic, since it is the preferred identification in all studied documentation, even when referring to criollas. I chose not to use the term "criolla" because as a construct of colonial discourse, it speaks more about

colonial categorization than personal identification. As Ralph Bauer and José Antonio Mazzotti state, "The idea of creolization usually carried pejorative implications" (5).

18. Asunción Lavrin refers to the long conflict in *Brides of Christ* 261–264.

19. The conflict at Nuestra Señora de Cosamaloapan will be analyzed in chapter 6.

20. The reform was intended to reverse the relaxed nature of the convents, particularly to reduce the number of servants and other relatives living in the cloister, and to have the nuns eat together in the refectory instead of using their own kitchens. For a more elaborate discussion, see Brading, *Church and State* 82–102; Kirk, *Convent Life* 81–126; and Chowning, *Rebellious Nuns*.

21. For more on the Convent of Nuestra Señora de los Ángeles, see Luis Castañeda Guzmán, *Templo de los Príncipes y monasterio de Nuestra Señora de los Ángeles*.

22. In her study of the Indian pueblos of Oaxaca, María de los Ángeles Romero analyzes the way in which the Indian nobility reinvented themselves through the rewriting of their histories, following the Spanish model of social stratification. Romero argues that among indigenous peoples the most important distinction was that of lineage (which possibly could have existed among commoners, as well), but pre-Hispanic and colonial documentation privileges a view of class distinction (36–43).

23. Two recent books from the field of history have been particularly influential in my concept of indigenous identities and the way the group of cacica nuns exercised agency in the conventual arena. The works of Yanna Yannakakis and Karen Graubart present a model of how historical analysis of subaltern groups is shifting, leading to a more nuanced understanding of ethnic and gendered identities. Yannakakis looks at the existence of native, male intermediaries in the Sierra Norte of Oaxaca and their political use of multiple identities. She analyzes the way these intermediaries conceptualized identities as fluid constructs that served to redefine the new colonial order and legitimize their pre-Hispanic power figure within this new system. Graubart studies indigenous women in Peru and the way they found agency in the material realm by quickly learning to use the new legal codes. Like Yannakakis, she contends that ethnic and social categories of identification were fluid and contestatory.

24. Informaciones, according to the *Diccionario de autoridades*, were the proofs provided regarding the quality and circumstances required of a person applying for a job or an honor. In a way, this kind of narrative is related to the *relaciones de méritos y servicios* (accounts of merits and services) and the *probanzas* (testimonies).

25. "Gender parallelism" and "complementarity" refer to the predominating paradigm in research "that sought to de-emphasize hierarchy and dominance and emphasize the centrality of separate gender roles" (van Deusen 144). See Louise Burkhart, "Mexica Women on the Home Front," and Susan Kellogg, "From Parallel and Equivalent." The groundbreaking work of Irene Silverblatt,

Moon, Sun and Witches: Gender and Class Ideologies under Inca and Spanish Rule (1987), also proposed this paradigm for pre-conquest Peru.

26. For example, Susan Kellogg's *Law and the Transformation of Aztec Culture* focuses on how law functioned as a new arena of cultural accommodation for Indians, who drew from both pre-Hispanic traditions and Spanish practices to participate in this contested terrain. Although men participated in larger numbers in this space, indigenous women from all classes left their mark on the legal record.

27. Yanna Yannakakis mentions this phenomenon as her reason for not including the study of women intermediaries in her book (26).

28. Martha Few's *Women Who Live Evil Lives* and Laura Lewis's *Hall of Mirrors* are good examples of this kind of study.

29. An *encomendera/o* was the holder of an *encomienda*, a grant of authority over a group of Indians as tribute payers or laborers. It was usually given to Spaniards as reward for their efforts during the conquest.

30. Patricia Seed, "Social Dimensions of Race," and John Chance, *Race and Class in Colonial Oaxaca*. For an earlier look at this issue, see Magnus Mörner, *Race Mixture in the History of Latin America*.

31. See Elizabeth Anne Kuznesof, "Ethnic and Gender Influences on 'Spanish' Creole Society in Colonial Spanish America," *Colonial Latin American Review* 4 (1995): 153–176.

32. The pattern of power established by the colonizer was based on the idea of difference. This ideological creation—and its subsequent consequences in the definition of the new identities of the native inhabitants of the Americas—meant the disavowal of their ethnic particularities. Aníbal Quijano refers to this creation of different spaces according to "race" as the coloniality of power (29). For a lengthier discussion of how limpieza de sangre traveled from Spain to the Americas, see María Elena Martínez, *Genealogical Fictions*.

33. Fisher and O'Hara's argument questions the commonly used categories of social difference in colonial society: "The debunking of race as a scientific discourse during the course of the twentieth century led many in the academic community to shift the discussion of social difference to the analytical categories of ethnicity or identity, terms that are perceived as more value-free, or at least more clearly divorced from the eugenics nightmare that culminated in the Nazi movement and the Holocaust" (7).

34. In 1989 Walter Mignolo and Rolena Adorno dedicated an edition of the journal *Dispositio* to the study and analysis of colonial discourse. In the "Afterword," Mignolo referenced Peter Hulme's contributions to colonial discourse, which according to him "comprehends all kinds of discursive production related to and produced in colonial situations from the Capitulations of 1492 to *The Tempest*, from Royal Orders and edicts to the most carefully written prose" ("Afterword" 333).

35. Rolena Adorno's 1988 article ends with this proposal. The same call to move in that direction in academia is proposed by Gustavo Verdesio in 2002 in his introduction to *Colonialism Past and Present*, although he identifies distinct types of intellectual colonization.

36. Myers, in "Crossing Boundaries: Defining the Field of Female Religious Writing in Colonial Latin America," states that by 1990 the writings of religious women had been legitimized, constituting a disciplinary subgenre of conventual literature.

37. Asunción Lavrin, "Religious Life of Mexican Women in the XVIII Century." Diss. Harvard University, 1963. Later, she published another article on Corpus Christi, this time focusing on the racial tensions in that convent. See Lavrin, "Indian Brides of Christ: Creating New Spaces for Indigenous Women in New Spain," *Mexican Studies/Estudios Mexicanos* 15 (1999): 225–60. Recently, a version of this article appeared as a chapter in her book *Brides of Christ*.

38. Ann Miriam Gallagher, "The Family Background of the Nuns of Two "Monasteries" in Colonial Mexico: Santa Clara, Querétaro; and Corpus Christi, Mexico City (1724–1822)." In a telephone conversation with Ann Miriam Gallagher, she mentioned to me that she had had the opportunity to live in the convent of Corpus Christi, which still exists, although not in the same place where it was founded. She had ample access to the convent's archives while she conducted her investigation at the end of the 1960s. Access to the convent archive is restricted presently because the Franciscan Nuns of Saint Claire's Order of Corpus Christi decided several years ago to guard more zealously the historic patrimony found in their archives.

39. Elisa Sampson Vera Tudela, *Colonial Angels: Narratives of Gender and Spirituality in Mexico 1580–1750*; Mariselle Meléndez, "El perfil económico de la identidad racial en los *Apuntes* de las indias caciques del convento de Corpus Christi"; María Justina Sarabia Viejo, "La Concepción y Corpus Christi: Raza y vida conventual femenina en México, siglo XVIII."

40. Manuel Ramos Medina, *Imagen de santidad en un mundo profano* and *Místicas y descalzas*; Jacqueline Holler, *Escogidas Plantas: Nuns and Beatas in Mexico City, 1531–1601*; and Margaret Chowning, *Rebellious Nuns: The Troubled History of a Mexican Convent, 1752–1863*.

41. Myers, "The Mystic Triad in Colonial Mexican Nuns' Discourse." See also *A Wild Country Out in the Garden* by the same author. The second chapter of the second part of the book discusses and compares the lives and lifestyles of both nuns and priests.

42. Kristine Ibsen, *Women's Spiritual Autobiography in Spanish America*; Kathryn Joy McKnight, *The Mystic of Tunja: The Writings of Madre Castillo 1671–1742*; Myers, Kathleen, and Kathleen Myers and Amanda Powell, *A Wild Country Out in the Garden: The Spiritual Journals of a Colonial Mexican Nun*; Jennifer Eich, *The Other Mexican Muse: Sor María Anna Águeda de San Ignacio, 1695–1765*; Stephanie L. Kirk,

Convent Life in Colonial Mexico: A Tale of Two Communities; and Kathleen Myers, *Neither Saints Nor Sinners: Writing the Lives of Women in Spanish America.*

43. The Real Audiencia of Mexico was the highest tribunal of the Spanish Crown, created in 1528 in response to complaints that had reached the Crown about Hernán Cortés and the abuses he committed in New Spain. The Audiencia had the authority to deal with both civil and criminal causes (Arregui 30).

Chapter 1. Indigenous Nobility and Conventual Foundations

1. The word "cacique" is of Arawak origin, the Spanish having adopted it in the Antilles during the fifteenth century and imposed its use in the case of New Spain (Gibson 36). Cacica is the female equivalent of cacique. In the discussion that follows, cacique refers to the individual, and cacicazgo to the entity governed by him. For a detailed analysis of native intermediaries, see Yanna Yannakakis, *The Art of Being In-Between.*

2. The term "macehual" (or "macehualli" in Nahuatl) translates literally as "human being," but it was used specifically to cordon off the rest of the population from the nobles. Macehual means plebeian and is used to refer to "the people" (Lockhart 96).

3. "Tlatoque" is the plural for "tlatoani," which means governor of an *altepetl*, a social unit of organization in the Nahuatl culture (Lockhart 14–15). Pipiltin is the plural for "pilli" and refers to the relatives of the tlatoque. "Cihuapilli" means noblewoman (Lockhart 95).

4. Examples of this phenomenon can be found in the informaciones presented in the Convent of Corpus Christi to demonstrate the noble lineage of candidates.

5. As demonstrated by María de los Ángeles Romero's research, some of these land titles and privileges were negotiated well into the colonial period and not necessarily owned originally from pre-Hispanic times. Romero refers to the rewriting of indigenous historiography with specific purposes in mind, as in the case of the señorío of Tututepec. In this señorío they kept a *códice* in which "someone" carefully erased complete figures of former governors and their names. They also added text in Mixtec language using Latin alphabet. The author emphasizes the conscientious effort of these Indian nobles to adapt their past to fit the colonial moment in the process of preparing legal documents to negotiate their land titles and other privileges with Spanish officials (112).

6. This assertion appears to generalize the characteristics of a group that were in no way uniform; later, Gibson will relent on this point, making evident the existing differences.

7. See, for example, Charles Gibson, *The Aztecs;* Delfina López Sarrelangue, *La nobleza indígena;* Ronald Spores, *The Mixtec Kings;* William Taylor, *Landlord and Peasant;* Nancy Farris, *Maya Society under Colonial Rule.*

8. The study of the ethnic identity of generations of indigenous nobles born once the colony had been established has been of interest to some

scholars, although from the standpoint of their written production. See, for example, Salvador Velazco, *Visiones de Anahuac*.

9. See Douglas Cope, *The Limits of Racial Domination*; Jonathan Israel, *Race, Class, and Politics*; Alan Knight, *Mexico*; and Steve Stern, *Peru's Indian Peoples*.

10. We should keep in mind, however, that this is a generalized picture and that there were in actuality considerable regional differences. See Chance, "Indian Elites."

11. As Yanna Yannakakis makes evident, the fact that a group of Indians finds accommodation within the system, rather than resisting colonial power openly, gives rise to conflicting academic opinions (5).

12. For a detailed discussion of this subject, see Soriano, *Lucha y resistencia* 98.

13. An example of this pedagogical undertaking is the creation of the Colegio de Santa Cruz de Tlatelolco, dedicated to educating the children of caciques and principales, with an eye to the future preparation of an indigenous clergy.

14. See Lino Gómez Canedo, *La educación de los marginados* (1982); and Elisa Ramírez Castañeda, *La educación indígena en México* (2006).

15. After the Royal Decree of 1774, the nuns in one of the more privileged and luxurious convents ("de vida privada") could vote to decide if they wanted to continue living that way or change to common life. The nuns of the Convent of Santa Clara de Jesús in Querétaro decided to maintain a lifestyle that would allow each nun to have a servant, except for some nuns who could have two, as well as live in private cells and have an allowance (Gallagher, "The Family Background" 84).

16. The nuns who entered these convents after the Royal Decree of 1774 had to adhere to the austere life prescribed by the king, despite entering a convent de vida privada.

17. As noted in the introduction, two nuns declared they were descendants of Juan Diego, María Micaela Escalona y Rojas and Gertrudis de Torres y Vásquez (Gallagher, "The Family Background" 162).

18. In the next chapters I hope to demonstrate the way the Indian nuns created alliances and communities to "challenge and reformulate" the impositions of the colonial Church (Kirk 14).

19. Although I contend that the term "racial identity" is inaccurate to explain the phenomenon of the Indian nobility, I find Patricia Seed's discussion useful to explain the concept of the caciques' identity; see "Social Dimensions of Race" (573).

Chapter 2. The Idea of Corpus Christi

1. Walter Mignolo in *The Darker Side of the Renaissance* explores at length the authority the Spanish bestowed on themselves through literacy and alphabetic writing and its relation to history and rhetoric (112).

2. Sara Castro-Klarén in "Historiography on the Ground: The Toledo Circle and Guamán Poma" studies this same dynamic in the case of the Andes,

focusing on the strategies the Spanish used to achieve colonial governing power (143–171).

3. See, for example, Francisco Javier Clavijero, *Historia antigua de México* (México: Porrúa, 1964).

4. These testimonials regarding ethnic issues have been studied by Asunción Lavrin in "Indian Brides of Christ," with a newer version in her book *Brides of Christ*, and by Elisa Sampson Vera Tudela in *Colonial Angels*, as well as by María Justina Sarabia Viejo in "La Concepción y Corpus Christi" and "Monacato femenino y problemática indígena en la Nueva España del siglo XVIII." Sampson's particular interest lies more in the question of gender than ethnic difference, and Sarabia Viejo limits herself to the presence of the Spanish novices and their expulsion from the convent. Asunción Lavrin includes other texts that appeared parallel to the debate over Corpus Christi, and her treatment of the topic focuses as much on gender as on race. The present study places these testimonials in a larger context and includes texts previously overlooked. It also expands the chronology of events and the magnitude of the debate on the opening of Corpus Christi and its subsequent years.

5. See, for example, Sarah Cline, "The Spiritual Conquest Reexamined: Baptism and Christian Marriage in Early Sixteenth-Century Mexico."

6. A calmecac was a learning center for the children of Aztec nobles.

7. In "The 'Indian Question' and the Case of Tlatelolco," Martin Austin Nesvig studies Spanish theologian Alfonso de Castro's defense of indigenous intellect, which was endorsed by Francisco Vitoria, known for his criticism of the enterprise of conquest in America. The article not only analyzes this topic, which has been ignored and largely forgotten, but it also tackles the broader issue regarding indigenous education and Christianization.

8. Indians, mestizos, and mulattos were admitted into seminaries and became priests, but a seminary exclusively for Indians was never opened.

9. In chapter 5, which focuses on the Convent of Cosamaloapan, the active role the nuns played in the conflict surrounding episcopal jurisdiction becomes evident.

10. Yanna Yannakakis notes that the use of the term "nación" (nation) reflected Iberian notions of difference (17).

11. This has been a pervasive idea, perpetuated even in scholarship. See, for example, Verena Stolcke, "Invaded Women" (1994); and Allan Greer, "Iroquois Virgin" (2003).

12. In the work of both Josefina Muriel and Ann Miriam Gallagher, we find statements about the different temperaments of Spanish and indigenous women. Part of this modern concept arises from the *indigenista* movements of the early twentieth century, which tried to appreciate indigenous people in their cultural environment and defend them from the *ladino* invasion. Ultimately, however, the Indian in the eyes of the *indigenista* is the Other.

13. According to ancient beliefs, human character and temperament were based on the four humors. Those with too much blood were sanguine and were

identified with the qualities of warmth and moistness. See Myers, "The Mystic Triad" (483).

14. Many of the indigenous women who wanted to take the veil had lived as servants in the Convent of San Juan de la Penitencia, where Sor Petra had taught them to read and write; others had entered as *donadas* (lay sisters of a religious community) to get an education in order to take the veil in the Convent of Corpus Christi.

15. All the convents mentioned by these priests are of the Order of Saint Claire, and the Spanish nuns who founded Corpus Christi were also from the convents of San Juan de la Penitencia, Santa Clara, and Santa Isabel.

16. Jo Ann McNamara explains that the Clarisses, although established as a separate order, were strictly subjected to legislation passed by the Franciscan friars: "They had to maintain a substantial number of friars as chaplains, advisers, and lay brothers." They also had friars appointed as annual visitors (399).

17. Allan Greer has dedicated an article and a monograph to the story of Catherine and the role that the publication of this hagiography played in this public debate. See "Iroquois Virgin: The Story of Catherine Tekakwitha in New France and New Spain" and *Mohawk Saint: Catherine Tekakwitha and the Jesuits*.

18. This is especially true of the more urban areas, where the presence of religious institutions and their many manifestations made it all but impossible for the indigenous population to escape their influence. Also, from early on in the colonization, to be Christian meant to be more Hispanicized, which had an effect on the forging of an Indian identity. Louise Burkhart writes: "By acting as Christians, Nahuas became Christians; they declared themselves to be Christians and Christianity to be what they did" (*Holy Wednesday* 81).

19. In reality, Iroquois territory was located in Canada and the northeastern United States, but Urtassum situated it closer to New Spain, perhaps with the intention of making it seem more real through proximity.

20. Antonio Rubial identifies the original sources of all the narratives: "The examples are taken from the literature of the seventeenth century: Juana de San Jerónimo, mentioned by Alonso Remón in *Vida de Fernando de Córdoba y Bocanegra*; Magdalena de Pátzcuaro, of whom Francisco de Florencia writes in his *Historia de la Compañía de Jesús en Nueva España*; . . . and one more (whose name is not given) about whom the Jesuit Guillermo Illing, a missionary among the *chilipas*, writes" ("La exaltación de los humillados" 5).

21. The visions and miracles experienced by Petronila and Francisca, like those in the vidas of other pious nuns, served as rewards for leading such exemplary lives.

22. It is important to note that Sigüenza y Góngora contributes to the text both as a compiler of facts and as a historian, noting: "Haciendo yo cuidadosas informaciones para escribir estas vidas con la verdad que se debe" ("I did careful research to write these lives with the truth owed them"; 287).

23. "Différance," or difference with an "a,"—Jacques Derrida's poststructuralist concept that means both "to differ" and "to defer"—is an ideal term to

signify the difference inherent in discourses about indigenous women. It connotes aspects of inequality, temporality, and spatiality, pivotal variables in definitive discursive constructions of subaltern women.

Chapter 3. Indigenous Women and Religious Life

1. As mentioned earlier, the nuns were criollas, but the documentation available concerning internal conflicts in the convents for noble Indian women, as well as the document cited, refers to them as Spanish women. For the sake of consistency throughout the present study, I refer to them as Spanish when alluding to the textual reference to these nuns, even when they were born in New Spain.

2. The royal decree indicates that the Papal Bull, issued in Rome on June 27, 1727, established that Corpus Christi was founded exclusively for Indian women from the families of ruling nobles. The principal issue of contention was not that the founding nuns were Spanish, but that the commissary general of the Franciscan order continued to accept Spanish novices into the convent.

3. Juan Ignacio de Castorena y Ursúa was the editor of Sor Juana Inés de la Cruz's *Fama y obras póstumas*, published in 1700.

4. One of New Spain's most notorious cases involved the intellectual dispute that occurred when Sor Juana Inés de la Cruz's *Carta atenagórica* was published (without her consent) and the saga of the *Respuesta a Sor Filotea*. See "Introduction" in *The Answer/La Respuesta*. Ed. and trans. Electa Arenal and Amanda Powell. New York: The Feminist P, 1994. 12–14.

5. David Sweet argues that mission history has suffered from placing missionaries on center stage and leaving Indians without agency: "We must reread their accounts more critically than has sometimes been done, with an eye primarily to what they have to say about the dimly viewed Indian "other"; and we must learn to distinguish their high ideals and aspirations, the inflated claims of their fundraising appeals, and the well-meaning instructions regularly sent by their superiors from what we can reconstruct of their actual practice" (9).

6. The genre of the hagiographic biography will be discussed at length in chapter 4. The biography is an account of a person's life narrated by a third person; the hagiography, an account of a saint's life; and the hagiographic biography, a hybrid that contains elements of both. For a discussion of this kind of hybrid text in autobiographical form, see Kate Greenspan, "The Autobiographic Tradition in Medieval Women's Devotional Writing," *Auto/hagiography Studies* 6 (1991): 157–168.

7. This text is featured in an analysis of a body of hagiographic works in Asunción Lavrin's "Indian Brides of Christ," along with the two vidas of indigenous women included in Sigüenza y Góngora's *Paraíso occidental* and the biographies included in *Las indias caciques de Corpus Chrsti* by Josefina Muriel.

8. This insight about colonial Spanish America stems from Frantz Fanon's description of colonial society as Manichean or a compartmentalized structure. Fanon concisely states: "Sometimes this Manichaeism reaches its logical conclusion and dehumanizes the colonized subject" (7).

9. Two exceptional cases of women who were subjects of hagiographical biographies but were neither nuns nor saints are the Third Order Dominican Rosa de Lima from Perú, canonized as the first saint of the Americas, and Catarina de San Juan, a beata from Puebla de los Ángeles. See Kathleen Myers, *Neither Saints nor Sinners* 23–68.

10. For instance, Andrés Xavier García and Pedro Malo de Villavicencio, both Jesuits, stated that Indian women lack the constancy of spirit needed for religious life and perpetual seclusion, suggesting that the life of a lay sister would be the best solution (AGN, Historia, vol. 109, exp. 2, fols. 36 and 53).

11. The parecer was an opinion and/or judgment included in a religious document that dealt with material treating theological matters. All documents, especially those of a religious-philosophical nature, were required to include at least one of these generally brief narratives, which usually dealt with issues raised and the fitness of the author to treat them. The emphasis is mine.

12. For a detailed discussion of the roots and debates of the concept in its two forms, the legal and the religious, see Paulino Castañeda Delgado, "La condición miserable del indio y sus privilegios," *Anuario de Estudios Americanos* 28 (1971): 245–258. In the Treinta proposiciones jurídicas (1552), Fray Bartolomé de las Casas provides legal-religious justification for the indoctrination of the Amerindians by the kings of Castile because of their "humble condition" (*Doctrina* 40).

13. Matthew O'Hara makes reference to a pastoral manual for parish priests authored by Alonso de la Peña Montenegro in 1668 that defines the concept of *miserable* as "one who has lost an earlier state of happiness and therefore deserves the pity of his fellow men" ("*Miserables* and Citizens" 15). María Elena Martínez places the concept of *miserable* together with that of *nuevamente convertidos* (recent converts); see *Genealogical Fictions* 102–104.

14. The term "semantic field," also known as "conceptual field," comes from lexicological analysis.

15. Fray Bartolomé de las Casas was one of the first religious figures to contribute to the prolific discourses on the "nature" of Amerindians; see Santa Arias 87–104.

16. Various testimonies mention that indigenous women ought to practice oral prayer only because they did not have the capacity for mental prayer and because of their simple nature it would be of no benefit for them, another illustration of the discursive ambivalence that defends these women even as it discriminates against them.

17. When the Marquis of Valero died, his heart was embalmed and given to the abbess in 1728. It was then buried in the convent's church (Amerlinck and Ramos 126).

18. In *The Interior Castle*, Teresa of Ávila writes: "A little more than four years ago I came to understand through experience that the mind (or imagination, to put it more clearly) is not the intellect. I asked a learned man and he told me that this was so; which brought me no small consolation. For since the intellect is one of the soul's faculties, it was an arduous thing for me that it should be so restless at times" (*Collected Works* 2:319).

19. See Osvaldo F. Pardo, *The Origins of Mexican Catholicism;* and Viviana Díaz Balsera, *The Pyramid under the Cross*.

20. The *Códice Mendoza* and the *Códice Aubin* show the image of the eagle perched on the cactus as a symbol of the place where Tenochtitlán was to be founded. Aubin includes the image that would later be adopted for the Mexican flag, the eagle devouring the serpent (Brotherston 55–57).

21. Both are included in *Visión de los vencidos: Relaciones indígenas de la conquista* (México: UNAM, 1992) 2–10.

22. In 1701 the new dynasty, the line of Bourbons, began with the reign of Philip V (1701–1746) in Spain. The coat of arms of the Hapsburgs with the double-headed eagle was a nostalgic reminiscence of a time lost. Just a few decades after the preaching of Castorena's sermon, Charles III (1759–1788) would expel all Jesuits from his dominions in Europe and America in 1767. The Church under the Bourbons was clearly losing political control. For a lengthier discussion, see David Brading, *Church and State* 3–19; and *First America* 492–513.

23. Similar to the way Santander y Torres refocused Augustinian María de San José's (1656–1719) autobiographical writings in order to create an official biography of an exemplary nun, Fray Joseph Valdés engaged in the "rescripting" of Sebastiana's writings (Myers, *Neither Saints* 84).

24. Both Kristine Ibsen in *Women's Spiritual Autobiography* and Elisa Sampson Vera Tudela in *Colonial Angels* dedicate a chapter to the analysis of Sebastiana's writings and mention the vida authored by Valdés. Both analyze the texts for their auto-hagiographic value, without exploring from the spiritual autobiography Sebastiana composed in her notebooks what could have been her actual life.

25. See Ann Miriam Gallagher, "The Family Background."

26. This is a reference to the Convent of Santa Clara in Querétaro.

27. Analysis of this and other panegyric sermons can be found in chapter 5 of this study.

28. A lengthier discussion of this passage can be found in chapter 4.

Chapter 4. Biographies and Hagiographies

1. Gerda Lerner explains that "autobiographers tell the story of their own life," whereas biographers have to rely on external evidence to write about another individual's life (*Living with History* 130–131).

2. Since 2000, the subfield of conventual writing, defined as such by Kathleen Myers in "Crossing Boundaries," has developed into a major area of study with interdisciplinary approaches that "thoroughly acknowledge the complex interplay of institutional and discursive practices, and the role of women and religion within them" ("Recent Trends" 291). These more recent studies have taken into consideration the gender approach I propose in this chapter, as well as a broader historical and cultural contextualization of nuns' writings.

3. Kathleen Myers, in her study of the life of María de San José, contends that the relationship between nun and confessor is not just bilateral, since the confessor is not the only one who has power over the nun: "Drawing on a tradition basic to Christian theology, María de San José tells her confessor that she experiences moments of direct divine intervention in her life and writings, and these sometimes cause her to deviate from the confessor's requirements" (*Word from New Spain* 33). Myers illustrates this concept with the structure of a triangle: God is at the apex, the nun at one corner of the base, and the priest at the other. As both nun and priest have direct access to God, the priest's intervention becomes unnecessary to her. This scenario causes a series of conflicts and frictions over the question of who has maximum authority over the nun, God or the priest.

4. Genre categories of colonial discourse overlap; indeed, one of the characteristics of colonial textuality is the open dialogue existing between genres. While studying these texts according to genre formation satisfies traditional literary interests, analysis should be extended to include a cultural studies approach that examines the impact of gender and ethnicity.

5. Jean Franco observes: "Confessors and biographers of 'mystical' nuns thus acted as publishers, examiners, and editors of material to which the women writers could not claim authorship" (14).

6. Some other themes and genres more frequently cultivated by men in colonial times that Sor Juana ventured to explore, as demonstrated by Grady Wray, are the theological commentary and debate in the *Carta atenagórica* ("Sacred Allusions" 66), and scientific discourse in the *Ejercicios devotos* (*The Devotional Exercises* 104). Other scholars have also studied her scientific speculation in *Primero sueño*.

7. In some instances, biographies were written by nuns for priests who would ask them to compose the life story of a deceased sister. Even when the nun did not write her spiritual autobiography, the same paradigm of dominance and submission is present in a relationship that required she reveal to the male reader the private life of her sister.

8. The writing nun depended on her confessor for spiritual guidance and endorsement in her writing exercise, and priests depended on the nun's writings to acquire material for their subsequent accounts of heroic virtues. For an excellent study of nun-confessor power relationships within the convent, see

Stephanie Kirk's *Convent Life in Colonial Mexico*, which affirms a slippage between the ideal community envisioned by the Church in Mexico and women's actual experience of convent life.

9. See the pioneering work of Josefina Ludmer, "Las tretas del débil." For a complete repertoire of these stratagems, see Arenal and Schlau, "Stratagems of the Strong, Stratagems of the Weak."

10. In "Autohagiography and Medieval Women's Spiritual Autobiography," Greenspan argues that spiritual autobiography, which resembles more the style of the hagiography than that of the autobiography, should be called autohagiography (218).

11. McKnight also adds that Pope Urban VIII established official rules for canonization by which all candidates for sainthood must meet three requirements: purity of doctrine, heroic virtue, and miraculous intercession after death.

12. See, for example, the works of Louise Burkhart, Jorge Klor de Alva, Susan Schroeder, and David Tavárez, among others.

13. This is a generalized picture of religious indoctrination, yet the gradual appropriation of religion as part of indigenous ethnic identity can be perceived, especially in the three geographical areas considered here: Central Mexico, Valladolid, and Oaxaca.

14. The original title of the manuscript, edited and paleographed by Muriel, is *Apuntes de varias vidas de las religiosas que han florecido en virtudes en este convento de Corpus Christi de indias caciques* (Notes on the Various Lives of the Religious Women Who Have Blossomed With Virtue in This Convent of Corpus Christi).

15. As a result of the investigation that began in 1981 in order to canonize Juan Diego, the Indian witness of the Guadalupe apparitions, the chronicler of the Villa of Guadalupe learned that two indigenous nuns of Corpus Christi claimed to be descendants of Juan Diego. A researcher on this particular issue, Arturo Rocha, who had ample access to the archives of the Convent of Corpus Christi, shared a copy of the *Apuntes* with me. In 1999 the nuns of the actual convent of Corpus Christi prepared a small exhibit of the *Apuntes* in the parlor of the convent.

16. Compared to the hagiographic biographies published by Josefina Muriel in the *Indias caciques*, the writings found in the archives of the Corpus Christi convent are less biographies than vignettes that contain biographical details and religious virtues.

17. This commentary in the hagiographic biography of Sor Antonia refers to conflict among nuns and their reluctance to accept others as normal occurrences in the convent. For example, in the vida of Madre Castillo, she portrays her struggles in the convent, where she was criticized, envied, and scorned by many of her sisters. At the same time, she received mercies from God in the form of mystical experiences.

18. Important writers of the era like Sor Juana Inés de la Cruz and, before her, Teresa of Ávila made use of metaphors in their writing; nevertheless, the general level of education of nuns in New Spain allowed only the use of simple metaphors drawn from common use, the Bible, or their daily prayers.

19. An interesting detail of this life story is that on page 12 of the *Apuntes*, we find thirteen lines that have been inked out, completely preventing us from reading this fragment. It is not known if this censorship was the work of the nun who wrote the biography, a confessor, or a reader.

20. *Carbunco* is an infectious illness caused by bacteria, known today as cutaneous anthrax.

21. The other nun identified as the descendant of Juan Diego was Sor María Antonia del Sacramento, whose name before taking the habit was María Micaela Gerónima de Escalona Rojas. As part of the investigation for Juan Diego's canonization, the team of researchers found the news about María Micaela joining the Convent of Corpus Christi in the colonial newspaper *La Gaceta de México*, which stated that she took the veil on May 24, 1739 (González Fernández 218).

22. Myers states that Santander y Torres even distorted the portrait that María had done of her sister in her own writings to create a more compelling story of the obstacles she confronted when entering the convent (84).

23. Teresa of Ávila is well known for mental prayer. In *The Interior Castle*, she defines mental prayer by using the castle as a metaphor. She writes in the Fourth Dwelling Places, chapter 3: "When God grants the favor it is a great help to seek Him within where He is found more easily and in a way more beneficial to us than when sought in creatures, as St. Augustine says after having looked for Him in many places. . . . But what I am speaking of comes in a different way. Sometimes before one begins to think of God, these people are already inside the castle" (*Collected Works* 2:328). Implicit in the prayer of recollection is the mystical experience.

24. Teresa of Avila writes in *The Interior Castle* in the Seventh Dwelling Places, chapter 4: "I repeat, it is necessary that your foundation consists of more than prayer and contemplation. If you do not strive for the virtues and practice them, you will always be dwarfs" (447). To explain the need to balance your time between prayer and doing good deeds, she uses the biblical example of Martha and Mary (Lk 10, 42).

25. Details about the life of Sor Petra of San Francisco will be considered more carefully in chapter 5 when analyzing the funeral sermon preached in her honor.

26. We have to take into consideration that priests and nuns held a specific place not just in the hierarchy of gender but also of the Church. We have already discussed the relationships of power established between these individuals, and the biographical texts of the Corpus Christi nuns illustrate the ways these are put into practice.

27. The emphasis is mine.

Chapter 5. Panegyric Sermons

1. Don Paul Abbott, in his study *Rhetoric in the New World*, illustrates the fundamental role of preaching in the colonization of America with this example.

2. For an analysis of the various aspects of sermon composing and preaching, see Hilary Dansey Smith, *Preaching in the Spanish Golden Age*.

3. Mikhail Bakhtin proposes that all verbal activity with definite thematic content, style, and structure can be considered speech genre ("The Problem of Speech Genres" 83).

4. Opinions about this nun vary. In "Religious Life of Mexican Women," Asunción Lavrin notes the existence of a letter written by Sor María Teresa de San José, as abbess of the Convent of Corpus Christi, to the Council of the Indies, asking for the expulsion of three Spanish novices (29). Nevertheless, María Justina Sarabia Viejo, in "La Concepción y Corpus Christi," indicates that Sor María Teresa de San José maintained a strong influence over the Convent of Corpus Christi, which impeded the indigenous inhabitants from taking control of their convent. The documents sent to the Council of the Indies mention the letter Lavrin indicates in which Sor María Teresa denies responsibility for the conflicts in the convent. Those scholars who believe Sor María Teresa was responsible because of her influence do not support Lavrin's position.

5. For example, the *relación* takes elements from the *historia* and the chronicle, which in turn has elements of the letter. See also Walter Mignolo, "Cartas, crónicas y relaciones del descubrimiento y la conquista."

6. As noted in chapter 2, some Franciscans supported the complaints of the Indian nuns who wanted to evict the Spanish women from the convent. There were also native leaders supporting their daughters from outside the convent walls. Asunción Lavrin provides us with some of their names: "Don Ambrosio de Mendoza, Florencio Calixto Ramírez y Mendoza, and Diego Torres Vázquez Quapoltoche" (*Brides of Christ* 262).

7. The funeral eulogies also served as vehicles of persuasion, as much for the community of nuns, who were supposed to learn about the exemplary life of the deceased nun, as for the general public, who listened to the sermon when it was preached or eventually read its published form.

8. Although this assertion by Cruz and Perry refers to the European context, we find a similar situation in the Americas. The colonial system tried to mirror the Spanish one but met different obstacles, like the robust ethnic diversity that, from the first years of the colony, existed in conjunction with hierarchical social difference. In the end, the results were similar both in the colony and in the metropolis. The debates and conflicts that provoked the establishing of convents for indigenous women in Mexico are a clear example of the effects of the imposition of alleged social order and religious control.

9. The relationship between confessors or spiritual directors and their religious daughters that inspired this literature has been analyzed by Jodi

Bilinkoff in "Confessors, Penitents, and the Construction of Identities." Bilinkoff argues that confessors used their relationships with exceptional religious women to affirm their roles as teachers and preachers. In addition, many were looking to grow the ranks of the faithful through discursive images, which they created in their sermons, spiritual biographies, and doctrinal treatises (89).

10. The three panegyric sermons dedicated to the three nuns are almost the same length, while sermons dedicated to men, such as the one preached for the death of Fray Joseph de Castro, vicar of the Convent of Corpus Christi, are much longer. The sermon for Fray Joseph is divided into nine sections which, according to most rhetoric manuals, was considered very extensive. Also, the sermons were not necessarily read; the *Retórica* of Fray Diego Valadés stresses memorization. Many preachers would write their sermons and memorize them for preaching. The written versions circulated later were specially prepared for publication and often different from the preached versions.

11. About the rhetorical structure of the sermon, divided into three parts, Hilary Smith observes that "there is always a single main text (*thema*), and always a division of the text, traditionally a tripartite one in honor of the Trinity" (44).

12. This structure is generally present in the panegyric funeral sermons dedicated to nuns; however, the sermon dedicated to Sor María Teodora, the founding indigenous nun, does not offer this information, even when it follows the same structure.

13. Sor María Teresa wrote a letter defending herself against the complaints filed against her by the indigenous nuns with the Council of the Indies. The image she constructs of herself is contrary to the one offered by the indigenous women in their documents and, more important, is consistent with the one constructed in the funeral panegyric sermon. In her letter, the nun defends her continuous support of the indigenous women and asks that more convents be established because so many Indian girls are not able to be admitted. It is, perhaps, because of this letter that her participation is mentioned in the founding of the Convent of Cosamaloapan (AINAH, FF, vol. 108, fol. 94).

14. Kathryn McKnight explains that Aquinas asserted that man possessed rational faculties, "while the inferior female body had a detrimental effect on woman's soul" (38). Still, women could "transgress" into a masculine domain by acquiring "virile" aptitudes. Fray Luis de León in *La perfecta casada* describes the perfect wife with that same qualifier: a *mujer varonil*.

15. In a recent study, Elizabeth Teresa Howe refers to Teresa of Ávila as "the New Judith." In reviewing St. Jerome's writings on women's education, Howe notes how Jerome described Judith: "A woman conquers men, chastity beheaded lust," adding that his choice of Judith as the virago also suggests other interpretations: "In her courageous defense of Betulia, Judith manifests the military acumen of the Amazons, as well as the virtues found among the *mulierum virtutes* praised by Plutarch" (6–7).

16. Artistic depictions of Judith beheading Holofernes reveal different interpretations of this story. The facial expression and the body positioning of the Judith by Caravaggio (circa 1598), for example, depict a certain distance between herself and the act of killing, which in a way justifies an act executed in God's name and to free the people from Bethulia.

17. Ecclesiastical authorities encouraged acts of penance, self-flagellation, and other bodily mortifications as long as they were closely monitored by the nun's confessor; see Stephanie Kirk, *Convent Life in Colonial Mexico* 40–46.

18. On the use of *imitatio Christi* for describing nun's obstacles and suffering in their path to perfection, see Kathleen Myers, "Sor Juana's *Respuesta*" 464–465.

19. For a detailed discussion of the 1692 riot, see Douglas Cope, *The Limits of Racial Domination* 125–160.

20. In Mexico City, a good number of Indians who lived and worked in the *traza*, the core of the colonial city, were forced to return to their Indian barrios after the riot.

21. Ixtlilxóchitl assumed an Indian identity even though his father was a Spaniard and his mother a mestiza. In his historiography, he appealed to the noble lineage of his great grandparents to defend his right to the cacicazgo of San Juan Teotihuacán (23). Yet Ixtlilxóchitl's Indian identity also integrates Christianity and pre-Hispanic history, and in this way, King Nezahualcoyotl appears like the biblical King David.

22. In 1811 the Convent of Nuestra Señora de Guadalupe, the last convent exclusively for Indian women, opened. It did not require purity of blood for admittance and had long been a school for Indian girls before its conversion into a convent of the Order of Mary. For an overview of the founding of the convent, see Muriel, *Conventos de monjas* 487–499.

23. As noted in chapter 4, by now the Indian nuns had adopted and adapted the religious rhetoric reinforcing difference to defend the ethnic character of their cloisters.

24. The *Memoriales* of Fray Toribio de Benavente Motolonía is an excellent example of the missionary discourse that supports the Indian isolation and their protection from the rest of Spanish society. Chapter 2 compares the ten plagues of Egypt narrated in Exodus 7–12 to the plagues brought by the conquest. Adhering to the Manichean model, Motolinía's line of argument separates the Spaniards into two groups, that of the "good" missionaries who came to save the Indians and that of the "mean" conquerors who were destroying their towns and peoples (138–146).

25. Michel de Certeau refers to *exempla* as those actions performed by the subject that furnish social models, located "at a crossroads between the evolution of the individual community in which they are elaborated and the sociocultural conjuncture that this evolution is traversing" (*The Writing of History* 278).

26. David Brading refers to "the ultra-baroque rhetoric" of the mendicant orders that influenced popular religion in Mexico (*Church and State* 37). This

approach to religion came under close scrutiny with the secularization of Indian parishes; see *First America* 492–502.

27. Matthew O'Hara has noted that in the years following Mexico's independence from Spain in 1821, the legal category of *indio* was eliminated. However, the distinction between Indians and non-Indians "continued to inform political thought, economic policy, local religious practices, and many other aspects of daily life" (*"Miserables* and Citizens" 15).

Chapter 6. Letters from the Convent

1. On the use of legal defense rhetoric, see McKnight 18; Slade 17; and Vollendorf 39.

2. See Lavrin and Loreto, *Diálogos espirituales* 263–383.

3. Sarah Owens's doctoral dissertation, "Subversive Obedience: Confessional Letters by Eighteenth-Century Mexican Colonial Nuns," studies this group of letters, as does a chapter of *Colonial Angels* by Elisa Sampson Vera Tudela, and the aforementioned article by Asunción Lavrin, "De su puño y letra." Owens studies the narratives of Sor Sebastiana within the epistolary genre, while Sampson Vera Tudela examines them within the genre of the *vida espiritual*.

4. Not necessarily correlated with the practice of epistolary confession, spiritual elements sometimes appear as part of the conventions of conventual genres in which the nun and a confessor establish a relationship of power and alleged dependency.

5. At the fifth annual conference on Women Writers on Medieval and Early Modern Spain and Colonial Latin America in October 2000, Asunción Lavrin presented a paper that considered the content of some of the letters studied in this chapter. Lavrin's historical approach offered a preliminary exploration of the conflicts within the convent and paved the way for the series of inquiries that drive this work.

6. Although here we focus on women who had the ability and training to write letters, in the case of an illiterate person who wished to have a written record, scribes were readily available in religious and secular spheres.

7. See Zamora, *Reading Columbus*.

8. This is particularly marked in a nun's letter addressed to a cleric because as Kathleen Myers has noted "her journals and letters reflect the cleric's requests for material, his comments on previous accounts, and the strength (or fragility) of their relationship" ("The Mystic Triad" 487).

9. Education was available to the majority of men and a small number of women. Lisa Vollendorf identifies men's literacy to be about 40 percent and women's 25 percent in sixteenth- and seventeenth-century Spain (4). Nevertheless, the cloister was one of the acknowledged intellectual centers, and for that reason, many women who found themselves in convents had access to

literature, especially the devotional variety, which exposed them to rhetoric. See Arenal and Schlau, "Leyendo yo" 214–215.

10. See Rosa Perelmuter, *Los límites de la femineidad* 17–24.

11. The term *captatio benevolentiae* refers to a rhetorical device that seeks to secure the good will of the reader or listener.

12. See Alison Weber for Teresa of Avila's use of the rhetoric of femininity.

13. Trueba Lawand notes stylistic differences between the two letters by Teresa of Ávila published in the *Epistolario*: The first, addressed to a postulant nun, is written in a high style, while the second, addressed to Father Báñez, is written in a medium and low style (116).

14. According to Walter Mignolo, the Cortés letters exemplify "the need and obligation to inform" in epistolary practices ("Cartas, crónicas y relaciones" 67). This double characteristic of need and obligation is evident in the letters analyzed in this chapter. The nuns of Cosamaloapan, and especially the abbess, had the obligation to inform about conditions in the convent, but at the same time, they needed to ask for the prelate's help. This "need" and "obligation" stem from the unequal relationship in which the letter-writing subject engages the recipient.

15. It is important to note that the skill possessed by the majority of the nuns in the Spanish colonies cannot compare to Sor Juana's mastery of rhetoric. In her *Respuesta*, she not only used classical rhetoric but also applied her vast literary and biblical knowledge. According to Kathleen Myers, Sor Juana also used the rhetorical possibilities of the confessional Vida; see "Sor Juana's Respuesta." Another key consideration in the *Respuesta* is the "double-tongued" rhetoric of a nun writing both to another supposed nun and to a male authority (the bishop of Puebla).

16. Susan Socolow asserts that women in colonial Spanish America lived in a patriarchal society, "a world in which men occupied positions of authority and power." Yet she also acknowledges the existence of a certain space for negotiation: "The culture of patriarchy was never as absolute in reality as it was in theory" (178). The Catholic Church allowed women certain privileges; maintaining their virginity allowed them to be more like men, but only men could occupy positions of power within the Church (see Jo Ann Kay McNamara 1–6).

17. Even though Perelmuter refers directly to Sor Juana's famous *Respuesta*, her observation is valid for other letters as well.

18. For further elaboration on the subject, see Josefina Ludmer, "Tricks of the Weak" 86–93.

19. The conventual conflict recorded in these letters persisted so long that the position of commissary general changed hands from Fray Pedro Navarrete, who was in office in 1743, to Fray Juan Fogueras, who became the Franciscan commissary general in 1745.

20. The epistolary exchange between the priest and Sor María Josefa is more extensive than what appears here; for the purposes of my discussion, I

preferred to give more space to the voices of the indigenous nuns. The letters that Sor María Josefa composed, although valuable for recreating the disputes among nuns, revolve mainly around her request for assistance to resolve the tension.

21. The letter was addressed to [Father] Don Juan de Altamirano, whose identity I have not yet been able to corroborate. Asunción Lavrin has also tried in vain to find other references to him (*Brides of Christ* 426).

22. According to Karen Graubart, at the turn of the seventeenth century Indians born in cities began calling themselves *indios criollos* (creole Indians) to distinguish their status from that of rural Indians, a term that according to Graubart appeared to mark cultural adaptation as well as place of birth (147).

23. I did not include the original Spanish version because it only lists the retinue that left the Convent of Corpus Christi to found the one in Valladolid.

24. For further elaboration on secularization, see David Brading, *Church and State* 62–81.

25. According to James Lockhart, in spite of all the lost lands, transformations, and name changes, Indian villages in the later colonial era still maintained a dynasty (or a number of them), a minority holding on to the prestige, education, and some of the riches related to the *tlatoque* of the sixteenth century (138).

26. About this incident, Asunción Lavrin notes that "one of the two Indian founders, a nun versed in Latin, was reported to be shunned and replaced in the conventual hierarchy by a white nun. It was possibly a punishment for having complained about the infiltration by white nuns" (*Brides of Christ* 266).

27. For a discussion of the bonds of solidarity among women living in a religious community, see Kirk 129; Arenal and Schlau, "Leyendo yo" 218; and Merrim xiii.

Epilogue

1. Entering the convent was another story, one made possible by the generosity of Professor Antonio Rubial and Fray Francisco Morales.

2. See Peter Guardino, *Peasants, Politics, and the Formation of Mexico's National State: Guerrero 1800–1857;* and Florencia Mallon, *Peasant and Nation: The Making of Postcolonial Mexico and Peru.*

3. For further discussion of the situation of indigenous women in present-day Latin America, see Kellogg, *Weaving the Past* 90–177. Today in Mexico, spaces still exist where Nahua women can exercise authority and power. Still, such actions are complementary as well as subordinated to the actions of men, primarily because the configuration of the Nahua family does not promote but rather undermines feminine agency (99).

4. Yanna Yannakakis identifies different categories of intermediaries: *indios conquistadores* (Indian conquerors), *indios principales* (Indian notables), and *indios ladinos* (Hispanized Indians) (17–18).

5. See Yannakakis 226–227.

6. Active agents of cultural transmission, indigenous women recreated their historical memory to fit the new order of things; see Graubart 1–9.

7. As Sherry Ortner notes, there are two modalities of agency, "one of which is closely related to ideas of power, including both domination and resistance, and another that is closely related to ideas of intention, to people's projects in the world and their ability to both formulate and enact them" (78). In the case of the Indian nuns, I see both modalities of agency in operation.

8. See Matthew O'Hara, *A Flock Divided*, chapter 2.

9. Indigenous nuns also seemed to be aware of the model of the indigenous ethnographer who played a role as cultural mediator through writing; see Rolena Adorno, "The Indigenous Ethnographer."

Bibliography

Primary Sources

Alva Ixtlilxóchitl, Fernando de. *Historia de la nación chichimeca.* Ed. Germán Vázquez Chamorro. Madrid: Dastin, 2000.

Anguita, Juan Uvaldo de. *El divino verbo grano, que sembrado en la tierra virgen de Maria santisima nuestra señora da por fructo una cosecha de vírgenes. Sermon panegyrico, que en el solemne ingreso de las Religiosas Indias Caziques de la primera Regla de Santa Clara, en el nuevo Convento de N. Señora de Cozamaloapan.* México, 1743.

Apuntes de algunas vidas de nuestras hermanas difuntas. México. ACC.

Castorena y Ursúa, Juan Ignacio. *Las indias entendidas, por estar religiosamente sacramentadas, en el convento, y templo de Corpus Christi de esta imperial corte de México, edifico el Exc. mo. señor don Baltasar de Zúñiga Guzmán Sotomayor y Mendoza, Marqués de Valero.* México, 1724.

Clavijero, Francisco Javier. *Historia antigua de México.* México: Porrúa, 1964.

De las Casas, Bartolomé Fray. *Brevísima relación de la destrucción de las Indias.* Ed. Andre Saint-Lu. México: Rei, 1994.

———. *Doctrina.* México: UNAM, 1992.

Durán, Fray Diego. *Historia de las indias de Nueva España e islas de la tierra firme.* Ed. Ángel María Garibay. México: Porrúa, 1967.

Granada, Fray Luis de. *Los seis libros de la retórica eclesiástica. Vertidos en español y dados a la luz de orden, y a costa del ilustrísimo señor Obispo de Barcelona.* Barcelona, 1770.

Guevara, Miguel Tadeo de. *Oración fúnebre en las exequias, que el religiosisimo Convento de Corpus Christi de México consagro a la venerable memoria de su exemplar* fundadora, y dignisima prelada la M. R. M. Sor Maria Teresa de Sr. S. Josef Betancourt. México, 1773.

Juana Inés de la Cruz, Sor. *The Answer/La Respuesta*. Ed. and trans. Electa Arenal and Amanda Powell. New York: Feminist P, 1994.

León Portilla, Miguel. *Visión de los vencidos: Relaciones indígenas de la conquista.* México: UNAM, 1992.

López, Joseph. *Piedra fundamental de la mystica Sion: El nuevo convento de señoras naturales, caziques, religiosas descalzas de Corpus Christi, la R. V. M. Sor Petra de San Francisco, su primera fundadora y abadesa.* México, 1727.

Mendieta, Fray Gerónimo de. *Historia eclesiástica indiana.* Ed. Francisco Solano y Pérez-Lila. Madrid, 1973.

Motolinía, Fray Toribio de Benavente. *Memoriales: Libro de oro* (MS JGI 31). Ed. Nancy Joe Dyer. México: El Colegio de México, 1996.

Paredes, Antonio de. *Carta edificante en que el P. Antonio de Paredes de la Compañía de Jesús, da noticia de la exemplar Vida, solidas virtudes, y santa muerte de la Hermana Salvadora de los Santos, India Otomí, Donada del Beaterio de las Carmelitas de la Ciudad de Querétaro.* México, 1762.

Quiñones, Nicolás. *Explicación de la primera regla de la esclarecida madre Santa Clara de Assis, virgen: Dispuesta para las religiosas descalzas del convento de Corpus Christi de México.* México, 1736.

Saint Augustine. *The Confessions.* Trans. John K. Ryan. New York: Doubleday, 1960.

Seoz, Juan Domingo de. *Suma manual de las ceremonias que deben observar las señoras religiosas descalzas del Convento título Corpus Christi.* México: 1737.

Sigüenza y Góngora, Carlos. *Paraíso occidental.* 1683. México: Consejo Nacional para la Cultura y las Artes, 1995.

Teresa of Ávila. *The Book of Her Life.* Trans. Kieran Kavanaugh and Otilio Rodriguez. Indianapolis: Hackett Publishing, 2008.

———. *The Collected Works of St. Teresa of Avila.* Vol. 2. Trans. Kieran Kavanaugh and Otilio Rodriguez. Washington: ICS Publications, 1980.

Urtassum, Juan de. *La gracia triunfante en la vida de Catharina Tegakovita, india iroquesa, y en las otras así de su nación como de esta Nueva España.* México, 1724.

Valadés, Fray Diego. *Retórica Cristiana.* Trans. Tarsicio Herrera Zapién. México: UNAM, FCE, 1989.

Valdés, Joseph Eugenio. *Vida de la venerable madre Sor Sebastiana Josepha de la SS. Trinidad, Religiosa de Coro, y Velo negro en el Sagrado Convento de San Juan de la Penitencia de Religiosas Clarisas de esta Ciudad de México.* México, 1765.

Ximenez de Arellano, Manuel. *Tiernos recuerdos, que excitan el llanto de las religiosas descalzas, indias caziques del convento de Corpus Christi de México, por la muerte del Rev. Padre fray Joseph de Castro.* México, 1753.

Secondary Sources

Abbott, Don Paul. *Rhetoric in the New World: Rhetorical Theory and Practice in Colonial Spanish America*. Columbia: U of South Carolina P, 1996.

Adorno, Rolena. "The Colonial Subject and the Cultural Construction of the Other." *Revista de Estudios Hispánicos* 17–18 (1990–1991): 149–165.

———. "The Indigenous Ethnographer: The "indio ladino" as Historian and Cultural Mediation." *Implicit Understandings: Observing, Reporting, and Reflecting on the Encounters between Europeans and Other Peoples in the Early Modern Era*. Ed. Stuart B. Schwartz. Cambridge: Cambridge UP, 1994. 378–402.

———. *Guaman Poma: Writing and Resistance in Colonial Peru*. Austin: U of Texas P, 1986.

———. "Nuevas perspectivas en los estudios literarios coloniales hispano-americanos." *Revista de Crítica Literaria Latinoamericana* 28 (1988): 11–27.

Aguirre Salvador, Rodolfo. "Un cacicazgo en disputa: Panoaya en el siglo XVIII." *El cacicazgo en Nueva España*. Ed. Margarita Menegus Bornemann and Rodolfo Aguirre Salvador. México: Plaza y Valdés, 2005. 87–135.

Ahlgren, Gillian. *Teresa of Avila and the Politics of Sanctity*. Ithaca: Cornell UP, 1996.

Alberro, Solange. "La iglesia como mediador cultural en la Nueva España, siglos XVI–XVII: La recuperación del complejo simbólico del águila y el nopal." *Entre dos mundos: Fronteras culturales y agentes mediadores*. Sevilla: Escuela de Estudios Hispano-Americanos de Sevilla, 1997. 393–414.

Amerlinck de Corsi, María Concepción, and Manuel Ramos Medina. *Conventos de monjas, fundaciones en el México virreinal*. México: CONDUMEX, 1995.

Araya Espinoza, Alejandra, Ximena Azúa Ríos, and Lucía Invernizzi. "El epistolario de Sor Josefa de los Dolores y Lillo." *Diálogos espirituales: Manuscritos femeninos hispanoamericanos, siglos XVI–XIX*. Ed. Asunción Lavrin and Rosalva Loreto. Puebla: Universidad de las Américas, 2006. 266–299.

Arenal, Electa, and Stacey Schlau. "Leyendo yo y escribiendo ella": The Convent as Intellectual Community." *Journal of Hispanic Philology* 13 (1989): 214–229.

———. "Stratagems of the Strong, Stratagems of the Weak: Autobiographical Prose of the Seventeenth-Century Hispanic Convent." *Tulsa Studies in Women's Literature* 9.1 (1990): 25–42.

———. *Untold Sisters: Hispanic Nuns in Their Own Works*. Trans. Amanda Powell. Albuquerque: U of New Mexico P, 1989.

Arias, Santa. *Retórica, historia y polémica: Bartolomé de las Casas y la tradición inte-lectual renacentista.* Lanham: UP of America, 2001.

Arregui Zamorano, Pilar. *La Audiencia de México según los visitadores: Siglos XVI y XVII.* México: UNAM, 1981.

Bakhtin, Mikhail. *The Dialogic Imagination.* Ed. Michael Holquist. Trans. Caryl Emerson and Michael Holquist. Austin: U of Texas P, 1981.

————. "The Problem of Speech Genres." *Modern Genre Theory.* Ed. David Duff. Essex: Pearson Education, 2000. 82–97.

Ballón Aguirre, Enrique. "Procedimientos discursivos en una epístola-poema colonial (a propósito de cierta carta de un minero peruano a una monja mexicana, siglo XVII)." *La cultura literaria en la América Virreinal: Concurrencias y diferencias.* Ed. José Pascual Buxó. México: UNAM, 1996. 43–99.

Barnes-Karol, Gwendolyn. "Religious Oratory in a Culture of Control." *Culture and Control in Counter-Reformation Spain.* Ed. Anne J. Cruz and Mary Elizabeth Perry. Minneapolis: U of Minnesota P, 1992. 51–77.

Baskes, Jeremy. *Indians, Merchants, and Markets: A Reinterpretation of the Repartimiento and Spanish-Indian Economic Relations in Colonial Oaxaca, 1750–1821.* Stanford: Stanford UP, 2000.

Bauer, Ralph, and José Antonio Mazzotti, eds. *Creole Subjects in the Colonial Americas: Empires, Texts, Identities.* Chapel Hill: U of North Carolina P, 2009.

Bhabha, Homi. *The Location of Culture.* London: Routledge, 1994.

————. "The Other Question: Difference, Discrimination and the Dis-course of Colonialism." *Literatures, Politics and Theory. Papers from the Essex Conference, 1976–84.* Ed. Francis Barker, Peter Hulme, Margaret Iversen, and Diana Loxley. London and New York: Methuen, 1986. 148–172.

Bilinkoff, Jodi. *The Avila of Saint Teresa: Religious Reform in a Sixteenth-Century City.* Ithaca: Cornell UP, 1989.

————. "Confessors, Penitents, and the Construction of Identities in Early Modern Avila." *Culture and Identity in Early Modern Europe, 1500–1800.* Ed. Barbara B. Diefendorf and Carla Hesse. Ann Arbor: U of Michigan P, 1994. 83–100.

Bleznick, Donald W. "Epistolography in Golden Age Spain." *Studies in Honor of Gerald E. Wade.* Ed. Sylvia Bowman et al. Madrid: José Porrúa Turanzas, 1979. 11–21.

Brading, David. *Church and State in Bourbon Mexico: The Diocese of Michoacán, 1749–1810.* Cambridge: Cambridge UP, 1994.

————. *The First America: The Spanish Monarchy, Creole Patriots, and the Liberal State, 1492–1867.* Cambridge: Cambridge UP, 1991.

————. *Mexican Phoenix: Our Lady of Guadalupe: Image and Tradition Across Five Centuries*. Cambridge: Cambridge UP, 2001.

————. *Miners and Merchants in Bourbon Mexico, 1763–1810*. Cambridge: Cambridge UP, 1971.

Bravo Arriaga, María Dolores. *La excepción y la regla: Estudios sobre espiritualidad y cultura en la Nueva España*. México: UNAM, 1997.

Briggs, Charles, and Richard Bauman. "Genre, Intertextuality, and Social Power." *Journal of Linguistic Anthropology* 2 (1992): 131–172.

Brotherston, Gordon. *Painted Books from Mexico*. London: British Museum P, 1995.

Burke, Peter. "How to Be a Counter-Reformation Saint." *Religion and Society in Early Modern Europe, 1500–1800*. Ed. Kaspar von Greyerz. London: George Allen and Unwin, 1984. 45–55.

Burkhart, Louise. *Holy Wednesday: A Nahua Drama from Early Colonial Mexico*. Philadelphia: U of Pennsylvania P, 1996.

————. "Mexica Women on the Home Front: Housework and Religion in Aztec Mexico." *Indian Women of Early Mexico*. Ed. Susan Schroeder, Stephanie Wood, and Robert Haskett. Norman: U of Oklahoma P, 1997. 25–54.

————. "Pious Performances: Christian Pageantry and Native Identity in Early Colonial Mexico." *Native Traditions in the Postconquest World*. Eds. Elizabeth Hill Boone and Tom Cummins. Washington, DC: Dumbarton Oaks Research Library, 1998. 361–381.

Burns, Kathryn. *Colonial Habits: Convents and the Spiritual Economy of Cuzco, Peru*. Durham: Duke UP, 1999.

————. "Unfixing Race." *Rereading the Black Legend: The Discourses of Religious and Racial Difference in the Renaissance Empires*. Ed. Margaret Greer, Walter Mignolo, and Maureen Quilligan. Chicago: U of Chicago P, 2007. 188–202.

Cahill, David. "Colour by Numbers: Racial and Ethnic Categories in the Viceroyalty of Peru, 1532–1824." *Journal of Latin American Studies* 26 (1994): 325–346.

Cañeque, Alejandro. *The King's Living Image: The Culture and Politics of Viceregal Power in Colonial Mexico*. New York: Routledge, 2004.

Carrera, Magali. *Imagining Identity in New Spain: Race, Lineage, and the Colonial Body in Portraiture and Casta Paintings*. Austin: U of Texas P, 2003.

Castañeda Delgado, Paulino. "La condición miserable del indio y sus privilegios." *Anuario de Estudios Americanos* 28 (1971): 245–258.

Castañeda Guzmán, Luis. *Templo de los príncipes y monasterio de Nuestra Señora de los Ángeles*. México: Instituto Oaxaqueño de las Culturas, 1993.

Castro-Klarén, Sara. "Historiography on the Ground: The Toledo Circle and Guamán Poma." *The Latin American Subaltern Studies Reader*. Ed. Ileana Rodríguez. Durham: Duke UP, 2001. 143–171.

Chance, John K. *Conquest of the Sierra: Spaniards and Indians in Colonial Oaxaca*. Norman: U of Oklahoma P, 1989.

———. "Indian Elites in Late Colonial Mesoamerica." *Caciques and Their People: A Volume in Honor of Ronald Spores*. Ed. Joyce Marcus and Judith F. Zeitlin. Ann Arbor: University of Michigan Museum of Anthropology, 1994. 45–65.

———. *Race and Class in Colonial Oaxaca*. Stanford: U of California P, 1978.

Chang-Rodríguez, Raquel. *El discurso disidente: Ensayos de literatura colonial peruana*. Lima: Pontificia Universidad Católica del Perú, 1991.

Chipman, Donald. *Moctezuma's Children: Aztec Royalty under Spanish Rule, 1520–1700*. Austin: U of Texas P, 2005.

Chowning, Margaret. *Rebellious Nuns: The Troubled History of a Mexican Convent, 1752–1863*. New York: Oxford UP, 2006.

Christian, William. *Local Religion in Sixteenth-Century Spain*. Princeton: Princeton UP, 1981.

Cline, Sarah. "The Spiritual Conquest Reexamined: Baptism and Christian Marriage in Early Sixteenth-Century Mexico." *The Church in Colonial Latin America*. Ed. John F. Schwaller. Wilmington: Scholarly Resources, 2000. 73–101.

Colie, Rosalie. "Genre-Systems and the Functions of Literature." *Modern Genre Theory*. Ed. David Duff. Essex: Pearson Education, 2000. 148–166.

———. *The Resources of Kind: Genre Theory in the Renaissance*. Berkeley: U of California P, 1973.

Cook, Elizabeth. *Epistolary Bodies: Gender and Genre in the Eighteenth-Century Republic of Letters*. Stanford: Stanford UP, 1996.

Cope, R. Douglas. *The Limits of Racial Domination: Plebeian Society in Colonial Mexico City, 1660–1720*. Madison: U of Wisconsin P, 1994.

Coronil, Fernando. "Listening to the Subaltern: The Poetics of Neocolonial States." *Poetics Today* 15 (1994): 643–658.

Cortés, Rocío. "(De)mystifying Sacred Geographical Spaces in Hernando de Alvarado Tezozomoc's *Crónica mexicana*. *Mapping Colonial Spanish America: Places and Commonplaces of Identity, Culture, and Experience*. Ed. Santa Arias and Mariselle Meléndez. Lewisburg: Bucknell UP, 2002. 68–83.

———. "Los estudios coloniales hispanoamericanos: Reconsideraciones y aperturas." *Revista de Estudios Hispánicos* 35 (2001): 577–583.

Cruz, Anne J., and Mary Elizabeth Perry, eds. "Introduction." *Culture and Control in Counter-Reformation Spain*. Minneapolis: U of Minnesota P, 1992. ix–xxiii.

Dean, Carolyn. *Inka Bodies and the Body of Christ: Corpus Christi in Colonial Cuzco, Peru*. Durham: Duke UP, 1999.

Dean, Carolyn, and Dana Leibsohn. "Hybridity and Its Discontents: Considering Visual Culture in Colonial Spanish America." *Colonial Latin American Review* 12.1 (2003): 5–35.

De Certeau, Michel. *The Mystic Fable*. Vol. 1. Chicago: U of Chicago P, 1992.

———. *The Writing of History*. New York: Columbia UP, 1988.

Delacampagne, Christian. "Racism and the West: From Praxis to Logos." *Anatomy of Racism*. Ed. David Theo Goldberg. Minneapolis: U of Minnesota P, 1990. 83–88.

De Lauretis, Teresa. *Technologies of Gender: Essays on Theory, Film, and Fiction*. Bloomington: Indiana UP, 1987.

Díaz, Mónica. "La identidad étnica de las monjas indígenas: Continuidad y ruptura desde el claustro." *Letras femeninas* 35.1 (2009): 255–274.

———. "The Indigenous Nuns of Corpus Christi: Race and Spirituality in Colonial Mexico." *Religion in New Spain*. Ed. Stafford Poole and Susan Schroeder. Albuquerque: U of New Mexico P, 2007. 179–192.

Díaz Balsera, Viviana. *The Pyramid under the Cross: Franciscan Discourses of Evangelization and the Nahua Christian Subject in Sixteenth-Century Mexico*. Tucson: U of Arizona P, 2005.

Diccionario de autoridades. Edición facsímil de 1737. Madrid: Gredos, 1963.

Donahue, Darcy. "Writing Lives: Nuns and Confessors as Auto/Biographers in Early Modern Spain." *Journal of Hispanic Philology* 13.3 (1989): 230–239.

Douay-Rheims Bible. Rockford: Tan Books, 2000.

Dubrow, Heather. *Genre*. London: Methuen, 1982.

Eagleton, Mary. "Genre and Gender." *Modern Genre Theory*. Ed. David Duff. Essex: Pearson Education, 2000. 250–262.

Eich, Jennifer. *The Other Mexican Muse: Sor María Anna Águeda de San Ignacio, 1695–1765*. New Orleans: UP of the South, 2004.

Eich, Jennifer, Jeanne Gillespie, and Lucia G. Harrison, eds. *Women's Voices and the Politics of the Spanish Empire: From Convent Cell to Imperial Court*. New Orleans, UP of the South, 2008.

Ennis, Arthur. "The Conflict between the Regular and Secular Clergy." Ed. Richard Greenleaf. *The Roman Catholic Church in Colonial Latin America*. New York: Knopf, 1971. 63–72.

Eriksen, Thomas H. "Ethnicity, Race, Class, and Nation." *Ethnicity*. Ed. John Hutchinson and Anthony D. Smith. Oxford: Oxford UP, 1996. 28–34.

Esteve Barba, Francisco. *Historiografía indiana*. España: Gredos, 1992.

Fanon, Frantz. *The Wretched of the Earth*. Trans. Richard Philcox. 1961. New York: Grove P, 2004.

Farris, Nancy. *Maya Society under Colonial Rule: The Collective Enterprise of Survival*. Princeton: Princeton UP, 1984.

Few, Martha. *Women Who Live Evil Lives: Gender, Religion, and the Politics of Power in Colonial Guatemala*. Austin: U of Texas P, 2002.

Finke, Laurie. *Feminist Theory, Women's Writing*. Ithaca: Cornell UP, 1992.

Fisher, Andrew, and Matthew O'Hara, eds. "Introduction." *Imperial Subjects: Race and Identity in Colonial Latin America*. Durham: Duke UP, 2009. 1–37.

Foucault, Michel. *The History of Sexuality*. Volume 1: *An Introduction*. Trans. Robert Hurley. New York: Pantheon Books, 1978.

———. *Power/Knowledge: Selected Interviews and Other Writings, 1972–1977*. Ed. and trans. Colin Gordon. New York: Pantheon Books, 1980.

Fowler, Alastair. *Kinds of Literature: An Introduction to the Theory of Genres and Modes*. Cambridge: Harvard UP, 1982.

Foz y Foz, Pilar. *La Revolución pedagógica en la Nueva España, 1754–1820*. Vol. 1. Madrid: Instituto de Estudios y Documentos Históricos, 1981.

Franco, Jean. *Plotting Women: Gender and Representation in Mexico*. New York: Columbia UP, 1989.

Frye, David. *Indians into Mexicans: History and Identity in a Mexican Town*. Austin: U of Texas P, 1996.

Gallagher, Ann Miriam. "The Family Background of the Nuns of Two Monasterios in Colonial Mexico: Santa Clara, Querétaro; and Corpus Christi, Mexico City (1724–1822)." Diss. Catholic University of America, 1972.

———. "Las monjas indígenas del monasterio de Corpus Christi de la ciudad de México: 1724–1821." *Las mujeres latinoamericanas: Perspectivas históricas*. Ed. Asunción Lavrin. México: FCE Tierra Firme, 1985. 177–201.

García Icazbalceta, Joaquín. *Documentos para la historia de México*. Vol. 1. México: Librería de J. M. Andrade, 1858.

Gibson, Charles. *The Aztecs under Spanish Rule*. Stanford: Stanford UP, 1964.

Giles, Mary, ed. "Introduction." *Women in the Inquisition: Spain and the New World*. Baltimore: Johns Hopkins UP, 1999. 1–15.

Gómez Canedo, Lino. *La educación de los marginados durante la época colonial: Escuelas y colegios para indios y mestizos en la Nueva España*. México: Porrúa, 1982.

Gonzalbo Aizpuru, Pilar. *Las mujeres en la Nueva España: Educación y vida cotidiana*. México: El Colegio de México, 1987.

———. "Tradición y ruptura en la educación femenina del siglo XVI." *Presencia y transparencia: La mujer en la historia de México*. Ed. Carmen Ramos Escandón. México: El Colegio de México, 1987. 33–59.

González Echevarría, Roberto. *Isla a su vuelo fugitiva: Ensayos críticos sobre literatura hispanoamericana*. Madrid: José Porrúa Turanzas, 1983.

González Fernández, Fidel, Eduardo Chávez Sánchez, and José Luis Guerrero Rosado. *El encuentro de la Virgen de Guadalupe y Juan Diego*. México: Porrúa, 2000.

González y González, Luis. *Atraídos por la Nueva España*. México: Clío, 1995.

Good, Catherine. "Indigenous Peoples in Central and Western Mexico." *Supplement to the Handbook of Middle American Indians*. Ed. John D. Monaghan. Austin: U of Texas P, 2000. 120–149.

Graubart, Karen B. *With Our Labor and Sweat: Indigenous Women and the Formation of Colonial Society in Peru, 1550–1700*. Stanford: Stanford UP, 2007.

Greenspan, Kate. "Autohagiography and Medieval Women's Spiritual Autobiography." *Gender and Text in the Later Middle Ages*. Ed. Jane Chance. Gainesville: UP of Florida, 1996. 216–236.

———. "The Autobiographic Tradition in Medieval Women's Devotional Writing." *Auto/hagiography Studies* 6 (1991): 157–168.

Greer, Allan. "Iroquois Virgin: The Story of Catherine Tekakwitha in New France and New Spain." *Colonial Saints: Discovering the Holy in the Americas, 1500–1800*. Ed. Allan Greer and Jodi Bilinkoff. New York: Routledge, 2003. 235–250.

———. *Mohawk Saint: Catherine Tekakwitha and the Jesuits*. Oxford: Oxford UP, 2005.

Gruzinski, Serge. *The Conquest of Mexico*. Cambridge: Polity P, 1993.

Guardino, Peter. *Peasants, Politics, and the Formation of Mexico's National State: Guerrero, 1800–1857*. Stanford: Stanford UP, 1996.

———. *The Time of Liberty: Popular Political Culture in Oaxaca, 1750–1850*. Durham, N.C.: Duke UP, 2005.

Hanks, William F. *Intertexts: Writings on Language, Utterance, and Context*. Lanham: Rowan & Littlefield, 2000.

Haskett, Robert. "Activist or Adulteress? The Life and Struggle of Doña Josefa María of Tepoztlan." *Indian Women of Early Mexico*. Ed. Susan Schroeder, Stephanie Wood, and Robert Haskett. Norman: U of Oklahoma P, 1997. 145–163.

Herpoel, Sonja. *A la zaga de Santa Teresa: Autobiografías por mandato*. Amsterdam: Rodopi, 1999.

Herrejón Peredo, Carlos. "Marcel Bataillon y el humanismo mexicano en el siglo XVI." *Relaciones: Estudios de Historia y Sociedad* 21 (2000): 187–199.

Hill, Ruth. *Hierarchy, Commerce, and Fraud in Bourbon Spanish America: A Postal Inspector's Exposé.* Nashville: Vanderbilt UP, 2005.

Holler, Jacqueline. *Escogidas Plantas: Nuns and Beatas in Mexico City, 1531–1601.* New York: Columbia UP, 2005.

Howe, Elizabeth Teresa. *Education and Women in the Early Modern Hispanic World.* Burlington: Ashgate, 2008.

Hulme, Peter. "Subversive Archipelagos: Colonial Discourse and the Break-Up of Continental Theory." *Dispositio* 14.36–38 (1989): 1–23.

Ibsen, Kristine. *Women's Spiritual Autobiography in Spanish America.* Gainesville: UP of Florida, 1999.

Israel, Jonathan. *Race, Class and Politics in Colonial Mexico, 1610–1670.* Oxford: Oxford UP, 1975.

Jaffary, Nora E., ed. "Introduction." *Gender, Race, and Religion in the Colonization of the Americas.* Burlington: Ashgate, 2007. 1–11.

JanMohamed, Abdul. "The Economy of Manichean Allegory." *The Post-Colonial Studies Reader.* Ed. Bill Ashcroft, Gareth Griffiths, and Helen Tiffin. London: Routledge, 1995. 18–23.

Karttunen, Frances. "Indigenous Writing as a Vehicle of Postconquest Continuity and Change in Mesoamerica." *Native Traditions in the Postconquest World.* Ed. Elizabeth Hill Boone and Tom Cummins. Washington, DC: Dumbarton Oaks Research Library, 1998. 421–447.

Katzew, Ilona. *Casta Painting: Images of Race in Eighteenth-Century Mexico.* New Haven: Yale UP, 2004.

Kellogg, Susan. "From Parallel and Equivalent to Separate but Unequal: Tenochca Mexica Women, 1500–1700." *Indian Women of Early Mexico.* Ed. Susan Schroeder, Stephanie Wood, and Robert Haskett. Norman: U of Oklahoma P, 1997. 123–143.

———. *Law and the Transformation of Aztec Culture, 1500–1700.* Norman: U of Oklahoma P, 1995.

———. *Weaving the Past: A History of Latin America's Indigenous Women from the Prehispanic Period to the Present.* Oxford: Oxford UP, 2005.

Kirk, Stephanie L. *Convent Life in Colonial Mexico: A Tale of Two Communities.* Gainesville: UP of Florida, 2007.

Klor de Alva, Jorge. "Aztec Spirituality and Nahuatized Christianity." *South and Meso-American Native Spirituality: From the Cult of the Feathered Serpent to the Theology of Liberation.* Ed. Gary H. Gossen. New York: Crossroad Publishing Co., 1997. 173–197.

Knight, Alan. *Mexico: The Colonial Era.* Cambridge: Cambridge UP, 2002.

Konetzke, Richard, ed. *Colección de documentos para la historia de la formación social de Hispanoamérica, 1493–1810.* Vol. 3. Madrid: Consejo Superior de Investigaciones Científicas, 1953.

Kuznesof, Elizabeth Anne. "Ethnic and Gender Influences on 'Spanish' Creole Society in Colonial Spanish America." *Colonial Latin American Review* 4 (1995): 153–176.

Lavrin, Asunción. *Brides of Christ: Conventual Life in Colonial Mexico.* Stanford: Stanford UP, 2008.

———. "De su puño y letra: Epístolas conventuales." *El monacato femenino en el imperio español.* Ed. Manuel Ramos Medina. México: Centro de Estudios de Historia de México, 1995. 43–61.

———. "Female Religious." *Cities and Society in Colonial Latin America.* Ed. Louisa S. Hoberman and Susan M. Socolow. Albuquerque: U of New Mexico P, 1986. 165–195.

———. "Indian Brides of Christ: Creating New Spaces for Indigenous Women in New Spain." *Mexican Studies/Estudios Mexicanos* 15 (1999): 225–260.

———. "Introduction." *Latin American Women: Historical Perspectives.* Ed. Asunción Lavrin. Westport: Greenwood P, 1978. 3–22.

———. "Religious Life of Mexican Women in the XVIII Century." Diss. Harvard University, 1963.

———. "Unlike Sor Juana? The Model Nun in the Religious Literature of Colonial Mexico." *Feminist Perspectives on Sor Juana Inés de la Cruz.* Ed. Stephanie Merrim. Detroit: Wayne State UP, 1991. 61–83.

———."La vida femenina como experiencia religiosa: Biografía y hagiografía en Hispanoamérica colonial." *Colonial Latin American Review* 2 (1993): 27–51.

———. "Women and Religion in Spanish America." *Women and Religion in America: The Colonial and Revolutionary Periods.* Vol. 2. Ed. Rosemary R. Ruether and Rosemary S. Keller. San Francisco: Harper & Row, 1981. 42–78.

Lavrin, Asunción, and Rosalva Loreto, eds. *Diálogos espirituales: Manuscritos femeninos hispanoamericanos, siglos XVI–XIX.* Puebla: U de las Américas, 2006.

Lerner, Gerda. *The Creation of Feminist Consciousness: From the Middle Ages to Eighteen-Seventy.* New York: Oxford UP, 1993.

———. *Living with History/Making Social Change.* Chapel Hill: U of North Carolina P, 2009.

Lewis, Laura A. *Hall of Mirrors: Power, Witchcraft, and Caste in Colonial Mexico.* Durham: Duke UP, 2003.

Llaguno, José. *La personalidad jurídica del indio en el III Concilio Provincial Mexicano, 1585*. México: Porrúa, 1963.

Lockhart, James. *The Nahuas after the Conquest: A Social and Cultural History of the Indians of Central Mexico, Sixteenth through Eighteenth Centuries*. Stanford: Stanford UP, 1992.

—————. *Nahuas and Spaniards: Postconquest Central Mexican History and Philology*. Los Angeles: Stanford UP, 1991.

López Sarrelangue, Delfina Esmeralda. *La nobleza indígena de Pátzcuaro en la época virreinal*. México: UNAM, 1965.

Ludmer, Josefina. "Las tretas del débil." *La sartén por el mango: Encuentro de escritoras latinoamericanas*. Ed. Patricia Elena González. Río Piedras: Huracán, 1984. 47–54.

—————. "Tricks of the Weak." *Feminist Perspectives on Sor Juana Inés de la Cruz*. Ed. Stephanie Merrim. Detroit: Wayne State UP, 1990. 86–93.

Luján, Ángel Luis. *Retóricas españolas del siglo XVI: El foco de Valencia*. Madrid: Consejo Superior de Investigaciones Científicas, 1999.

Lynch, John. *Bourbon Spain, 1700–1808*. London: Blackwell, 1989.

Machuca, Laura. "Como la sal en el agua": La decadencia del cacicazgo de Tehuantepec (siglos XVI–XVIII)." *El cacicazgo en Nueva España y Filipinas*. Ed. Margarita Menegus Bornemann and Rodolfo Aguirre Salvador. México: Plaza y Valdés, 2005. 165–195.

Majfud, Jorge. *La narración de lo invisible: Los significados ideológicos de América Latina*. Alicante: Biblioteca Virtual Miguel de Cervantes, 2007.

Mallon, Florencia. *Peasant and Nation: The Making of Postcolonial Mexico and Peru*. Berkeley: U of California P, 1995.

—————. "The Promise and Dilemma of Subaltern Studies: Perspectives from Latin American History." *American Historical Review* 99.5 (1994): 1491–1515.

Martínez, María Elena. *Genealogical Fictions: Limpieza de Sangre, Religion, and Gender in Colonial Mexico*. Stanford: Stanford UP, 2008.

Mazín Gómez, Óscar. *El Cabildo Catedral de Valladolid de Michoacán*. México: El Colegio de Michoacán, 1996.

McKnight, Kathryn Joy. *The Mystic of Tunja: The Writings of Madre Castillo, 1671–1742*. Amherst: U of Massachusetts P, 1997.

McNamara, Jo Ann Kay. *Sisters in Arms: Catholic Nuns through Two Millennia*. Cambridge: Harvard UP, 1996.

McNay, Lois. *Gender and Agency: Reconfiguring the Subject in Feminist and Social Theory*. Cambridge: Blackwell, 2000.

Meléndez, Mariselle. "Eighteenth Century Spanish America: Historical Dimensions and New Theoretical Approaches." *Revista de Estudios Hispánicos* 34 (2001): 615–632.

————."El perfil económico de la identidad racial en los *Apuntes* de las indias caciques del convento de Corpus Christi." *Revista de Crítica Literaria Latinoamericana* 46 (1997): 115–133.

Menegus Bornemann, Margarita. "El cacicazgo en Nueva España." *El cacicazgo en Nueva España y Filipinas*. Ed. Margarita Menegus Bornemann and Rodolfo Aguirre Salvador. México: Plaza y Valdés, 2005. 13–69.

————. "El Colegio de San Carlos Borromeo: Un proyecto para la creación de un clero indígena en el siglo XVIII." *Saber y poder en México: Siglos XVI al XX*. Ed. Margarita Menegus. México: UNAM, 1997. 197–243.

Merrim, Stephanie. *Early Modern Women's Writing and Sor Juana Inés de la Cruz*. Nashville: Vanderbilt UP, 1999.

Mignolo, Walter. "Afterword: From Colonial Discourse to Colonial Semiosis." *Dispositio* 36–38 (1989): 333–337.

————. "Cartas, crónicas y relaciones del descubrimiento y la conquista." *Historia de la literatura hispanoamericana*. Ed. Luis Iñigo Madrigal. Vol 1. Madrid: Cátedra, 1982. 57–80.

————. "Colonial and Postcolonial Discourse: Cultural Critique or Academic Colonialism?" *Latin American Research Review* 28.3 (1993): 120–134.

————. *The Darker Side of the Renaissance: Literacy, Territoriality, and Colonization*. Ann Arbor: U of Michigan P, 1995.

————. *The Idea of Latin America*. Malden: Blackwell, 2005.

————. "La lengua, la letra, el territorio o la crisis de los estudios literarios coloniales." *Dispositio* 28–29 (1986): 137–160.

————. *Local Histories/Global Designs*. Princeton: Princeton UP, 2000.

Miller, Carolyn R. "Genre as Social Action." *Genre and the New Rhetoric*. Ed. Aviva Freedman and Peter Medway. London: Taylor and Francis, 1994. 23–42.

Moraña, Mabel. "Sor Juana y sus otros: Núñez de Miranda o el amor del censor." *Sor Juana Inés de la Cruz y sus contemporáneos*. Ed. Margo Glantz. México: UNAM/CONDUMEX, 1998. 319–331.

————. *Viaje al silencio: Exploraciones del discurso barroco*. México: UNAM, 1998.

Mörner, Magnus. *Race Mixture in the History of Latin America*. Boston:Little, Brown, 1967.

Muriel, Josefina. *Conventos de monjas en la Nueva España*. 1946. México: Jus, 1995.

————. *Cultura femenina novohispana*. México: UNAM, 1994.

————. *Las indias caciques de Corpus Christi*. México: UNAM, 1963.

Murphy, James. *Rhetoric in the Middle Ages: A History of Rhetorical Theory from Saint Augustine to the Renaissance*. Berkeley: U of California P, 1974.

Myers, Kathleen. "Crossing Boundaries: Defining the Field of Female Religious Writing in Colonial Latin America." *Colonial Latin American Review* 9 (2000): 151–165.

———. "The Mystic Triad in Colonial Mexican Nuns' Discourse: Divine Author, Visionary Scribe, and Clerical Mediator." *Colonial Latin American Historical Review* 6 (1997): 479–524.

———. *Neither Saints nor Sinners: Writing the Lives of Women in Spanish America*. Oxford: Oxford UP, 2003.

———. "Recent Trends in the Study of Women and Religion in Colonial Mexico." *Latin American Research Review* 43.2 (2008): 290–301.

———. "Sor Juana's *Respuesta*: Rewriting the *Vitae*." *Revista Canadiense de Estudios Hispánicos* 14.3 (1990): 459–471.

———. "Sor Juana y su mundo: La influencia mediativa del clero en las vidas de religiosos y monjas." *Revista de Literatura* 61 (1999): 35–59.

———. "Testimony for Canonization or Proof of Blasphemy? The New Spanish Inquisition and the Hagiographic Biography of Catarina de San Juan." *Women and the Inquisition*. Ed. Mary E. Giles. Johns Hopkins UP, 1993.

———. *Word from New Spain: The Spiritual Autobiography of Madre María de San José, 1656–1719*. Liverpool: Liverpool UP, 1993.

Myers, Kathleen, and Amanda Powell. *A Wild Country Out in the Garden: The Spiritual Journals of a Colonial Mexican Nun*. Bloomington: Indiana UP, 1999.

Nesvig, Martin Austin. "The 'Indian Question' and the Case of Tlatelolco." *Local Religion in Colonial Mexico*. Ed. Martin Austin Nesvig. Albuquerque: U of New Mexico P, 2006. 63–89.

———. "Introduction." *Local Religion in Colonial Mexico*. Albuquerque: U of New Mexico P, 2006. xvii–xxvii.

O'Hara, Mattthew. *A Flock Divided: Race, Religion, and Politics in Mexico*. Durham: Duke UP, 2010.

———. "*Miserables* and Citizens: Indians, Legal Pluralism, and Religious Practice in Early Republican Mexico." *Religious Culture in Modern Mexico*. Ed. Martin Austin Nesvig. Lanham: Rowman and Littlefield, 2007. 14–34.

O'Malley, John. "Content and Rhetorical Forms in Sixteenth-Century Treatises on Preaching." *Renaissance Eloquence: Studies in the Theory and Practice of Renaissance Rhetoric*. Ed. James Murphy. Berkeley: U of California P, 1983. 283–252.

Ortiz, Fernando. *Contrapunteo cubano del tabaco y el azúcar*. Caracas: Biblioteca Ayacucho, 1978.

Ortner, Sherry. "Specifying Agency: The Comaroffs and Their Critics." *Interventions* 3 (2001): 76–84.

Osowski, Edward W. "Carriers of Saints: Traveling Alms Collectors and Nahua Gender Roles." *Local Religion in Colonial Mexico*. Ed. Martin Austin Nesvig. Albuquerque: U of New Mexico P, 2006. 155–186.

Owens, Sarah. "Subversive Obedience: Confessional Letters by Eighteenth-Century Mexican Colonial Nuns." Diss. University of Arizona, 2000.

Pardo, Osvaldo F. *The Origins of Mexican Catholicism: Nahua Rituals and Christian Sacraments in Sixteenth-Century Mexico*. Ann Arbor: U of Michigan P, 2006.

Pastor, Rodolfo. *Campesinos y reformas: La mixteca, 1700–1856*. México: El Colegio de México, 1987.

Perelmuter Pérez, Rosa. "La estructura retórica de la *Respuesta a Sor Filotea*." *Hispanic Review* 51 (1983): 147–158.

———. *Los límites de la femineidad en Sor Juana Inés de la Cruz*. Madrid: Iberoamericana, 2004.

Perry, Mary Elizabeth. *Gender and Disorder in Early Modern Seville*. Princeton: Princeton UP, 1990.

Phelan, John Leddy. *The Millennial Kingdom of the Franciscans in the New World*. Berkeley: U of California P, 1970.

Picón Salas, Mariano. *De la conquista a la independencia*. México: FCE, 1994.

Poole, Stafford. "Church Law on the Ordination of Indians and Castas in New Spain." *Hispanic American Historical Review* 61 (1981): 637–650.

———. "The Declining Image of the Indian among Churchmen in Sixteenth-Century New Spain." *Indian Religious Relations in Colonial Spanish America*. Ed. Susan Ramírez. Syracuse: Maxwell School of Citizenship and Public Affaires, 1989. 11–19.

Powers, Karen Vieira. *Women in the Crucible of Conquest: The Gendered Genesis of Spanish American Society, 1500–1600*. Albuquerque: U of New Mexico P, 2005.

Prakash, Gyan. "La imposibilidad de la historia subalterna." *Convergencia de tiempos: Estudios subalternos/contextos latinoamericanos estado, cultura, subalternidad*. Ed. Ileana Rodríguez. Amsterdam: Rodopi, 2001. 61–69.

———. "Subaltern Studies as Postcolonial Criticism." *American Historical Review* 99.5 (1994): 1475–1490.

Pratt, Mary Louise. *Imperial Eyes: Travel Writing and Transculturation*. London: Routledge, 1992.

Quijano, Aníbal. "La colonialidad del poder y la experiencia cultural latinoamericana." *Pueblo, época y desarrollo: La sociología de América Latina*. Ed. Roberto Briceño-León and Heinz R. Sonntag. Caracas: Nueva Sociedad, 1998. 27–38.

Quispe-Agnoli, Rocío. *La fe andida en la escritura: Resistencia e identidad en la obra de Guaman Poma de Ayala.* Lima: Universidad Nacional Mayor de San Marcos, 2006.

Rabasa, José. *Inventing America: Spanish Historiography and the Formation of Eurocentrism.* Norman: U of Oklahoma P, 1993.

———. "Of Zapatismo: Reflections on the Folkloric and the Impossible in a Subaltern Insurection." *The Politics of Culture in the Shadow of Capital.* Ed. Lisa Lowe and David Lloyd. Durham: Duke UP, 1997. 399–432.

Ramírez Castañeda, Elisa. *La educación indígena en México.* México: UNAM, 2006.

Ramos Medina, Manuel. *Imagen de santidad en un mundo profano.* México: Iberoamericana, 1990.

———. *Místicas y descalzas.* México: CONDUMEX, 1997.

Ricard, Robert. *The Spiritual Conquest of Mexico.* Berkeley: U of California P, 1966.

Rivera, Luis. "The Theological Juridical Debate." *The Church in Colonial Latin America.* Ed. John F. Schwaller. Wilmington: Scholarly Resources, 2000. 3–26.

Rodríguez, Ileana. "Reading Subalterns across Texts, Disciplines, and Theories: From Representation to Recognition." *The Latin American Subaltern Studies Reader.* Ed. Ileana Rodríguez. Durham: Duke UP, 2001. 1–32.

Rodríguez Garrido, José Antonio. "Espinoza Medrano: La recepción del sermón barroco y la defensa de los americanos." *Relecturas del Barroco de Indias.* Ed. Mabel Moraña. Hanover: Ediciones del Norte, 1994. 149–169.

Romero, María de los Ángeles. *El sol y la cruz: Los pueblos indios de Oaxaca colonial.* México: CIESAS, 1996.

Ross, Kathleen. *The Baroque Narrative of Carlos de Sigüenza y Góngora: A New Paradise.* Cambridge: Cambridge UP, 1993.

Routt, Kristin Eva. "Authorizing Orthodoxy: The Body and the *Camino de perfección* in Spanish American Colonial Convent Writings." Diss. Indiana University, 1998.

Rubial García, Antonio. "Espejo de virtudes, sabrosa narración, emulación patriótica: La literatura hagiográfica sobre los venerables no canonizados de la Nueva España." *La literatura novohispana.* Ed. José Pascual Buxó y Arnulfo Herrera. México: UNAM, 1994. 89–110.

———. "La exaltación de los humillados: Indios y santidad en las ciudades novohispanas del siglo XVIII." *Actas del III Congreso Internacional Mediadores Culturales: Ciudades mestizas: Intercambios y continuidades en la expansión occidental, siglos XVI al XIX.* México: CONDUMEX/INAH, 2001. 139–155.

Said, Edward. *Culture and Imperialism*. New York: Knopf, 1994.

———. *Orientalism*. New York: Pantheon, 1978.

Sampson Vera Tudela, Elisa. *Colonial Angels: Narratives of Gender and Spirituality in México, 1580–1750*. Austin: U of Texas P, 2000.

———. "Fashioning a Cacique Nun: From Saint's Lives to Indian Lives in Spanish America." *Gender & History* 9 (1997): 171–200.

Sarabia Viejo, María Justina. "La Concepción y Corpus Christi: Raza y vida conventual femenina en México, siglo XVIII." *Manifestaciones religiosas en el mundo colonial americano*. Ed. Clara García Ayluardo and Manuel Ramos Medina. México: INAH/UIA/CONDUMEX, 1997. 179–192.

———. "Monacato femenino y problemática indígena en la Nueva España del siglo XVIII." *Congreso Internacional del monacato femenino en España, Portugal y America, 1492–1992*. Madrid: U de León, 1993. 173–200.

Schlau, Stacey. *Spanish American Women's Use of the Word: Colonial through Contemporary Narratives*. Tucson: U of Arizona P, 2001.

Schroeder, Susan. "Introduction." *Indian Women of Early Mexico*. Ed. Susan Schroeder, Stephanie Wood, and Robert Haskett. Norman: U of Oklahoma P, 1997. 3–22.

Schwaller, John Frederick. "The Ordenanza del Patronazgo in New Spain, 1574–1600." *The Americas* 42.3 (1986): 253–274.

Seed, Patricia. "Colonial and Postcolonial Discourse." *Latin American Research Review* 26. 3 (1991): 181–200.

———. "Social Dimensions of Race: Mexico City, 1753." *Hispanic American Historical Review* 62 (1982): 569–606.

Silverblatt, Irene. *Moon, Sun and Witches: Gender Ideologies and Class in Inca and Colonial Peru*. Princeton: Princeton UP, 1987.

Slade, Carole. *St. Teresa of Avila: Author of a Heroic Life*. Berkeley: U of California P, 1995.

Smith, Anthony D. *National Identity*. Reno: U of Nevada P, 1991.

Smith, Hilary Dansey. *Preaching in the Spanish Golden Age: A Study of Some Preachers of the Reign of Philip III*. Oxford: Oxford UP, 1978.

Socolow, Susan Migden. *The Women of Colonial Latin America*. Cambridge: Cambridge UP, 2000.

Soriano Hernández, Silvia. *Lucha y resistencia indígena en el México colonial*. México: UNAM, 1994.

Spivak, Gayatri. "Can the Subaltern Speak?" *Marxism and the Interpretation of Culture*. Ed. Cary Nelson and Lawrence Grossberg. Urbana: U of Illinois P, 1988. 271–313.

Spores, Ronald. *The Mixtec Kings and Their People*. Norman: U of Oklahoma P, 1967.

————. "Mixteca Cacicas." *Indian Women of Early Mexico*. Ed. Susan Schroeder, Stephanie Wood, and Robert Haskett. Norman: U of Oklahoma P, 1997. 185–197.

Stern, Steve J. *Peru's Indian Peoples and the Challenge of Spanish Conquest: Huamanga to 1640*. Madison: U of Wisconsin P, 1993.

————. *The Secret History of Gender: Women, Men, and Power in Late Colonial Mexico*. Chapel Hill: U of North Carolina P, 1995.

Stolcke, Verena. "Invaded Women: Gender, Race, and Class in the Formation of Colonial Society." *Women, "Race," and Writing in the Early Modern Period*. Ed. Margo Hendricks and Patricia Parker. London: Routledge, 1994. 272–365.

Sweet, David. "The Ibero-American Frontier Mission in Native American History." *The New Latin American Mission History*. Lincoln: U of Nebraska P, 1995. 1–48.

Tavárez, David. "Legally Indian: Inquisitorial Readings of Indigenous Identity in New Spain." *Imperial Subjects: Race and Identity in Colonial Latin America*. Ed. Andrew Fisher and Matthew O'Hara. Durham, N.C.: Duke UP, 2009. 81–100.

Taylor, William. *Landlord and Peasant in Colonial Oaxaca*. Stanford: Stanford UP, 1972.

————. *Magistrates of the Sacred: Priests and Parishioners in Eighteenth-Century Mexico*. Stanford: Stanford UP, 1996.

Thompson, Elbert N. S. *Literary Bypaths of the Renaissance*. New Haven: Yale UP, 1973.

Townsend, Camilla. *Malintzin's Choices: An Indian Woman in the Conquest of Mexico*. Albuquerque: U of New Mexico P, 2006.

Trueba Lawand, Jamile. *El arte epistolar en el renacimiento español*. Madrid: Tamesis, 1996.

van Deusen, Nancy. "Recent Studies on Gender Relations in Colonial Native Andean History." *New World, First Nations: Native Peoples of Mesoamerica and the Andes under Colonial Rule*. Ed. David Cahill and Blanca Tovías. Brighton: Sussex Academic P, 2006. 144–166.

Van Young, Eric. "The New Cultural History Comes to Old Mexico." *Hispanic American Historical Review* 79. 2 (1999): 211–247.

Velazco, Salvador. *Visiones de Anahuac: Reconstrucciones historiográficas y etnicidades emergentes en el México colonial*. Guadalajara: U de Guadalajara, 2003.

Verástique, Bernardino. *Michoacán and Eden: Vasco de Quiroga and the Evangelization of Western Mexico*. Austin: U of Texas P, 2000.

Verdesio, Gustavo. "Colonialism Now and Then: Colonial Latin American Studies in the Light of the Predicament of Latin Americanism." *Colonialism*

Past and Present: Reading and Writing about Colonial Latin America Today. Ed. Álvaro Félix Bolaños and Gustavo Verdesio. Albany: State U of New York P, 2002. 1–17.

Vidal, Hernán. "The Concept of Colonial and Postcolonial Discourse: A Perspective from Literary Criticism." *Latin American Research Review* 28.3 (1993): 113–119.

Vollendorf, Lisa. *The Lives of Women: A New History of Inquisitional Spain*. Nashville: Vanderbilt UP, 2005.

Warren, Benedict. *The Conquest of Michoacán: The Spanish Domination of the Tarascan Kingdom in Western Mexico, 1521–1530*. Norman: U of Oklahoma P, 1985.

Weber, Alison. *Teresa of Avila and the Rhetoric of Femininity*. Princeton: Princeton UP, 1990.

Wray, Grady. *The Devotional Exercises/Los Ejercicios Devotos of Sor Juana Inés de la Cruz, Mexico's Prodigious Nun (1648/51–1695): A Critical Study and Bilingual Annotated Edition*. Lewiston: Edwin Mellen P, 2005.

———. "Sacred Allusions: Theology in Sor Juana's Work." *Approaches to Teaching the Works of Sor Juana Inés de la Cruz*. Ed. Emilie L. Bergmann and Stacey Schlau. New York: Modern Language Association, 2007. 65–76.

Yannakakis, Yanna. *The Art of Being In-Between: Native Intermediaries, Indian Identity, and Local Rule in Colonial Oaxaca*. Durham: Duke UP, 2008.

Zahino Peñafort, Luisa. "La fundación del convento para indias cacicas de Nuestra Señora de los Ángeles en Oaxaca." *El monacato femenino en el imperio español: Monaterios, beaterios, recogimientos y colegios*. Ed. Manuel Ramos Medina. México: CONDUMEX, 1995. 331–337.

Zamora, Margarita. *Language, Authority, and Indigenous History in the Comentarios Reales de los Incas*. Cambridge: Cambridge UP, 1988.

———. *Reading Columbus*. Berkeley: U of California P, 1993.

Index

11, 32, 125; subordination in, 15, 68, 71, 133, 156–57

Concepción, Petronila de la, 58–60

confessors, 145, 151–52. *See also* priests; nuns' relation to, 85–88, 90, 129, 136, 140, 195n3, 198n9; nuns' writings and, 85, 90–91, 101, 105–6, 114, 195n5, 195n7

conquest, 74, 104–5

conquistadores, 4, 10, 25, 34, 200n24

Convent of Corpus Christi, 7–8, 20, 37, 91, 113, 147, 187n38, 196n15, 196n16; abbesses of, 76, 82–83, 106–8, 111, 126–31, 198n4; biographies of nuns in, 86, 94; controversy over, 49–50, 52–58, 62, 68; entrance requirements, 100, 106; ethnic conflicts in, 105–9, 128–29; histories of, 93–96; opening sermon for, 64, 71–76, 126; selection of nuns for, 8, 12, 26–27, 34–36, 55, 63, 154; Spanish nuns in, 38–39, 63–64, 76–84, 148

Convent of Nuestra Señora de la Purísima Concepción de Cosamaloapan, 1, 9, 121, 147; abbesses of, 143–44, 150–51; ethnic conflict in, 63, 83, 135–37, 140, 142–53, 202n19; opening sermon for, 23, 111, 126–28

Convent of Nuestra Señora de los Ángeles, 9, 63, 154

Convent of San Juan de la Penitencia, 37–38, 79, 106–7, 124–26, 128

Convent of Santa Clara, 54, 81, 189n15

Convent of Santa María de los Ángeles, 111, 130–31

convents, 20, 24, 38, 53, 111, 115, 122, 148–49, 150, 185n20, 196n17; administration of, 150–51, 189n15; characteristics of candidates for, 32–36; entrance requirements for, 32, 55, 77, 80, 124–25, 191n14, 200n22; ethnicity in, 6, 34–36, 55, 63; ethnic tensions in, 51, 77–79, 82–83, 113–14; Indians as servants in, 6–7, 38, 52, 54, 59, 61, 67–68, 191n14; Indians' suitability for, 6, 42–43, 49, 193n10; Indian *vs.* non-Indian, 1–2, 6, 8; locations of, 2, *3*

convents for indigenous women, 30, 92–93, 111, 114, 157. *See also* specific convents; controversy over, 42, 48, 50–53, 104–5, 113; efforts to defend autonomy of, 71, 135, 137, 143; entrance into, 8, 93, 102;

founding of, 5, 8–9, 22, 43, 142, 153, 184n14; Indians not thought capable of governing, 8–9, 76, 81–83, 107, 113; Spanish nuns barred from, 148, 192n2; Spanish nuns in, 8–9, 23, 33, 38–39, 106–8, 113

conventual writings, 16–17, 20, 85–86, 195n2, 197n18; conventions of, 107, 135; genres of, 85, 91, 107, 135, 139–41

conversion, 46, 65; effects of, 92, 105, 191n18; quickness of, 4, 10, 34, 39, 74, 111, 158

Cope, Douglas, 14, 31, 125

Cortés, 13, 202n13

Council of the Indies, 72; indigenous nuns' complaints to, 64, 82–83, 128–29, 198n4; Spanish nuns' defenses to, 83, 199n13

Council of Trent, 110, 114–15

Counter-Reformation, 7, 113–14

criollos, 6, 34, 184n17, 192n1, 203n22. *See also* nuns, Spanish; in convents, 35, 63, 81, 92–93, 113; in convents for indigenous women, 8, 33, 76, 106–8, 113, 129, 136, 142–43

Crown, Spanish, 2–3, 30, 53, 79, 188n43. *See also* colonialism; Church and, 5, 47, 54–55, 69, 72, 75–76, 148–49; Indian solidarity against, 31, 33; indigenous nobles and, 26–28, 30; paternalism toward Indians, 4, 69

culture: continuity and change in, 10–12, 32; Hispanization of, 11, 28, 31, 44–45, 93

Dominicans, 3–4, 45

dowry, to enter convents, 55, 77, 80, 124

education, 5, 137–39, 197n18, 201n9; in convents, 6, 38, 81–82; to enter convents, 100, 106, 191n14; for indigenous elite, 5, 33–34, 46, 123, 157

ethnic identity, 23, 30, 33, 40–41, 156–57, 196n13; efforts to maintain, 108–9, 157; indigenous nuns using, 76, 136–37, 149–50, 153; race *vs.*, 15–16; religion and, 105, 130

First Rule of Saint Claire, 8, 37–38, 55

Fisher, Andrew, 15, 186n33

Fogueras, Fray Juan, 136, 142, 144, 150, 202n19

Franciscans, 5, 8, 40, 43. *See also* missionaries;
  on Convent of Corpus Christi, 49–50, 52,
  56–57; ethnic conflict in convents and, 63,
  77, 143–53, 198n6; evangelizing by, 3–4,
  45; jurisdiction over convents, 37–38, 149,
  191n16
Franco, Jean, 17, 90
funeral panegyrics, 199n10; conventions of,
  112, 115, 118–25, 133, 199n12; examples
  of, 111–12, 123–26, 129, 131–34; goals of,
  118–19, 124, 198n7; hagiography and, 115,
  123–24, 129–30, 133; as performed event
  and text, 110–11, 115, 118–19

Gallagher, Sister Ann Miriam, 20, 35–36, 50–
  51, 55, 187n38
gender, 14, 85–86, 152, 155; construction of,
  23, 62; in religious roles, 5–6, 91, 121,
  199n14; women's texts and, 90–91, 143,
  157
gender differences, 50, 53, 141, 157,
  199n14, 201n9; ideology of difference and,
  34, 48–49; in religious genres, 18, 21–22,
  195n6; in religious writings, 18–19, 87–89,
  96–99, 199n10; in writing styles, 90, 96,
  105–6
gender relations, 14, 113, 141, 203n3;
  complementarity, 12–13, 185n25; power
  in, 157, 202n16; within convents, 111,
  144–45
Gertrudis del Señor San José, Sor, 94, 100
Gibson, Charles, 4, 26–29, 65
*Gracia triunfante en la vida de Catharina Tegakovita,
  La* (Colonee), 56–58, 61, 68, 77
languages, 46, 51, 71; native, 3, 5, 27, 45, 65;
  Spanish, 5, 10, 99, 156, 189n1
Granada, Fray Luis de, 110, 116–17
Graubart, Karen, 13, 185n23, 203n22
Guevara, Joseph María, 52–53, 104, 121

hagiographic biographies, 64, 66, 76–80, 84,
  86, 100–101, 123–24, 136, 193n9, 196n17;
  motives for writing, 67–68, 77, 114–15;
  structure of, 91, 102
hagiography, 56, 58; conventions of, 97, 102,
  106, 114–15, 119, 123, 129–30, 133; other
  genres *vs.*, 87, 129–30, 192n6
Holler, Jacqueline, 7, 8, 20
humanism, 110, 113, 137–38

Ibsen, Kristine, 21, 49, 67, 77, 194n24
identity, 14–16, 25–28, 93. *See also* ethnic
  identity; construction of, 9–10, 15, 158,
  183n4, 185n22, 188n5, 200n21; continuity
  and change in, 10–11, 24, 154–56; Indian,
  12, 183n1, 185n23, 201n27; influence of
  Church on, 92, 191n18; retention of Indian,
  25, 28, 30–31, 41, 93; solidarity from, 31,
  33, 43; women's, 9–10, 23, 64, 93, 141–42
ideology of difference, 14–15, 22, 25, 65, 68–
  69, 76, 155, 186n32; in colonial discourse,
  30–31, 33, 42, 44; in funeral panegyrics,
  112, 125; gender and, 48–49; indigenous
  nuns' use of, 41, 71, 135, 137, 200n22;
  indigenous women and, 38, 50, 190n12,
  191n23; in religious discourse, 128, 133–34
Indians: characterizations of, 4–5, 45–46, 50,
  52–55, 57–61, 64, 68–71, 193n13; under
  colonialism, 5–6, 84, 153, 156; descriptions
  of, 15, 203n22; difference emphasized, 45–
  46, 149–50, 191n23; identity as, 154–56,
  183n1, 201n27; living conditions of, 46–47,
  125; oral tradition of, 99, 107–8; religion
  of, 92, 126–28; separation of, 1–3, 6,
  200n20; solidarity of, 31, 41, 146, 155;
  spiritual capacity of, 42–43, 48, 72–76,
  193n16; stereotypes of, 50, 65, 104–5, 118,
  125, 129, 132, 153, 193n13
Indias caciques de Corpus Christi, Las (Muriel), 20,
  36, 93–96, 100, 196n14; *Apuntes de algunas
  vidas* compared to, 86, 96–109; Sor Petra's
  biography in, 111, 123–24
Indias entendidas por estar religiosamente, Las
  (Castorena), 72–76

JanMohamed, Abdul, 65, 74
Jesuits, 43, 49–50, 52–53, 56–57, 61, 67–68
Juana Inés de la Cruz, Sor, 49, 89, 140–41,
  192n3, 192n4, 202n15

Karttunen, Frances, 10, 156
Klor de Alva, Jorge, 45, 47, 92

Lavrin, Asunción, 17, 67, 90, 93, 138, 142,
  190n4; on conflicts in convents, 144,
  198n4; on convents, 8, 20, 52, 56, 126
letters, 23, 77, 152; as acceptable genre for
  women, 89–90, 135; in colonial discourse,
  137–42; nuns' uses of, 135, 142–53; in

About the Author

Mónica Díaz is an assistant professor at Georgia State University, where she teaches colonial Latin American literature and culture. She completed a dual PhD in Hispanic literature and Latin American history from Indiana University in 2002. Her research interests include Latin American history and culture, gender and ethnicity in colonial discourse, post-colonial theory, and women's literature. She has published several articles in journals and edited volumes on gender and indigenous writing.